Christianizing Death

Illuminated initial *P* of *Proficiscere* in the Gellone manuscript
(Paris, Bibliothèque Nationale, MS lat. 12048, fol. 246v.) Photo Bibliothèque Nationale.

†

Christianizing Death

*The Creation of a Ritual Process
in Early Medieval Europe*

Frederick S. Paxton

Cornell University Press

ITHACA AND LONDON

Copyright © 1990 by Cornell University

First published 1990 by Cornell University Press.

International Standard Book Number 0-8014-2492-5
Library of Congress Catalog Card Number 90-34072
Printed in the United States of America
*Librarians: Library of Congress cataloging information
appears on the last page of the book.*

To my parents

Contents

Rituals

Tables

ix

Acknowledgments

I was first drawn to medieval rituals for the dead and dying as a fledgling graduate student under Caroline Walker Bynum at the University of Washington in 1979. Her humanity and scholarship remain my strongest source of inspiration. I thank Thomas N. Bisson, Gerard Caspary, Stephan Kuttner, and Peter Brown for their guidance and support during my years at the University of California, Berkeley, and ever since. Work on this book was greatly facilitated by a year (1987–88) as an Andrew W. Mellon Faculty Fellow in the Humanities at Harvard University. I thank the Mellon Foundation and their representatives at Harvard, Richard Hunt and Amy Gazin-Schwartz, for their support. My thanks go as well to the other Mellon Fellows who shared that year at Harvard and to my students, both in Cambridge and in New London, who stimulated my thinking in so many ways. R. Francis Johnson, Dean of the Faculty (Emeritus), Connecticut College, deserves my special gratitude for making it possible to take my family with me to Cambridge that year, as do my wife and children, for whom that was only part of the journey that has produced this book. I also thank the Kungliga Biblioteket, Stockholm; the Pierpont Morgan Library, New York; the Zentralbibliothek, Zürich; the Bibliothèque Nationale, Paris; and the Robbins Collection and the Institute of Medieval Canon Law at the University of California, Berkeley, for access to manuscripts or photocopies of manuscripts.

I owe a great deal to Susan A. Keefe, who read and commented on all of this book in an earlier form. I thank as well Geoffrey Koziol, who commented on most of it; Joseph Lynch and Roger A. Reynolds, who gave it an extraordinarily thorough reading; and Carole Straw, who checked the translations. Any mistakes or infelicities that remain are my own. Finally, I thank Barbara H. Salazar for her elegant editing and John G. Ackerman for his support and encouragement.

FREDERICK S. PAXTON

New London, Connecticut

Abbreviations and Short Titles

AESC	*Annales: Economies, sociétés, civilisations*
ALW	*Archiv für Liturgiewissenschaft*
Autun	*Liber sacramentorum Augustudonensis,* ed. Odilo Heiming
Bobbio	*The Bobbio Missal: A Gallican Mass-book,* ed. Elias A. Lowe et al.
c.	*capitula*
CCCM	Corpus christianorum, continuatio medievalis
CCL	Corpus christianorum, series latina
CCM	Corpus consuetudinum monasticarum
CLLA	Klaus Gamber, *Codices liturgici latini antiquiores*
CSEL	Corpus scriptorum ecclesiasticorum latinorum
DACL	*Dictionnaire d'archéologie chrétienne et de liturgie*
DHGE	*Dictionnaire d'histoire et de géographie ecclésiastiques*
DMA	*Dictionary of the Middle Ages*
EL	*Ephemerides liturgicae*
FS	*Frühmittelalterliche Studien*
Gallicanum vetus	*Missale Gallicanum vetus,* ed. Leo Cunibert Mohlberg
Gelasian	*Liber sacramentorum Romanae ordinis anni circuli,* ed. Leo Cunibert Mohlberg
Gellone	*Liber sacramentorum Gellonensis,* ed. Antoine Dumas
Gothicum	*Missale Gothicum,* ed. Leo Cunibert Mohlberg
Gregorian	*Le sacramentaire grégorien,* ed. Jean Deshusses
Hadrianum	*Le sacramentaire grégorien,* ed. Jean Deshusses, 1.83– 348
HBS	Henry Bradshaw Society

JTS   *Journal of Theological Studies*

Liber ordinum   *Le liber ordinum en usage dans l'église wisigothique et mozarabe d'Espagne du cinquième au onzième siècle,* ed. Mario Férotin

Liber ordinum
sacerdotal   *Liber ordinum sacerdotal,* ed. José Janini

LQF   Liturgiewissenschaftliche Quellen und Forschungen

MGH   Monumenta Germaniae historica

  SRM   Scriptorum rerum Merovingicarum

  Concilia 1   *Concilia aevi Merovingici,* ed. F. Maasen

  Concilia 2   *Concilia aevi Karolini,* ed. A. Werminghoff

  Concilia 3   *Concilia aevi Karolini DCCCXLIII–DCCCLIX,* ed. W. Hartmann

  Capitularia 1   *Capitularia regum Francorum 1,* ed. A. Boretius

  Capitularia 2   *Capitularia regum Francorum 2,* ed. A. Boretius and V. Krause

  Capitula epis-
    coporum   *Capitula episcoporum,* pt. 1, ed. Peter Brommer

Missale
  Francorum   *Missale Francorum,* ed. Leo Cunibert Mohlberg

NCE   *New Catholic Encyclopedia*

PL   *Patrologia latina,* ed. J.-P. Migne

RB   *Revue bénédictine*

RED   Rerum ecclesiasticarum documenta

Rheinau   *Sacramentarium Rhenaugiense,* ed. Anton Hänggi and Alfons Schönherr

SF   Spicilegium Friburgense

St. Gall   *Ein St. Galler Sakramentar-Fragment,* ed. Georg Manz

Stowe   *The Stowe Missal,* ed. George F. Warner

Supplement   *Le sacramentaire grégorien,* ed. Jean Deshusses, 1:351–605

Verona   *Sacramentarium Veronense,* ed. Leo Cunibert Mohlberg

Christianizing Death

History and Ritual

M ost areas of religious life in Christian Europe were characterized more by diversity than by uniformity before the
twelfth century. The hard realities of time and distance, the scar-
city of written texts, and the conflicting demands of tradition and
authority ensured that the experience of Christianity varied from
place to place and among various groups—laymen, clerics, monks,
nuns, townspeople, and country folk. Nevertheless, the end of the
ninth century saw the culmination of a centuries-long process of
ritual creation in the Latin West as early medieval people struggled
with the problem of human mortality within the limits of their
Christian world view. Funerals and mortuary ceremonies are always rites of passage, yet the complex of prayers and gestures that
emerged in written texts and ritual practice shortly before the year
900 made up a rite of passage that was to see Christian Europeans
to the grave and beyond throughout the Middle Ages and long
afterward. This ritual complex began before death, with rites of
purification and separation; it accompanied the agony and the moment of death, the laying out, the vigils, and the burial; and it
continued for many years in commemorative ceremonies that affected the state of the soul in the other world and bound together
the communities of the living and the dead. Its various pieces
originated in the separate Christian communities of late imperial
Rome, Visigothic Spain, early medieval Ireland, Anglo-Saxon England, and Gaul under the Merovingian and Carolingian kings.

Their synthesis in the later ninth century was the result of the peculiar historical circumstances engendered by the reform of church and society undertaken by the leaders of the Carolingian realm between A.D. 750 and 850. The history of this ritual complex—the creation and interaction over time of its constitutive parts and the process by which they came to characterize the response to death among Christians in western Europe—is the subject of this book.

Thus, this is not a complete guide to death, dying, and the dead in the early Middle Ages but a historical study of the formation of a peculiar set of ritual responses to death in the Christian society of the medieval West.[1] Its sources are literary (legal texts, letters, rules for living the Christian life, biographies, and saints' lives) and for the most part liturgical—the remains of books created by and for the clergy to record and transmit the prayers of Christian worship and, to a lesser extent, their accompanying gestures. The central act of Christian worship was the mass, and collections of mass prayers form the core of many of the ritual books—usually called sacramentaries—cited in the pages that follow. These "sacramentaries," however, came early on to include prayers and directions pertaining to the noneucharistic activities of the clergy as well, especially the performance of pastoral work, and it is among these materials that much of the evidence concerning rites for the dead and dying lies.[2]

Like all bodies of historical sources, the liturgical remains from the early Middle Ages present difficulties.[3] Since the main purpose of liturgical books was utilitarian, those that were most used are often least likely to have survived. Many that remain do so because they were splendid copies meant more for display than for use.

1. In the words of Paul-Albert Février, it is concerned with the historical process by which the "death of a Christian became a Christian death"; Février, "La mort chrétienne," in *Segni e riti nella chiesa altomedievale occidentale*, 2 vols., Settimane di studio del centro italiano di studi sull'alto medioevo 33 (Spoleto, 1987), 2.881.

2. On sacramentaries, see Roger Reynolds, "Sacramentary," DMA 10.605–6; Jean Deshusses, "Les sacramentaires: Etat actuel de la recherche," ALW 24 (1982): 19–46; and Cyrille Vogel, *Medieval Liturgy: An Introduction to the Sources*, rev. and trans. William G. Storey and Niels Krogh Rasmussen (Washington, D.C., 1986), 64–110. On other early medieval ritual books, especially the old Spanish *Libri ordinum*, see Vogel, *Medieval Liturgy*, and below, chap. 2.

3. See Vogel, *Medieval Liturgy*, 62–64. The standard guide to early medieval liturgical manuscripts is Klaus Gamber, *Codices liturgici latini antiquiores*, 2d ed., Spicilegii Friburgensis subsidia 1 (Fribourg, 1968), but Gamber's typology is controversial and his remarks on individual manuscripts often need revising on the basis of recent work.

Others exist because they record the usages of monastic communities whose libraries have survived the ravages of time better than others. Furthermore, as most manuscripts contain a mixture of material from more than one time and place, they call for careful analysis before one can arrive at conclusions about current practice at any particular time. The oldest of these books go back no further than the seventh century, and earlier practices must be reconstructed by analysis and inference from later texts. Finally, because the early medieval ritual books were created for and by the clergy, they often present only an outline of practices within a circumscribed monastic community or an ideal to be pursued. Thus they sometimes illuminate the ritual life of the cloister only indirectly and shed even less light on that of the populace as a whole.

Some of these difficulties can be overcome, others cannot, but most derive from the very circumstances that also make the liturgical records of the period a rich source for the historian interested in ritual. Because of the basically utilitarian nature of the manuscripts, even display copies often reflected or had an effect on actual practice, preserving and transmitting prayers and gestures that were or could be used in a ritual setting. The mixture of elements in the manuscripts from various times and places is the result of interchange among cultural traditions, and careful attention to the changing contents of groups of prayers or ritual orders reveals the degree to which materials from one tradition were accepted or rejected by another. As to the essentially clerical nature of the documents, four things must be said. First of all, very little is known about non-Christian ritual among the indigenous cultures of the early medieval West. Pagan practices survived, of course, and are sometimes referred to in Christian sources, usually by way of condemnation.[4] Archaeological finds are rich, but anthropologists and archaeologists have not solved the vexing problems of the relations between ritual behavior and mortuary remains or between religious change and forms of burial. In neither case is there an easy way to derive the former from the latter.[5] Even were this not

---

4. W. Boudriot, *Die altgermanische Religion in der amtlichen Literatur des Abendlandes vom 5.–11. Jahrhundert* (Bonn, 1928; repr. Darmstadt, 1964), 48–51.

5. See Lewis R. Binford, "Mortuary Practices: Their Study and Their Potential," *American Antiquity* 36 (1971): 6–29; Ellen-Jane Pader, *Symbolism, Social Relations, and the Interpretation of Mortuary Remains* (Oxford, 1982), esp. 196–97; and Brad Bartel, "A Historical Review of Ethnological and Archaeological Analyses of Mortuary Practice," *Journal of Anthropological Archaeology* 1 (1982): 32–58. On the difficulty of correlating changes in burial practices with the process of Christianization in the period covered by this study, see Bailey Young, "Paganisme, chris-

the case, the history of ritual change within the literate circles of the clergy has its own coherence and merits a separate discussion. The Christian clergy of the early Middle Ages were impresarios of ritual, using it to weld various linguistic, ethnic, and legal groups into some form of unified society. Second, the clergy of the early Middle Ages were not so very different from the populace as a whole as their counterparts in later centuries. Education was minimal; there were no universities, and no sophisticated scholastic theology created a sense that monks, priests, and the laity were separate bodies. It is true that Latin was a foreign language in Britain and Ireland and among many of the barbarian peoples who became Christian in the late Roman period and afterward, but the language of liturgy and ritual was simple and direct and when heard repeatedly over a lifetime must have seemed a familiar, if only partially understood, idiom to most men and women. In any case, its accompanying gestures and symbols were fully comprehensible. Third, the prayers and the structure of the rituals in early liturgical sources are, for the most part, the work of generations of anonymous men and women. The composite and cumulative nature of the sacramentaries and other books, and their non-canonical status, gave room for the inclusion of new material as well as the excision, alteration, and adaptation of old prayers and directions, and nearly every manuscript has been reworked in part by the people who wrote and used it. Thus the ritual books have some claim to being collective—not representative of society as a whole perhaps, but at least representative of the people who strove to make sense of their experience within the structures of Christian symbolism and meaning. Finally, though monks, nuns, and clerics developed and experienced many of the rituals that are the subject of this book, the rituals are almost never presented as the exclusive province of religious.[6] On the contrary, letters, sermons, and the decrees of bishops, popes, kings, and councils all attest to the desire to bring the benefits of Christian ritual directly to the people. Though it is difficult to judge the success of this endeavor,

---

tianisation et rites funéraires mérovingiens," *Archéologie médiévale* 7 (1977): 5–81; Edward James, "Merovingian Cemetery Studies and Some Implications for Anglo-Saxon England," in *Anglo-Saxon Cemeteries, 1979,* ed. P. Rahtz, T. Dickinson, and L. Watts (Oxford, 1980), 40; and Février, "Mort chrétienne," 916–18.

6. Cf. Thierry Maertens and Louis Heuschen, *Die Sterbeliturgie der katholischen Kirche: Glaubenslehre und Seelsorge* (Paderborn, 1959), 48.

the intention is clear, and the creation of ritual was closely bound up with the work of forging a Christian society as a whole.

In one sense the problem of clerical/lay participation in rituals for death and dying has determined the chronological limits of this book. The study begins in late antiquity with a consideration of the rites that might be performed for any Christian in the Roman West, lay or clerical. Some of the rituals that originated in Gaul, Spain, and Ireland in the sixth, seventh, and eighth centuries, such as the burial service associated with the rule for nuns devised by Bishop Caesarius of Arles, were created for use in convents; others, such as the old Spanish rite for granting penance to the dying, were clearly meant for use among the laity. The ritual innovations and syntheses of the Carolingian age most often arose out of the peculiar conditions of life in the cloister, where dying could be closely monitored and where active participation in rituals around the deathbed and afterward was ensured by the stability of the community and its commitment to the care of its members. Nonetheless, the constant pressure of the Carolingian reformers to extend the benefits of Christian ritual to the whole community kept the clergy in touch with the wider population, at least its more powerful and visible members. Thus the final stage in the development of the death rituals in the later ninth century coincided with significant moves to expand the availability of the rites, both old and new, beyond the limits of the cloister. The legacy of the Carolingians comprised not only the specific rituals created by the clergy but also the conviction that all Christians should benefit from them. This factor as much as any other, explains their long-term success within the medieval church and Christian culture in the West.

This book is primarily a work of history, but it is informed by closely related fields that have a claim on its subject matter, especially anthropology and the new field of ritual studies.[7] To anthropology it owes the fundamental insight that death rituals have a structure, above all the tripartite structure of rites of passage first defined by Arnold van Gennep.[8] In van Gennep's formulation,

7. Ronald L. Grimes, *Research in Ritual Studies: A Programmatic Essay and Bibliography* (Metuchen, N.J., 1985); idem, "Ritual Studies," in *The Encyclopedia of Religion*, ed. Mircea Eliade (New York/London, 1987), 12.422–25.

8. Arnold van Gennep, *The Rites of Passage*, trans. Monika B. Vizedom and Gabrielle L. Caffee (Chicago, 1960; first published Paris, 1909). For discussions of

death rituals, like other rites of passage, accompany and effect a change in the person or persons involved by which they pass "from one cosmic or social world to another." The whole process comprises three subsets of ritual action: (preliminal) rites of separation, (liminal) rites of transition, and (postliminal) rites of incorporation.[9] Rites of separation are generally marked by "symbolic behavior signifying a detachment of the individual or the group from either an earlier fixed point in the social structure or an established set of cultural conditions ('a state')," and often include "washings, anointings, and rites of purification in general."[10] The liminal (from the Latin word *limen*, threshold) stage of rites of passage is often marked by actions at portals and symbols of portals. But it also has profound effects on the participants in the ritual. At funerals, the liminal rites entail the suspension of social life and the setting apart of the mourning group, whose condition is analogous to that of the deceased, suspended between the worlds of the living and the dead. It is a condition fraught with possibilities and danger. Incorporation rituals often mirror the acts and gestures of separation rites. They close gaps and reinstate the normal conditions of social life, often by means of communal meals.[11]

Attention to the structural schema of rites of passage lies behind much of the organization of this book. That is why, for example, I give so much attention to ritual responses to sickness even when

---

van Gennep's insights, see Monika Vizedom, *Rites and Relationships: Rites of Passage and Contemporary Anthropology* (Beverly Hills and London, 1976), and Richard Huntington and Peter Metcalf, *Celebrations of Death: The Anthropology of Mortuary Ritual* (Cambridge, Eng., 1979), 8–13, 97–98. Historians are perhaps most familiar with the middle term of van Gennep's schema, thanks to the work of Victor Turner, who developed it independently into an interpretive tool in the social anthropology of religion. See, e.g., Victor Turner, *The Forest of Symbols: Aspects of Ndembu Ritual* (Ithaca, N.Y., 1967), 93–111; *The Ritual Process: Structure and Anti-Structure* (Chicago, 1969), esp. 94–97, 166–67; and *Dramas, Fields, and Metaphors: Symbolic Action in Human Society* (Ithaca, N.Y., 1974), 231–71 and index, s.v. "liminality."

9. Van Gennep, *Rites of Passage*, 10–12, 21, and passim.

10. Turner, *Dramas, Fields, and Metaphors*, 232; van Gennep, *Rites of Passage*, 164.

11. Van Gennep, *Rites of Passage*, 15–25, 147, 164–65. It is Robert Hertz, however, and not van Gennep, who first saw the deep symbolic connections between the activities of the living and the state of the deceased. See Robert Hertz, "A Contribution to the Study of the Collective Representation of Death," in his *Death and The Right Hand*, trans. R. and C. Needham (Glencoe, Ill., 1960), first published in *Année Sociologique* 10 (1907): 48–137; and Huntington and Metcalf, *Celebrations of Death*, 13–17, 61–67.

death was not imminent, for an essential part of the ritual history that I am tracing concerns the way in which rituals of healing became transformed into rituals of preparation for death—that is, rites of separation. Indeed, the development of an elaborate set of separation rituals is one of the most distinctive features of the historical process that culminated in the ritual synthesis of the later ninth century. Van Gennep's remark that "on first considering funeral ceremonies, one expects rites of separation to be their most prominent component" almost certainly derives from his native familiarity with the Christian European tradition, for it came as a surprise to him that the ethnographic literature on death rituals in other cultures showed separation rites to be "few . . . and very simple."[12]

My focus on ritual structure in accordance with van Gennep's tripartite schema has also led me to go beyond the funeral ceremonies themselves to investigate the history of commemorative services for the dead, for ritual activity did not end at death or even when a body was laid in a grave, but could continue long afterward at regular intervals as a form of aid to the incorporation of the soul into the other world. Once separated by preliminal rituals (and then finally by death) from the physical body and the "body" of the living, the dead person was accompanied by words and actions aimed at the twofold task of incorporating the physical remains among those of the earlier dead and of aiding the soul in its journey to and inclusion in the community of the dead in the other world. During most of that process, the fate of the soul was somewhat in question and the demands placed on the living were heavy. Attention to these aspects of the ritual process has enabled me to trace the interplay of a variety of ritual approaches and traditions over time and has revealed the significance of the eighth and ninth centuries as a decisive period in the creation of a Christian response to death and dying in the incipient society of medieval Europe.

Another debt to anthropology, and to ritual studies in general, concerns the function and meaning of ritual in living societies. Rituals do things. They are performances, participatory activities that involve groups of people—people who learn things through their participation in rituals. They can model the way in which

12. Van Gennep, *Rites of Passage,* 146; but cf. the remark on p. 11 that "rites of separation are prominent in funeral ceremonies." Was he referring there to familiar Christian European practices?

crisis or change has been met in the past and suggest ways to meet it in the future.[13] They can, as Theodore Jennings points out, be "one of the ways in which human beings construe and construct their world."[14] They are social actions that reveal, enhance, and sometimes even alter the relations among members of the society in which they are acted out. In tracing the historical development of the ritual complex around death, dying, and the dead in the early medieval West, I have kept an eye on these aspects of ritual as well. They are not so central in my presentation as they might be, on two accounts. On the one hand, the problems and insights involved in the creation and transmission of the texts that recorded the rites presented itself as the most pressing historical task. On the other, I am hesitant to overstate the case for the link between the written sources and the experience of the actual ritual performance, as the ways people have experienced their lives are less accessible to the historian than to the student of contemporary societies.[15]

It is this hesitancy that has kept me as well from generalizing too broadly about attitudes toward death among the early medieval communities that developed and used the rituals under discussion here. That is not to say that no such generalizations are possible or that I avoid them entirely.[16] The literary remains that are the main source of this study and their reception and treatment by the people who used them and passed them on give eloquent testimony to the hopes and fears of late antique and early medieval men and women. But in this formative period such feelings were not universal, and operated more often as an ideal to be striven for than a model of collective "mentalities."[17] Thus I have concentrated on presenting the evidence for the ritual history as clearly as possible. If I have been less hesitant to tackle questions of the social and

13. On rituals as "cultural performances" and as models both of and for the world, see Clifford Geertz, *The Interpretation of Cultures* (New York, 1973), 112–18.

14. Theodore Jennings, "On Ritual Knowledge," *Journal of Religion* 62 (1982): 111–27, at 112.

15. See Grimes's criticisms of narrowly textual approaches to the study of ritual in *Research in Ritual Studies*, 4.

16. For a discussion of the methodological problems inherent in the study of attitudes toward death, see Michel Vovelle, "Les attitudes devant la mort: Problèmes de méthode, approches et lectures différentes," AESC 31 (1976): 120–32.

17. Cf. the provocative discussion on pain and death by Jacques Paul in *L'église et la culture en occident, ix*^e*–xii*^e *siècles*, 2 vols. (Paris, 1986), 2.674–83; and on violence and death by Michel Rouche in *A History of Private Life*, vol. 1, *From Pagan Rome to Byzantium*, ed. Paul Veyne, trans. Arthur Goldhammer (Cambridge, Mass., 1987), 485–517.

ecclesio-political contexts of the rituals under discussion, that is because their development was so often clearly linked to specific, identifiable circumstances. These circumstances range from the particular concerns of Irish reformers whose reading of Old Testament law led them to avoid contact with the dead, and hence to elaborate rituals for the dying, to the general concerns of popes, kings, and bishops to define membership in Christian society through access to death rituals. The social context is most apparent in the process by which participatory aspects of deathbed rituals grew apace with the system of commemorative services and "confraternities of prayer" in the eighth and ninth centuries. The elaboration of these portions of the ritual process both created and mirrored bonds not only between the living and the dying but between the living and the dead, and played an important role in the definition of the family and community in the tenth and eleventh centuries and throughout the Middle Ages.[18]

Van Gennep's schema is thus only a beginning. As one anthropologist has put it,

> Van Gennep's notion that a funeral ritual can be seen as a transition that begins with the separation of the deceased from life and ends with his incorporation into the world of the dead is merely a vague truism unless it is positively related to the values of the particular culture. The continued relevance of Van Gennep's notion is not due to the tripartite analytical scheme (separation, liminality, reincorporation) itself, but to the creative way it can be combined with cultural values to grasp the conceptual vitality of each ritual.[19]

As a historian, I have set out not only to grasp the conceptual vitality of individual rituals but also to trace their emergence and development over time and within a variety of cultural settings, keeping an eye on continuities as well as changes of emphasis, shifts in interest, and responses to new needs. Accordingly, my greatest debt is to historians of the liturgy, whose patient labors at sorting out, dating, and editing the documentary remains of the

---

18. Gerd Tellenbach, "Die historische Dimensionen der liturgischen Commemoratio im Mittelalter," in *Memoria: Der geschichtliche Zeugniswert des liturgischen Gedenkens im Mittelalter*, ed. K. Schmid and J. Wollasch, Münstersche Mittelalter-Schriften 48 (Munich, 1984), 200–214; Gerd Althoff, *Adels- und Königsfamilien im Spiegel ihrer Memorialüberlieferung*, Münstersche Mittelalter-Schriften 47 (Munich, 1984).

19. Huntington and Metcalf, *Celebrations of Death*, 98.

period and whose extensive writings on the history of the mass and the rites for the sick, the penitent, and the dead are fundamental to my investigations. Since this scholarly tradition has generally remained outside the mainstream of medieval historiography, and since it is so fundamental to this study, it might be helpful to give a brief introduction to its history and tendencies, and to the ways in which my work attends to and diverges from its proper concerns.[20]

Although the modern study of the medieval liturgy goes back to the sixteenth century, its origins in Reformation-era controversies over the "purity" or "antiquity" of the traditions handed down from the Middle Ages have often caused its results to stop short of full historical explanations. For example, at the turn of the twentieth century F. W. Puller sought to trace the history of the rite of anointing the sick or dying in order to argue for a return to the ancient practice of administering it to heal and not to prepare the recipient for death.[21] As an Anglican, he wished to discredit the medieval form of the rite in favor of what he felt was, as more primitive, the truer form. In so doing, he was able to pinpoint rather closely the point at which ritual anointing took on new elements and began to approach the medieval sacrament of extreme unction—that is, in the ninth century. But there he stopped. For his purposes he had only to show that (a) there was an ancient practice of anointing the sick and (b) it had become something else in the Middle Ages. What that something else was, how it came to be and why, and what it meant to the people whose creation it was were questions in which Puller had no interest. Moreover, any attempt he might have made to answer them would have been confused by the general lack of knowledge of the provenances and dates of composition of the manuscripts that contained the material he had studied. The manuscripts are so numerous and their interrelationships so complex that the energies of generations of scholars have been needed to construct even the main lines of development.

Fortunately, even before Puller's time scholars had begun the scientific investigation of liturgical manuscripts which would

20. Although Giles Constable's remarks on the marginal status of monastic history in respect to medieval history as a whole ("The Study of Monastic History Today," in *Essays on the Reconstruction of Medieval History*, ed. V. Murdoch and G. S. Couse [Montreal/London, 1974], 21–51) have happily lost some of their urgency, they are still applicable to the study of the liturgy. The best guides in English to liturgical scholarship are Richard W. Pfaff, *Medieval Latin Liturgy: A Select Bibliography* (Toronto, 1982), and Vogel, *Medieval Liturgy*.

21. F. W. Puller, *The Anointing of the Sick in Scripture and Tradition* (London, 1904).

form the basis for an objective appreciation of the history of ritual in the Middle Ages. In the seventeenth century Dom H. Ménard had published a Gregorian sacramentary with copious notes containing comparable passages from similar books.[22] At the same time, another monk of the Congregation of St-Maur, Edmond Martène, compiled in three volumes a large number of texts of the medieval liturgy (to which he later added a fourth on monastic rituals) which until recently remained standard tools for historians.[23] For Germany a less satisfactory collection of texts was compiled in the eighteenth century by the Benedictine M. Gerbert.[24] In England in the nineteenth century, the Surtees Society and the Henry Bradshaw Society began to edit and publish critical editions of liturgical books from the British Isles.[25] With good texts available, scholars such as Edmund Bishop could begin the scientific reconstruction of the history of the liturgy which has continued to the present day.[26] During this century, progress has accelerated as highly scientific editions of liturgical texts have appeared on a regular basis.[27] These modern editions have been essential to my investigations. I have consulted manuscripts directly when necessary, yet the liturgical remains of the period are so vast and so scattered among the libraries of Europe that without published critical editions these investigations would not have been possible.

On particular historical questions relevant to this book, the work of the last two generations has been extraordinary. The pub-

22. *Divi Gregorii papae I liber sacramentorum*, ed. H. Ménard (Paris, 1642; repr. PL 78.26–240). For other short surveys of liturgical scholarship, see William J. O'Shea, "Liturgiology," in NCE 8.919–27, and Louis Bouyer, *Liturgical Piety* (Notre Dame, Ind., 1955), 272–81.

23. Edmond Martène, *De antiquis ecclesiae ritibus*, 3 vols. (Rouen, 1700–1702; 2d ed., 4 vols. Antwerp, 1736–38, repr. Hildesheim, 1967–69). For precise identifications of the manuscripts consulted by Martène, see A. G. Martimort, *La documentation liturgique de Dom Edmond Martène: Etude codicologique* (Vatican City, 1978).

24. *Monumenta veteris liturgiae allemannicae*, ed. M. Gerbert, 2 vols. (St-Blaise, 1777–79; repr. Hildesheim, 1967).

25. The Surtees Society was founded in 1834, the Henry Bradshaw Society in 1890. The work of the first was largely superseded by that of the second.

26. See the collected articles of Edmund Bishop in *Liturgica Historica* (Oxford, 1918; repr. 1962), still an indispensable book.

27. New editions have regularly appeared in such series as Rerum ecclesiasticarum documenta, under the general direction of L. C. Mohlberg (Rome, 1956–); Spicilegium Friburgense, under the general editorship of G. G. Meersseman, A. Hänggi, and P. Ladner (Fribourg, 1957–); and the Corpus christianorum (Turnhout, 1953–). A comprehensive bibliography of new publications in all fields of liturgical studies can be found in the pages of the journal *Archiv für Liturgiewissenschaft*, published by the Abtei Maria Laach (Regensburg, 1950–).

lication of Michel Andrieu's studies and editions of the Roman ritual "orders" (ordines) and pontificals form, among much else, the basis of the study of the Roman *ordo defunctorum* and its transmission—of which much will appear in these pages.[28] Antoine Chavasse's investigations of the anointing of the sick and of the nature and history of the "Gelasian" sacramentary are of fundamental importance.[29] Quite recently the study of the Gregorian sacramentary and its history has been set on a new level by the publications of Jean Deshusses. Deshusses's "comparative" edition of the ninth-century manuscripts of the Gregorian sacramentary, which in effect has made nearly fifty manuscripts available to scholarly research, is the basis for many of the findings in Chapters 4 and 5 of this book.[30] Finally, Damien Sicard's monumental study of the prayers and rubrics of the funeral liturgy up to the year 800 has to be a starting point for any investigation concerned with death and burial in the Christian tradition of the early medieval West.[31]

My research proceeds along the lines laid out in this scientific tradition of liturgical scholarship insofar as it rests on the analysis of the contents of manuscripts. Its conclusions are drawn from the manner in which rites and prayers were transmitted and from the evidence of choices for and against available materials made by the people involved in the process of transmission. That methodology has allowed me to determine with some precision the stages of the process of ritual creation and transmission before and during the Carolingian period and to discover the point of synthesis in the later ninth century.

Given the long history and the quality of work in this field, one

28. Les "Ordines Romani" du haut moyen âge, ed. Michel Andrieu, 5 vols. (Louvain, 1931–61; repr. 1960–65); Le pontifical romain au moyen-âge, ed. Michel Andrieu, 4 vols. (Vatican City, 1938–41).

29. Antoine Chavasse, Etude sur l'onction des infirmes dans l'église latine du iiie au xie siècle, vol. 1, Du iiie siècle à la réforme carolingienne (Lyons, 1942), and Le sacramentaire gélasien (Vatican Reginensis 316): Sacramentaire presbytéral en usage dans les titres romains au viie siècle (Paris/Tournai/New York/Rome, 1958). The second volume of Chavasse's study of anointing the sick was never published, but his conclusions are summarized in his "Prières pour les malades et onction sacramentelle," in L'église en prière: Introduction à la liturgie, ed. A. G. Martimort (Paris/Tournai/New York/Rome, 1961), 580–94, and by Placid Murray, "The Liturgical History of Extreme Unction," in Studies in Pastoral Liturgy II, ed. Vincent Ryan (Dublin, 1963), 18–35.

30. Le sacramentaire grégorien: Ses principales formes d'après les plus anciens manuscrits, ed. Jean Deshusses, comparative ed., 3 vols. (Fribourg, 1971–82). On the Gregorian sacramentary as a type, see Vogel, Medieval Liturgy, 79–102.

31. Damien Sicard, La liturgie de la mort dans l'église latine des origines à la réforme carolingienne, LQF 63 (Münster, 1978).

might wonder why this discovery was not made earlier. There are three reasons. First, it is only recently that codicological research has progressed to the point where most liturgical manuscripts can be confidently located in time and place, an essential prerequisite for their use in detailed analysis of change over time. Second, the very antiquity of the field has led to overspecialization, which is evident in even the most recent work. The (mostly Catholic) historians who have worked on these issues have followed the practice of treating the various rites as distinct sacraments, each with its own history. Yet the sacramental system that underlies that approach was the product of high-medieval scholastic theology. During late antiquity and the early Middle Ages in the West, ritual life was more fluid. Thus, although much has been written on the separate rites of the sick, the dying, and the dead, and although it has been clear for some time that the eighth and ninth centuries were critical for the introduction of anointing and penance as rites for the dying and of the old Roman rite for death and funerals into the mainstream of ritual tradition, they have never been addressed as a whole, and seldom with an eye to the social and cultural context in which they developed. Finally, the history of the liturgy has inevitably been closely allied with what is known as "liturgics" or "liturgiology," a branch of systematic theology which aims to study the ritual of the past in order to enhance present forms of worship.[32] This goal has kept alive some of the tendencies noted in Puller's book on anointing, especially the tendency to equate antiquity with "correctness" or to consider the traditions of Rome and the Roman church as of paramount importance. In either case, the cultural creations of the non-Roman Middle Ages often get short shrift. For example, even the best of the recent work on the liturgy of the dead tends to regard the Roman tradition as the central factor to which all other traditions accommodated themselves. This tendency has obscured the complex interaction of various ritual traditions that fed into the cultural stream of Europe, especially in the critical period during and after the Carolingian reform of the eighth and ninth centuries. When viewed from the perspective of the whole ritual process, the Roman contribution to the medieval Latin death ritual emerges as important but by no means central.

Therein lies the value as a heuristic device of the anthropologi-

32. Grimes, "Ritual Studies," 423; cf. O'Shea, "Liturgiology"; and Theodore W. Jennings, "Ritual Studies and Liturgical Theology: An Invitation to Dialogue," *Journal of Ritual Studies* 1 (1987): 35–56.

cal schema of rites of passage. By expanding the field of analysis, it highlights previously unseen relationships. Because it derives from the tradition of the social rather than the ecclesiastical sciences, it permits us to explore and understand the Christian tradition without concern for questions of the theological "correctness" of a ritual practice or its relation to a ritual tradition unconnected with Rome. In any case, it is only against the background of change and continuity in a whole complex of related rites and prayers that the historical significance of early medieval developments stands out. In matters concerning the ritual care of the dying and the dead in medieval Europe, the contributions of Spain, Ireland, and Francia weigh more heavily than those of Rome and Anglo-Saxon England, and unity, when achieved, was due less to adherence to the traditions of Rome or the stated goals of the Carolingian reform than to the persistent attempts of numerous Christian communities to construct a ritual response to death which made sense in terms of both their antique inheritance and their own experience.

This book has, accordingly, three main goals. The primary goal is to explore and interpret the process by which Christian Europeans in the Latin West came to ritualize death, dying, and the commemoration of the dead in a way quite peculiar to themselves, their religion, and their society. My explorations end in the late ninth century because by that time, although the rites continued to develop, their basic structural components were in place both in practice and within the mainstream of book production, so that their transmission to later generations was assured. The second goal is to build a bridge between the specialized study of the liturgy and broader programs of research. In order to do so, I have tried to preserve the careful attention to the construction and transmission of texts, and of the manuscripts that preserve them, which is the hallmark of research in liturgical history. I have also tried, however, to situate the texts, and their production and transmission, within the contexts of social, political, and religious change in order to exhibit the richness of this field for more general understandings of medieval cultural development. Finally, I hope to throw new light on the special qualities and contributions of the Carolingian period to the development of European Christendom in the Middle Ages. The Carolingian age witnessed a burst of creativity in many fields, not least of which was the development of Christian forms of worship and ritual. Much has been written on the reform of the church in Carolingian Francia and the attempts of the Frankish kings to conform to the ritual life of Rome. In part, this book is about the failure to achieve such conformity and its impossibility in regard to the ritual care of the dying and the dead.[33] Early medieval Christians needed a ritual response to death which conformed not to a model from the past but to the shape of their own social structures and of their own understanding of Christianity. This book shows some of the ways in which they satisfied that need.

Chapter 1 lays the background for what follows. It is concerned with the emergence of specifically Christian ritual responses to sickness, dying, and death in Mediterranean antiquity. After a short survey of the connections and disjunctions between Christian ritual behavior and that of Jews and pagans, I look at the evidence for a peculiarly Roman ritual attitude and response to sickness in the Christian community. Although in their original context these responses had nothing to do with death and dying, later associations between anointing the sick and the dying and the tension created by the confluence of Roman and non-Roman ritual approaches to the sick in the eighth and ninth centuries necessitate their presentation from the start. I then turn to rites in preparation for death, especially to forms of baptism and reconciliation resorted to in emergencies. The final section presents a hypothetical model of the earliest Latin ritual for death and burial. Like the prayers and rites for the sick, the oldest manuscript evidence for this Roman *ordo defunctorum* does not predate the eighth century, but its origins lie in the period between the fourth century and the sixth.

In Chapter 2 I look to the rituals of Latin Christian communities that formed from the merging of Romans and barbarians and the conversion of new peoples to Christianity between the sixth century and the middle of the eighth. I begin with Caesarius, bishop of Arles, in southeastern Gaul, in the first half of the sixth century, because his writings and his work on ecclesiastical discipline reveal much about the transition between antique traditions and those of the early Middle Ages, and because his legacy was variously received in later centuries in those areas most affected by it—Merovingian Gaul, Visigothic Spain, and Ireland. The rest of the chapter looks at the ritual remains of these three areas and presents their most distinctive productions: Gallican prayers for

---

33. For a comprehensive assessment of the state of Carolingian studies, see Richard E. Sullivan, "The Carolingian Age: Reflections on Its Place in the History of the Middle Ages," *Speculum* 64 (1989): 267–306.

the sick and for death and burial, a Visigothic rite for granting penance to the dying, Irish and Visigothic rites for the sick, and new forms of commemorating the dead.

Chapters 3 and 4 look closely at developments during the century or so of intense activity under the Frankish kings (roughly 750–850) known as the Carolingian reform. The greater detail and depth of analysis are themselves consequences of the reform, which touched every level of society but was aimed particularly at the education and organization of the clergy. As the resources of Carolingian society were marshaled toward the goal of raising the level of Christian learning among the clergy and people, the number of centers at which manuscripts were produced rose sharply. As a result, a correspondingly more precise picture of change and development emerges. But the extra precision is a function not just of the quantity of evidence but of the manner in which material was received, produced, and transmitted. Although guided by a desire for ritual unity, individual scribes and clerics were not bound by it, nor would they have been able to achieve it even if they had been so bound. The production of texts was directly dependent on the laborious copying of other texts and thus on what was available at a given time and place. And what was available was most often the remembered or written traditions of that place, supplemented by new materials brought in from other centers or temporarily on loan. Thus the ritual remains of this period throw a much brighter light on local developments than those of preceding centuries do. The common thrust of subtle changes in recorded rituals in different locales then becomes all the more significant. In Chapter 3 I contrast the rites for the sick, the dying, and the dead in two types of Frankish sacramentary, the first represented by the Vatican "Gelasian" sacramentary (Vatican MS Reg. Lat. 316), compiled shortly before the year 750, and the second by a group of sacramentaries created just before the year 800. The comparative analysis reveals a number of innovations and trends in ritual life characteristic of the early reform period. They are placed against the background of religious and social change that marked the coming to power of the Carolingian rulers and the reform and reorganization of the Christian church in their expanding realm. Chapter 4 focuses on the work of one man, Benedict of Aniane, whose ritual productions acted to stall the process of ritual development and draw it into new channels, but only temporarily. By the middle of the ninth century, Benedict's work was caught up in a larger process of change and subject to reworking and reinscription by later liturgists.

Chapter 5 reveals how, in a final burst of activity, Carolingian clerics synthesized the diverse materials inherited from the past into a coherent ritual structure extending from grave sickness through death and burial to the incorporation of the soul into the next world. The synthesis was achieved in both the literary and the active senses. The ritual books of the later ninth century, especially a remarkable and influential series of sacramentaries from the monastery of St-Amand in Picardy, blend essential elements of the antique Roman death ritual with others from Irish, Visigothic, and Gallican sources. This synthesis of word and act coincided with an extension of commemorative services beyond the exclusive domain of the clergy—rites of separation and transition developed apace with rites of incorporation. Thus, while the ritual synthesis around death and burial was the work of liturgists, it took place within a social context of increasing emphasis on collective participation in rites and prayers for the dead and dying. By the end of the ninth century they formed a unified complex whose essential features would persist throughout the Middle Ages and well beyond.

Because of the state of Latin during the period covered by this book and the state of the manuscripts that are its sources, the spelling and grammar of many of the texts are quite irregular. When translating, I have tried to be as faithful to the actual wording as possible, even if the result is English less graceful than it might otherwise be. When transcribing texts in the notes, I have tried to be exactly faithful to the source cited, whether an edition or a manuscript, presenting the text exactly as it stands. I signal an irregularity with *sic* only when it is a particularly glaring error in Latin usage. Except where I have noted otherwise, references to the Bible are to the Latin Vulgate form.

Philippe Ariès was the first scholar to demonstrate the historical unity in the period from the beginning of the fifth to the end of the eighteenth centuries in Europe when that period is viewed from the perspective of the relations between the living and the dead. During those long centuries, the living and the dead coexisted in close proximity, and in many ways death was seen as a natural part of life, accepted and understood. Ariès's most powerful example of this relationship was the repositioning of the cemetery vis-à-vis the abodes of the living. In ancient Mediterranean cultures the dead were not allowed within the precincts of the living; only with the triumph of Christianity and the desire for burial near the bodies of the saints did the ancient divisions dissolve and the living come to cohabit the same space as the dead.[34] Peter Brown has shown in a characteristically suggestive manner the deep social significance of this joining of two worlds and its precise underpinnings in the relations of power and dependence which dominated late Roman society. He has also noted, however, that the peculiar form thus taken by late antique Christianity prevented it from reaching out to the whole of society. "A universal and exclusive religion, Christianity claimed to have spread to every region of the known world. In fact, having spread, it lay around the shrines of the saints like pools of water on a drying surface."[35] The joining of heaven and earth at the graves of the saints was not the end but the beginning of a process of "socializing" death and the dead in Latin Christianity.[36] The rituals that are the subject of this book saw that process through. The living and the dead could not become one Christian society without a means of safe passage from the one group to the other. For medieval Europeans, the complex of rituals that took definitive shape in late ninth-century Francia was the means to that end.

34. Philippe Ariès, *The Hour of Our Death*, trans. Helen Weaver (New York, 1981), 29–42; and see below, chap. 1.

35. Peter Brown, *The Cult of the Saints: Its Rise and Function in Latin Christianity* (Chicago, 1981), 124.

36. The other end of this historical process—the "dechristianization" or "desocialization" of death in eighteenth- and nineteenth-century Europe—has been much discussed by Michel Vovelle, *Piété baroque et déchristianisation en Provence au xviiie siècle: Les attitudes devant la mort d'après les clauses des testaments* (Paris, 1973); John McManners, "Death and the French Historians," in *Mirrors of Mortality: Studies in the Social History of Death*, ed. Joachim Whaley (London, 1981), 124–26; and Otto Gerhard Oexle, "Die Gegenwart der Toten," in *Death in the Middle Ages*, ed. Herman Braet and Werner Verbecke (Leuven, 1983), 72.

CHAPTER ONE

The Mediterranean Background
to the Sixth Century

Jews, Pagans, and Christians

Christian ritual practices and attitudes toward death, dying, and the dead did not emerge simply by a process of differentiation from a static background of Jewish and pagan custom. Neither Judaism nor paganism was a monolithic, unchanging system; each was a part of and contributor to large processes of religious change in the Mediterranean world of antiquity as a whole.[1] The most well-understood area of change—the complex of beliefs about the state of the soul in the afterlife—reveals a layering of old and new conceptions. The Jews' experience of exile in the sixth century B.C. and the struggle against Greek cultural and political hegemony in the second century led to the erosion of the ancient conception of a shadowy afterlife in She'ol and the first expressions of expectations of a personal judgment and the resurrection of the just at the end of the time.[2] But even in the first century A.D. Jews had reached no consensus on such issues. The Pharisees, for exam-

---

1. On the place of Christianity within the religious climate of Mediterranean antiquity, see Luther H. Martin, *Hellenistic Religions: An Introduction* (New York/Oxford, 1987), esp. 90–133; and Robin Lane Fox, *Pagans and Christians* (San Francisco, 1986).

2. S. G. F. Brandon, *The Judgment of the Dead: The Idea of Life after Death in the Major Religions* (New York, 1967), 56–75; Joanne E. McWilliam Dewart, *Death and Resurrection* (Wilmington, Del., 1986), 15–27.

ple, had accepted the idea of an individual afterlife and the resurrection of the just as doctrine, but the Sadducees had not, and apocalyptic writing kept alive images of She'ol, often mixed with Greek or Egyptian ideas. The spread of Greek philosophical and scientific ideas during the same period led some pagans to such a profound skepticism that they saw death as simple termination, best summed up in the sepulchral inscription "I was not, I was, I am not, I don't care" (non fui, fui, non sum, non curo).[3] The popularity of mystery religions and such quasi-philosophical systems as Neo-Pythagoreanism fostered in others the hope of personal immortality and replaced the old images of insubstantial shades wandering in Hades with souls ascending to a blessed afterlife in the heavens.[4] The growing interest in the fate of the soul in the afterlife among both Jews and pagans accompanied a shift away from fear of the dead to fear for their welfare in the afterlife.[5] Yet the coexistence of new and old attitudes and beliefs ensured that funeral rituals could work to both ends—protecting the living from the wrath of the dead and the dead from demons that might hinder their ascent to the upper regions. In such circumstances, people could interpret new ideas within both old and new cultural frameworks. Robin Lane Fox has pointed out how this mechanism might operate among initiates to mystery religions. "In mystery cults, initiations offered reassurance, whatever the fate of the soul after death. If it ascended to the heavens, initiation helped ensure its safe passage through the opposing powers. . . . If it went down into a literal underworld, initiation spared the dead the chillier terrors and the gloomier halls of residence."[6] In matters of burial practice, there is the still puzzling shift away from cremation as a form of disposal of bodily remains which is everywhere evident in the Ro-

3. *Inscriptiones latinae selectae,* ed. Hermann Dessau (Berlin, 1892–1916; repr. 1954–55), nos. 8162–64; cf. nos. 8165–66. This sentiment was so common on gravestones that it was sometimes reduced to "nf f ns nc." See also J. M. C. Toynbee, *Death and Burial in the Roman World* (Ithaca, N.Y., 1971), 34; and Keith Hopkins, *Death and Renewal* (Cambridge, Eng., 1983), 230.

4. Franz Cumont, *After Life in Roman Paganism* (New Haven, Conn., 1922). See also Toynbee, *Death and Burial,* 33–42; Hopkins, *Death and Renewal,* 226–32.

5. Joseph Ntedika, *L'évocation de l'au-delà dans la prière pour les morts* (Louvain/Paris, 1971), 15–21 (Jews); Johannes Quasten, *Music and Worship in Pagan and Christian Antiquity,* trans. Boniface Ramsey (Washington, D.C., 1983), 158–60 (pagans).

6. Lane Fox, *Pagans and Christians,* 97. In general, however, Lane Fox wishes to put the emphasis on the motivating power of fear of the dead in pagan cult practices during the whole of antiquity (98).

man world from the second century A.D.[7] In the same period, rabbis effected a turn away from ostentatious funerals out of deference to poor Jews who could not afford them.[8] Such changes reveal the historical dynamic of attitude and belief in living societies, especially those that participated in a multicultural system such as the Roman Empire, which fostered cultural mixing and the transmission of ideas among its many communities.

Christianity emerged and developed as part of this multicultural system. Although the Christian attitude toward death was in some ways a radical break with the past, the Christian communities of antiquity did not immediately develop distinctive ritual practices around the care of the dying and the dead, but continued in the ways of their Jewish or pagan ancestors. The New Testament accounts record the persistence of Jewish patterns of burial and treatment of the corpse in Palestine.[9] After death, the body was washed and anointed and wrapped in linen cloth, sometimes along with aromatic herbs. Because bodies decomposed rapidly in Palestine's hot climate, burial followed quickly, most often in a rock-hewn grave.[10] Jewish ritual mourning followed a precise schedule: "three 'days of weeping'; a period up to the seventh day, with abstention from work and any personal care and adornment; and finally a period of slightly mitigated formal mourning down to the thirtieth day."[11] The initial three-day period of mourning had its roots in a popular Near Eastern belief that the soul lingered near the corpse for three days after death, hoping to reenter the body. Only when the soul observed the face of the corpse begin to change in the process of decay did it give up hope and go on its way.[12] This belief may explain Jesus' rather odd delay in going to Bethany after hearing of the illness that would lead to the death of his friend Lazarus (John 11:6). When Jesus finally did stand before the tomb of Lazarus and ask that the stone be rolled away from the cave where

---

7. A. D. Nock, "Cremation and Burial in the Roman Empire," *Harvard Theological Review* 25 (1932): 321–59, repr. in idem, *Essays on Religion in the Ancient World*, ed. Z. Stewart, 2 vols. (Cambridge, Mass., 1972), 1.277–307. See also Toynbee, *Death and Burial*, 39–42.

8. Geoffrey Rowell, *The Liturgy of Christian Burial* (London, 1977), 5.

9. Ibid., 3–8.

10. On eastern rock tombs in Roman imperial times, see Toynbee, *Death and Burial*, 188–99.

11. Rowell, *Liturgy of Christian Burial*, 4.

12. Emil Freistedt, *Altchristliche Totengedächtnistage und ihre Beziehung zum Jenseitsglauben und Totenkultus der Antike*, LQF 24 (Münster, 1928), 53–72.

the body lay, the dead man's sister Martha protested, "Lord, by now he stinks, for it is the fourth day" (John 11:39). The power of Jesus' act in raising Lazarus from the dead on the fourth day had the greater effect on the Jews who witnessed it for their belief that the soul of the dead man would have deserted its body by that time.[13]

There is no record of the prayers that might have been spoken at a Jewish or early Christian burial ceremony. The ancient Jewish traditions of prayer were transmitted orally, so no records survive of the words that accompanied the ritual action surrounding death and burial in the period when Christianity emerged. Nonetheless, later sources suggest that they were constructed around "a basic pattern of strongly biblical prayer" emphasizing the righteousness of God and, in some circles, expressing the hope that God would raise up the just again at the end of time.[14] These sentiments are expressed in the oldest extant Christian prayer over a corpse, from the prayerbook of Bishop Serapion of Thmuis (mid-fourth century):

> God, you who have the power of life and death, God of the spirits and lord of all flesh, God, you who kill and make alive, you who lead down to the gate of Hades and lead back up, you who create the spirit of man within and receive and refresh the souls of the saints, you who change and transform and transfigure your creatures, as is right and proper, being yourself alone incorruptible, unalterable, and eternal, we beseech you for the repose and rest of this your servant or this your handmaiden: refresh her soul and spirit in green pastures, in chambers of rest with Abraham and Isaac and Jacob and all your saints; and raise up the body in the day which you have ordained, in accordance with your trustworthy promises, that you may render to it also its fitting inheritances in your holy pastures. Remember not her transgressions and sins; cause her going forth to be prepared and blessed; heal the griefs of her relatives with the spirit of consolation; and grant unto us all a good end through your only-begotten Jesus Christ, through whom to you are glory and strength in the Holy Spirit for ever and ever, Amen.[15]

---

13. Ibid., 61. It should be noted also that the raising of Lazarus appears only in the Gospel of John, where it is represented as the cause of the decision by the Jewish authorities to see to Jesus' death (John 11:45–53).

14. Rowell, *Liturgy of Christian Burial*, 6–8.

15. *Sacramentum Serapionis*, XXX, in *Didascalia et Constitutiones Apostolorum*, ed. Franz X. Funk, 2 vols. (Paderborn, 1905), 2.193–94: "Deus, qui vitae et mortis potestatem habes, Deus spirituum et dominus omnis carnis, Deus, qui mortificas et vivificas, qui deducis ad portas inferorum et reducis, qui creas spiritum hominis in ipso et suscipis sanctorum animas ac recreas, qui mutas ac transformas et transfiguras creaturas tuas, prout iustum et utile est, cum ipse solus incorrup-

The addition of a Christian ending does not obscure the Jewish origin and character of this prayer.[16]

A considerable amount is known about the rituals around death and dying among pagan Romans under the early empire. These people made no ritual preparations for death, but a close relative might try to catch the last breath of the dying or give a final kiss as a sign of affection. After death, the eyes and mouth were closed and those present loudly called out the name of the dead person as a precaution against the false appearance of death. This *conclamatio mortis* was repeated throughout the ceremonies. Then the corpse was washed, anointed, and laid out, usually in a white toga but often in rich garments of linen, clothing befitting its rank in life, or with a funeral crown. The funeral itself could be an occasion for much exuberant lamentation and ritual display of grief as well as a public display of the social status of the dead person and his or her family. Female relatives or hired mourners wailed and lacerated their cheeks, and the procession was accompanied by trumpets and flutes. If the dead person were a man of high status, the procession might include the slaves freed by his last testament and actors wearing masks representing his ancestors. The corpse was cremated, but the rites ended only with the interment of a small portion of the body (the *os resectum*), removed before the rest was burned. At the grave site the mourners bade a final farewell; if the dead person had been a public figure, someone gave a formal funeral oration.[17]

Roman pagans held elaborate commemorative services for their dead. The first of many meals served in honor of the dead was eaten at the grave on the day of the funeral. Others were eaten on the ninth and fortieth days, on the anniversary of the dead person's birth, and during the festivals of the dead, especially the Parentalia

---

tibilis et immutabilis et aeternus sis; oramus te pro dormitione et requie huius servi tui vel huius servae tuae: animam et spiritum eius recrea in locis pascuae, in cubilibus recreationis cum Abraham et Isaac et Iacob et omnibus sanctis tuis; corpus vero resuscita in die, quam definisti secundum promissiones tuas haud dubias, ut et hereditates ei convenientes retribuas in sanctis tuis pascuis. Delictorum eius ac peccatorum ne memineris; exitum eius fac paratum et benedictum esse; tristitias superstitum spiritu consolationis sana et nobis omnibus finem bonum dona per unigenitum tuum Iesum Christum, per quem tibi gloria et imperium in sancto spiritu in saecula saeculorum, amen."

16. Rowell, *Liturgy of Christian Burial*, 21.

17. Toynbee, *Death and Burial*, 43–61; A. C. Rush, *Death and Burial in Christian Antiquity* (Washington, D.C., 1941; repr. 1977). See also Hopkins, *Death and Renewal*, 12–14, 217–21 (on death and social status), 201, 255–56 (on masks).

(February 13–21).[18] The centrality of eating in these commemorative acts links them with similar rites of incorporation observed in many societies around the world, for eating symbolizes the reestablishment of the integrity of the family in the wake of the death of one of its members as well as the incorporation of the dead into their new home in the tomb or into the society of the other world.[19] The timing of the commemorative feasts may have derived from ancient understandings of conception and prenatal development, so that the period after death was inversely related to the maturing of the embryo in the womb.[20] The essential function of the feasts, however, was to mark the transition of the dead person from the society of the living to the society of the dead and to organize the process of grief and mourning among the survivors.

Above all else, what distinguished an early Christian funeral from a contemporary Jewish or pagan ceremony was the presence among the mourners of a new sense of the meaning of death and of the place of the dead vis-à-vis the community of the living. New Testament writings betray much uncertainty about the nature of the resurrection of persons baptized in the name of Christ, but they are unanimous on one point: Jesus rose from the dead not at the end of time but in time, and by his resurrection death had been overcome and the access to paradise lost through Adam's sin regained.[21] In the immediate aftermath of that event, there was little interest in the death of "Christians," for it was expected that Jesus would return before the present generation had passed away. As the second coming began to fade into an unknown future, however, attention began to focus on the resurrection of the dead and their care in the indefinite interim that would precede it. It was then that Christians began to distance themselves from pagan and Jewish ritual practices that conflicted with their new conception of death. This process took centuries, of course, and there must always have been a gap between the ideal behavior expressed by learned clerics and that of many ordinary Christians. Indeed, more

18. Toynbee, *Death and Burial*, 50–52, 61–64; Hopkins, *Death and Renewal*, 233–35.

19. Van Gennep, *Rites of Passage*, 20–24, 164–65. Quasten points out that the mystery religions "portrayed the life of the blessed as a continual banquet": *Music and Worship*, 156. The rites were no doubt also sometimes regarded as a means of placating the spirits of the dead; see Quasten, *Music and Worship*, 157–60, and Hopkins, *Death and Renewal*, 234.

20. Freistedt, *Altchristliche Totengedächtnistage*, 172–97; Rowell, *Liturgy of Christian Burial*, 12.

21. McWilliam Dewart, *Death and Resurrection*, 25–35.

often than not our evidence for the ideal is directly dependent on the failure to live up to it, for most surviving texts were generated in order to correct abuses and bring behavior into line with doctrine. As time passed, however, ideal and practice usually met in a process of mutual adaptation. For example, while some Christians opposed the use of torches at funerals as a pagan encroachment on the peace of the dead, the festive associations of torches eventually ensured them a place within Christian ceremony.[22]

For devout Christians, death was the door to salvation, and the bodies of the dead represented souls that had passed through it. Unlike Jews and pagans both, for whom contact with corpses brought about a state of ritual pollution, Christians regarded the bodies of their dead as sacred and holy, and were urged to handle them freely and without fear.[23] Not that Christians honored the ordinary dead. They opposed the pagan practice of placing a crown on the dead as idolatry, and reserved all honors to those saints who had won the crown of martyrdom.[24] The glorious deaths of the martyrs ensured the present residence of their souls in paradise, and their graves became the focal points for the community of the dead.[25] At the beginning of the third century, some Christian communities had their own cemeteries, usually organized around the tomb of a martyred saint. After the peace of the church, graves began to cluster around the tombs of the saints as Christians sought burial *ad sanctos*.[26] This behavior could express contradictory impulses, denoting sometimes a sense that ordinary people shared in the glory attained by the martyrs and sometimes the need for intercession and advocacy.[27] In any case, between the

22. Rush, *Death and Burial*, 224–28.
23. *Didascalia et Constitutiones Apostolorum*, ed. Funk, 1.376, Const. Apost. 6.22 (28)5: "Unde ergo eos, qui requiescunt, sine observatione tangentes nolite abominari, et quod in consuetudinibus est, id nolite segregare." On the separation of the dead from the living, see Rush, *Death and Burial*, 17, 103 (Israel); Brown, *Cult of the Saints*, 6–8 (Rome).
24. Rush, *Death and Burial*, 137–49.
25. Victor Saxer, *Morts martyrs reliques en Afrique chrétienne aux premiers siècles: Les témoignages de Tertullian, Cyprien et Augustin à la lumière de l'archéologie africaine*, Théologie historique 55 (Paris, 1980); Brown, *Cult of the Saints*.
26. J. Stevenson, *The Catacombs: Rediscovered Monuments of Early Christianity* (London, 1978), 7–44; Ariès, *Hour of Our Death*, 29–42; and the works cited in n. 25 above.
27. Février, "Mort chrétienne," 918–23, 931–32; and see also idem, "Vie et mort dans le 'Epigrammata Damasiana,'" in *Saeculum Damasiana*, 89–111, Studi de antichità cristiana 39 (Vatican City, 1986); and "La mort chrétienne: Images et vécu collectif," in *Histoire vécue du peuple chrétien*, ed. Jean Delumeau, 2 vols. (Toulouse, 1979), 1.75–104.

fourth and the sixth centuries, the creation of holy sites dedicated to the martyrs completely transformed the urban topography of the western Mediterranean and became the focus of a new sense of community, radiating out from the "very special dead" to include the whole Christian populace, especially those most often excluded from ritual care, the powerless and the poor.[28]

This new sense of community can best be seen in Christian commemorative rituals. As we have seen, Jewish and pagan commemorations of the dead were closely connected with the mourning process and tended to concentrate around certain sequences of days: the third, ninth, thirtieth, and fortieth days and the birthday of the deceased or the anniversary of his or her death. The various Christian communities of antiquity followed their own sequences of commemorative services, but all reinterpreted their meanings in Christian or at least biblical terms.[29] In the Latin West, Augustine argued against commemoration on the ninth day because of associations with Roman pagan custom.[30] Likewise, birthday celebrations were replaced by commemorations of the anniversary of a death, which was seen as a new *dies natalis*, a birth into eternal life.[31] But the greatest change had to do with the manner of celebration. As late as the end of the fourth century, Christians still regularly attended pagan commemorative celebrations. The Syriac *Apostolic Constitutions* (ca. 380), for example, warned Christians not to overindulge at such events, but did not proscribe then.[32] Under such circumstances, it is no wonder that Christians continued to celebrate with food and drink, song and dance, during commemorations for Christian dead, especially for martyrs and saints. In the West, Augustine tried to alter such behavior. His strategy was to raise the issue whether the dead could really be aided by the living and to redirect the outlay of food and drink away from the grave site toward the living poor. In his tract on care of the dead, he argued that the acts of the living are more for their own benefit than for the good of the dead, and in a letter to Bishop Aurelius of Carthage he suggested that "if anyone for the sake of

28. Brown, *Cult of the Saints*, 23–49. On the treatment of the dead poor in imperial Rome, see Hopkins, *Death and Renewal*, 207–11.

29. Rowell, *Liturgy of Christian Burial*, 12–13; Freistedt, *Altchristliche Totengedächtnistage*, 1–52.

30. Freistedt, *Altchristliche Totengedächtnistage*, 146.

31. Rush, *Death and Burial*, 72–87.

32. *Didascalia et Constitutiones Apostolorum*, ed. Funk, 1.555, 8.44: "in mortuorum vera memoriis invitati, cum moderatione ac Dei metu epulamini."

religion should wish to offer something of money, let it be paid out directly to the poor."[33] Thus he expressly linked care for the dead with care for the living poor, bringing together, in a sense, two "invisible" ends of the community and transforming a private, familial matter into a public, communal one.[34]

Over time Christian innovations in modes of commemoration were matched by new rituals for the sick, around the deathbed, and for burial. Once embedded in the liturgical and canonical writings of the church, such rituals encoded the new sense of community and of the meaning of death which emerged in Christian antiquity and provided a means for their transmission to other communities at other times.

The Ritual Care of the Sick

The Christian communities of Roman antiquity developed two basic responses to the presence of sickness among their members: prayer for their recovery, in the context of either a mass or a visit to the sickbed; and, in accordance with certain scriptural texts, the performance of rituals of healing, through either the laying on of hands or anointing with oil, of course always accompanied by prayer. Both of these ritual gestures are attested in the Gospels and in the Acts of the Apostles, and James explicitly recommended anointing with oil (James 5:14–15): "Is any among you sick? Let him call for the elders of the church, and let them pray over him, anointing him with oil in the name of the Lord; and the prayer of faith will save the sick man; and the Lord will raise him up; and if he has committed sins, he will be forgiven."[35]

The recommendation of oil for use in a healing ritual is not fortuitous. Oil had a long tradition of medical and ritual uses in Mediterranean antiquity and became central to a variety of Chris-

33. Augustine, *De cura pro mortuis gerenda,* ed. Joseph Zycha, CSEL 41 (Vienna, 1900), 623; and *Epistulae,* ed. A. Goldbacher, CSEL 34 (Vienna, 1895), 1.59 letter 22.6: "sed si quis pro religione aliquid pecuniae offerre uoluerit, in praesenti pauperibus eroget."

34. See Oexle, "Die Gegenwart der Toten," in *Death in the Middle Ages,* ed. Braet and Verbeke, 48–57.

35. See H. Frankenmölle, "Krankensalbung im Neuen Testament," in *Heilssorge für die Kranken und Hilfen zur Erneuerung eines missverstandenen Sakraments,* ed. Manfred Probst and Klemens Richter (Freiburg, 1975), 28–38; the text from the epistle of St. James is quoted according to the Revised Standard Version of the Bible (New York, 1946).

tian rites, above all baptism.[36] The connection that James made
between sickness and sinfulness is no more fortuitous. The religious communities of the Near East had long believed in a causal
connection between sinfulness and sickness. Sin was equated with
ritual impurity, and oil (as well as water) was a purifying agent.[37]
Thus bodily health would naturally follow upon ritual purification. Jesus criticized such attitudes, but his healing miracles often
included forgiveness of sins along with restoration of health, and in
one instance he is said to have told a man whom he had cured not
to sin again or something even worse might happen to him.[38] This
double nature of Jesus' treatment of the sick formed an unstable
core for later ritual attitudes as they developed within various
Christian communities over time.[39] Some ritual traditions tended
to emphasize the forgiveness of sins, others the cure of the body,
still others both. At times, the old attitude that sickness was the
result of sin reappeared, especially in cases of madness, or demonic
possession, as it was usually considered.[40] At other times the purificatory aspect of ritual anointing was understood primarily as a
complement to the forgiveness of sin—an aid to spiritual rather
than physical healing. Ultimately, this last attitude was to account
for the incorporation of anointing in rites of preparation for death,
but for the Roman church of the early centuries of the Christian
era the ritual care of the sick was centered on the restoration of
physical health and the return of the sick to the living community
in this world.

Although the evidence of actual practice in the early church
regarding the care of the sick is limited, enough survives to suggest
that the basic approach was in general pragmatic and that specific
rites emerged only slowly. To the extent that Christian ritual re-

36. On the myriad medical uses of oil in antiquity, see A. Pauly, G. Wissowa, and
W. Kroll, *Real-Enzyklopädie der klassischen Altertumswissenschaft*, 17 (Stuttgart,
1937), 2.2013–14, s.v. "Ölbaum, medezinische Verwendung"; on the liturgical use
of oil in the Christian traditions, see Philipp Hofmeister, *Die heiligen Öle in der
morgen- und abendländischen Kirche*, "Östliche Christentum, n.s. 6/7 (Würzburg,
1948).

37. Frankenmölle, "Krankensalbung"; Gerhard Fichtner, "Christus als Arzt:
Ursprunge und Wirkungen eines Motivs," FS 16 (1982): 3–5; Annette Niederhellmann, *Arzt und Heilkunde in den frühmittelalterlichen Leges* (Berlin/New York,
1983), 41–42.

38. John 5:14; see Niederhellmann, *Arzt und Heilkunde*, 47–48, though Niederhellmann accepts uncritically the notion that sickness was generally equated with
sin in late antiquity.

39. A.-G. Martimort, "Prières pour les malades et onction sacramentelle," in
L'église en prière, ed. Martimort, new ed. (Paris, 1984), 3.133.

40. Niederhellmann, *Arzt und Heilkunde*, 47–50.

sponses to sickness did develop, they did so less in opposition to the practice of Greco-Roman medicine than as a specifically religious adjunct to it.[41] Care for the sick was delegated to deacons and deaconesses, and by the third century bishops were setting up hospitals.[42] Polycarpus of Smyrna, writing in the third century, urged bishops and priests to visit the sick, and Augustine in his time made such visits a regular practice of his episcopal ministry.[43] The oldest liturgical evidence concerns the act of blessing oil for anointing the sick. The *Apostolic Tradition* of Hippolytus, written at the beginning of the third century and extant in Latin in a fifth-century copy, preserves a prayer for that purpose. It asks God to grant comfort to all who taste the oil and health to all who use it.[44] From the late fourth century, the *Apostolic Constitutions* record a benediction of water and oil asking God to confer on them the power of "producing health, chasing out sickness, putting demons to flight, and overcoming all snares."[45] Although such formulas imply an organized rite for blessing the oil, its actual use was a more casual affair, even in the fifth century. Pope Innocent I, writing in 416 in reference to the text from the letter of James, remarked that the oil blessed by the bishop for the anointing of the sick could be used not only by priests but by all Christians when they were oppressed by sickness.[46]

Antoine Chavasse's analysis of the texts preserved in the earliest surviving liturgical books led him to conclude that a formula for blessing the oil for the sick in the Roman sacramentaries could be

41. Stephen d'Irsay, "Patristic Medicine," *Annals of Medical History* 9 (1927): 364–78; idem, "Christian Medicine and Science in the Third Century," *Journal of Religion* 10 (1930): 515–44.

42. Martimort, "Prières pour les malades," 138; Alfred Stuiber, "Der Tod des Aurelius Augustinus," in *Jenseitsvorstellungen in Antike und Christentum*, Jahrbuch für Antike und Christentum, Ergänzungsband 9 (Münster, 1982), 5.

43. Fichtner, "Christus als Arzt," 6.

44. *La Tradition Apostolique de Saint Hippolyte*, ed. Bernard Botte, LQF 39 (Münster, 1963), 18: "Ut oleum hoc . . . omnibus gustantibus confortationem et sanitatem utentibus illud praebeat"; cf. Chavasse, *Etude*, 29–39.

45. Martimort, "Prières pour les malades," 135; *Didascalia et Constitutiones Apostolorum*, ed. Funk, 1.533, Const. Apost. 8.29: "Domine . . . per Christum sanctifica hanc aquam atque hoc oleum . . . et da vim effectricem sanitatis, morborum expultricem, daemonum fugatricem, omnium insidiarum profligatricem." Cf. the similar blessing in *Sacramentum Serapionis*, 2.179–81.

46. R. Cabié, *La lettre du Pape Innocent Ier à Décentius de Gubbio*, Bibliothèque de la Revue d'Histoire Ecclésiastique 58 (Louvain, 1973), 30: "Quod non est dubium de fidelibus aegrotantibus accipi vel intelligi debere qui sancto oleo chrismatis perungui possunt quod ab episcopo confectum non solum sacerdotibus sed et omnibus uti christianis licet, in sua aut in suorum necessitate unguendum." Cf. ibid., 56–61, and Chavasse, *Etude*, 89–99.

traced back to the fourth century.[47] In its early form, that formula indicated that the oil was ingested as well as applied, and that it was understood exclusively as a means to physical health. According to Chavasse's reconstruction, the Roman blessing of the oil for the sick asked God to send the Holy Spirit from heaven into the oil to make of it a *tutamentum corporis*—that is, a guardian, defender, protector of the body.

> Lord, send down from heaven the Holy Spirit your Paraclete into this olive oil, which you have seen fit to produce from living wood for the restoration of the body, so that through your holy benediction it may be a defender of the body to all using it as an ointment, drinking, or touching it, for the ridding of all pains, all weaknesses, and every sickness of the body; your perfect chrism, Lord, blessed by you, from which you anointed prophets, priests, kings and martyrs, remaining in our inmost parts.[48]

The other remains of the ancient Roman liturgy concerning the ritual treatment of the sick reveal the same attention to the restoration of physical health. The prayers in the mass for the sick in the Vatican "Gelasian" sacramentary may derive from an early Roman sacramentary of the sixth century, and are probably somewhat older.[49] The mass in the Vatican Gelasian could be said in the name of more than one person (*illis*) and for people of both sexes (*famulorum et famularumque*).[50] The prayers of this mass call

47. Chavasse, *Etude*, 40–51, esp. 41; Martimort, "Prières pour les malades," 136.

48. Chavasse, *Etude*, 42–43: "Emitte Domine spiritum sanctum tuum paraclitum de coelis in hanc pinguidinem olivae, quam de viridi ligno producere dignatus es ad refectionem corporis ut tua sancta benedictio sit omni ungenti, gustanti, tangenti, tutamentum corporis ad evacuandos omnes dolores, omnesque infirmitates, omnem aegritudinem corporis, unde unxisti sacerdotes, reges, prophetas, et martyres, chrisma tuum perfectum Domine a te benedictum permanens in visceribus nostris." According to Chavasse (45–46), in the Gelasian and Gregorian sacramentaries the words *mentis et* appear as a later interpolation not present in the original text, and in the Gregorian the word *gustanti* has disappeared; cf. Gelasian, no. 382, and Gregorian, no. 334.

49. Gelasian, nos. 1539–42; see Chavasse, *Sacramentaire gélasien*, 460–61, where he attributes these prayers, among others, to a hypothetical "pre-Gelasian" Roman sacramentary. Although there has been no general agreement that such a book existed, the argument for the antiquity of the formulas under discussion is corroborated by the other evidence presented here. On this and related matters, see Vogel, *Medieval Liturgy*, 64–70; Deshusses, "Sacramentaires," 26–28; and below, chap. 3. To distinguish this sacramentary from others called "Gelasian," I refer to it as the Vatican Gelasian, from its sole manuscript witness (Vatican MS Reg. lat. 316).

50. Chavasse (*Sacramentaire gélasien*, 461) argued that this indicates the presence of some sort of hospital served by a priest: "Une telle situation exclut une maison particulière et fait penser à une hospice, groupent des malades des deux

upon God's mercy and aid to heal the sick so that they may reenter the community of the faithful in this world: "All-powerful and eternal God, everlasting health of believers, hear us, for these your servants, for whom we implore the aid of your mercy, so that, restored to themselves in health, they may give thanks to you in your church."[51] And again: "Omnipotent eternal God, who can remove the sicknesses of souls and bodies, reveal the virtue of your succor upon our sick, so that through the aid of your mercy they may be restored to all the duties of your devotion."[52] The prayers of the congregation express the desire to see their sick brothers and sisters restored to the living community, where they can participate in the worship of God. This same attitude is expressed in the prayer for the return of health which follows the mass prayers in the Gelasian: "Lord . . . with your right hand may you raise up this your servant freed from sickness and granted health; in virtue strengthen [him], with power guard [him], and restore [him] to your church and your holy altars, with all desired health."[53]

An early eighth-century North Italian book known as the Bobbio Missal preserves a mass for the sick based on the same old Roman source as the mass in the Vatican Gelasian.[54] Like all the masses in the Bobbio Missal, this one is preceded by accompanying readings. The first is the text from the Epistle of James which was always the basis for the ritual anointing of the sick (James 5:13–16). The second is Luke 4:38–40, which records an incident in which Jesus cured Peter's mother-in-law of a fever. Significantly, this Gospel

---

sexes et bénéficiant du ministre d'une église particulière, à laquelle il est rattaché." Although that may have been the case, there seem to be no real grounds for such a conclusion. A simpler explanation is that the prayers and the mass express the congregation's concern for its sick members (*infirmos nostros*).

51. Gelasian, no. 1539: "Omnipotens sempiternae deus, salus aeternae credentium, exaudi nos pro famulis tuis *illis* pro quibus misericordiae tuae inploramus auxilio, ut reddita sibi sanitate gratiarum tibi in aecclesia tua referant actionem."

52. Gelasian, no. 1540: "Omnipotens sempiterne deus, qui egritudinis et animorum depellis et corporum, auxilii tui super infirmos nostros ostende uirtutem, ut ope misericordiae tuae ad omnia pietatis tuae reparentur officia." This language is repeated in the "secret" and the "postcommunion" prayers of the mass, nos. 1541–42.

53. Gelasian, no. 1543: "Domine . . . hunc famulum tuum liberatam egritudinem et sanitate donatam dextera tua erigas, uirtute confirmes, potestate tuearis, ecclesiae tuae sanctisquae altaribus tuis cum omni desiderata prosperitate restituas."

54. Bobbio, nos. 377–83. On the Bobbio Missal, see J. F. Kenney, *Sources for the Early History of Ireland*, vol. 1, *Ecclesiastical* (New York, 1929), 691–92; and CLLA 220. On the Roman source for their mass, see Chavasse, *Sacramentaire gélasien*, 676–77.

text does not mention anointing or the forgiveness of sins; it ends abruptly in the midst of describing the many cures that Jesus later performed through the laying on of his hands (*manus imponens*), a characteristic of the ritual care of the sick in the North Italian (Ambrosian) liturgy.[55] The prayers in the Bobbio mass, the first two of which appear as well in a group of four prayers "over a sick person in the home" in the Vatican Gelasian, continue the emphasis on physical healing.[56] They beg God to restore the patient to "the perfect grace of his former health" so that "having been put to flight by illnesses and recalled to men, he may immediately in renewed health bless your holy name."[57] The rest of the mass continues in the same vein. The prayer after the reading of the names is a construct from two of the mass prayers in the Vatican Gelasian, and the "Preface" (here *Contestatio*), the only clearly non-Roman prayer in the mass, reiterates the message of the second reading: "May you visit him in your heavenly visitation, just as you saw fit to visit the mother-in-law of Peter."[58]

Thus the late antique Roman church did not dwell on the relation between sin and sickness, but sought the cure of its sick members through visitation, communal prayer, and the distribution and use of sanctified oil. While the benediction of the oil was a liturgical act, its application was not, and its use was regarded as a means to the restoration of physical health and the return of the sick to an active life in the church.

Rituals for the Dying

Communion as Viaticum

The central act of preparation for death in the Roman church of antiquity was the reception of the Eucharist under one or both

55. Achille M. Triacca, "Le rite de l'"impositio manuum super infirmum' dans l'ancienne liturgie ambrosienne," in *La maladie et la mort du chrétien* (Rome, 1975), 339–60.

56. Bobbio, nos. 379–80 = Gelasian, nos. 1538, 1537, although the Latin of the Bobbio prayers is deficient. The visitation ritual and two prayers in the Vatican Gelasian not shared with the Bobbio Missal are discussed in chap. 3.

57. Bobbio, no. 379, with variants in the Gelasian in brackets: "gracia in eum [gratia in eo] pristine sanitatis perfecta reparitur [reparetur]"; and no. 380: "ut fugatis infirmitatibus et uiribus reparatis nomine sancto tuo instaurato [reuocatis nomen sanctum tuum instaurata], protinus sanitate benedicas [benedicat]."

58. Bobbio, no. 383: "uisites eum uisitacione tua celeste sicut uisitare dignatus est socrum petri." On the *post nomina* prayer, see Chavasse, *Sacramentaire gélasien*, 677.

forms as a "viaticum"—that is, a provision for the journey to the other world.[59] A person would receive the body and blood of Christ while on his or her deathbed, as close to death as possible. The earliest textual reference to the practice is the death scene in Paulinus's life of St. Ambrose, but there is no question that it was a long-established custom by that time.[60] Among Roman pagans the Latin term *viaticum*, related to the Greek *epodion*, had referred to the practice of placing a coin in the mouth of the dead as payment to Charon, who ferried shades over the river Styx to the underworld. The Christian understanding of the viaticum of course differed from the pagan conception out of which it grew. The Eucharist received at death was a sign of the full membership of the recipient in the community of Christians and of the saving grace first received in baptism. Nevertheless, the importance of its reception must be related to the comfort derived from a ritual action that maintained a connection with the practices of generations of men and women in antiquity. It is in this light that we can understand the tendency to administer it even to corpses, a practice first condemned in 393 at a North African council and as late as the end of the sixth century at a council in Auxerre.[61]

The general practice of giving the Eucharist to the dying did create difficulties, however, for in order to receive it one had to be a full member of the Christian community. Thus in some instances

59. Rush, *Death and Burial*, 92–99; idem, "The Eucharist: The Sacrament of the Dying in Christian Antiquity," *Jurist* 34 (1974): 10–35; Peter Browe, "Die Sterbekommunion im Altertum and Mittelalter," *Zeitschrift für Katholische Theologie* 60 (1936): 1–54, 210–40; Gregory Grabka, "Christian Viaticum: A Study of Its Cultural Background," *Traditio* 9 (1953): 1–43.

60. Damien Sicard, "La mort du chrétien," in *L'église en prière*, ed. Martimort, 3.244; Février, "Mort chrétienne," 884–85; Pierre Boglioni, "La scène de la mort dans les premières hagiographies latines," in *Essais sur la mort*, ed. G. Couturier, A. Charon, and G. Durand (Montreal, 1985), 278–79.

61. *Concilia Africae a. 345–a. 525*, ed. C. Munier (Turnhout, 1974), 21, Concilium Hipponense, c. 4: "partem Corporis sancti cum exanimi cadauere communicare arbitror prohibendum"; *Concilia Galliae a. 511–a. 695*, ed. Carlo de Clercq (Turnhout, 1963), 267, Synodus dioecesana Autissiodorensis, c. 12: "Non licet mortuis nec eucharistia nec usculum tradi nec de uela uel pallas corpora eorum inuolui." See also Février, "Mort chrétienne," 885, 918; and Rush, *Death and Burial*, 99–101. The reference to kissing the corpse recalls the pagan Roman custom of the last kiss; see Rush, 101–5. Richard Rutherford, *The Death of a Christian: The Rite of Funerals* (New York, 1980), 25, points out that most of the practices concerning the treatment of corpses condemned by conciliar decree in the fourth through the sixth centuries—those referred to in the canons cited as well as the tendency to bury corpses as close to an altar as possible—are related by the common desire to associate the dead with the Eucharist, either by giving it to them, by wrapping them in cloths used in the mass, or by burying them near the place where bread and wine are transformed.

other ritual practices took place around the deathbed, notably emergency baptism and the reconciliation of penitents.

Emergency Baptism

In the earliest Christian communities of the apostolic age, baptism often followed immediately upon conversion; it was the sign of the acceptance of the new faith.[62] During the second and third centuries, the practice developed of preparing for baptism during a more or less extended period of time as a catechumen. Although there is some evidence that infants were baptized in this period, by the fourth century it was not uncommon to spend much of one's adult life as a catechumen. St. Ambrose was not baptized until he was thirty-four, and then as part of the ceremony by which he was elevated to the episcopacy. Augustine was baptized at thirty-four, and Jerome was over twenty years old. The emperor Constantine did not receive baptism until the end of his life.[63] This tendency to postpone baptism derived from the fear of failing to live up to the standards of Christian living and made the granting of emergency baptism a necessary and common event in the fourth century. Augustine's mother, Monica, had everything prepared for an emergency baptism when Augustine was sick as a child, but postponed the ritual when she saw that he was recovering. Augustine himself witnessed such a rite when one of his friends became seriously ill.[64] Some clerics did not grant such "clinical" baptism the same efficacy as regular baptism, which took place on the Saturday before Easter in a church ceremony, but it was defended in the third century by Cyprian of Carthage and in the fifth by Pope Leo I, who upbraided the bishops of southern Gaul for denying baptism to the dying: "We do not at any time deny this the only safeguard of true salvation to anyone in danger of death, in the crisis of a siege, in the distress of persecution, in the fear of shipwreck."[65] Thus it would

---

62. R. Cabié, "L'initiation chrétienne," in *L'église en prière*, ed. Martimort, 3.25; Henry F. Brown, *Baptism through the Centuries* (Mountain View, Calif./Omaha, 1965), 23.

63. Brown, *Baptism*, 26.

64. F. van der Meer, *Augustine the Bishop: Religion and Society at the Dawn of the Middle Ages*, trans. B. Battershaw and G. R. Lamb (New York, 1961), 350–52.

65. Leo I, letter 16 (A.D. 447), c. 5 (PL 54.701): "in mortis periculo, in obsidionis discrimine, in persecutionis angustiis, in timore naufragii, nullo tempore, hoc verae salutis singulare praesidium cuiquam denegemus." See also Cyprian, letter 69, cc. 12–13, CSEL 3 (Vienna, 1871), 760–63. It is probable that in the hundred years after the pontificate of Leo I, a shortened form of the baptismal ritual was incorporated into the early forms of the Roman sacramentaries; Chavasse, *Sacramentaire gélasien*, 168–69, 172–76.

not have been unusual during these centuries for a deathbed ceremony to comprise the ritual actions of baptism—a confession of faith, aspersion with exorcised and blessed water, and an anointing with chrism in the sign of the cross. When baptism was received in this manner, the communion that followed the aspersion and anointing stood as the viaticum.[66]

Deathbed Reconciliation

By the later fifth century and the beginning of the sixth, chiefly under the influence of Augustine, infant baptism was increasingly the normal means of initiation into the Christian community.[67] Thus deathbed baptisms became less common events. But the same reasons that had led fourth-century Christians to postpone baptism led many in the fifth century to postpone the penitential ritual that was the church's means of forgiving sins committed after baptism and reconciling fallen Christians to full membership in the community. The ancient penitential discipline of the church was severe. It was public, marking the penitent through dress, ritual distance, and the denial of full participation in the worship of the community.[68] And it was not repeatable. The church could not and would not help a former penitent who fell into sin again. Thus such people were encouraged not to engage in economic, military, or sexual conduct—if necessary for the rest of their lives. In a small, intense religious community, this degree of strictness was possible, but in the imperial church of the fourth and fifth centuries, and afterward when the barbarian peoples of the north became Christian, alterations had to be made.

The system of public penance for grave sins had developed slowly during the second and third centuries of the Christian era. It did not at first encompass certain crimes that God might forgive but that the church could not: idolatry, adultery, homicide. As time went on, individuals differed on the church's ability to pardon capital crimes, especially apostasy. Disagreement over this question came to a head in the middle of the third century, during the persecution under the emperor Decius. Large numbers of Chris-

---

66. See Gelasian, no. 612, and chap. 2 below.
67. Van der Meer, *Augustine the Bishop*, 350–51.
68. O. D. Watkins, *A History of Penance*, vol. 1 (London, 1920); Cyrille Vogel, *La discipline pénitentielle en Gaule des origines à la fin du viie siècle* (Paris, 1952), 21–28; Herbert Vorgrimler, *Busse und Krankensalbung*, Handbuch der Dogmengeschichte 4.3 (Freiburg/Basel/Vienna, 1978), 1–69; P. M. Gy, "La pénitence et la réconciliation," in *L'église en prière*, ed. Martimort, 3.116–23.

tians who lapsed under pressure and sacrificed to the pagan gods later sought reconciliaticn with the church. Yet many members of the Christian community refused reconciliation to these *lapsi*. Such people became associated with Novatian, a Roman cleric, who formed a schismatic church that lasted for centuries. But Novatian's rigorist position was the last stand for the old view that certain sins were unforgivable in this life. Cyprian of Carthage, when faced with the large numbers of *lapsi* in the North African church, argued for the granting of penance and reconciliation to *lapsi*, especially on their deathbeds, so that they could receive a final communion.[69] The debate over the issue continued into the early fourth century, when the rigorist position was most fully expressed at a Spanish council at Elvira which denied communion at death to over a dozen categories of sinners.[70] A few years later, when the first general council of the church met in Nicaea, the fathers laid down a definitive ruling that no one should die without viaticum, no matter what his or her status in the church.[71]

Though the decree of the Council of Nicaea did not immediately put an end to the controversy, it defined viaticum as the central rite for the dying and paved the way for the granting of rites of deathbed penance and reconciliation for anyone who requested them. And people did request them. Because penance and reconciliation could be granted only once, many people who took on the penitential state postponed their reconciliation until their deaths, and many others did not request penance at all until they felt that death was near. Pope Innocent I, in 416, allowed priests the episcopal power to reconcile penitents in an emergency, and Pope Celestine I, in 428, condemned those who refused to grant penance to the dying. When penance was administered at death, the rite involved confession, admission to the status of a penitent, and reconciliation at least through the Eucharist if not also through the imposition of hands.[72] A canon from the late fifth-century collection known as the *Statuta ecclesiae antiqua* describes what was

69. Watkins, *History of Penance*, 1.143–221; Vogel, *Discipline pénitentielle*, 47–54. Cf. Vorgrimler, *Busse und Krankensalbung*, 53–58.

70. *Concilios visigóticos e hispano-romanos*, ed. José Vives, España cristiana, textos 1 (Barcelona/Madrid, 1963), 1–15; F. Javier Lozano Sebastián, "La legislación canónica sobre la penitencia en la España romano y visigoda (s. iv–vii)," *Burgense* 19 (1978): 402–6.

71. *Conciliorum oecumenicorum decreta*, ed. Joseph Alberigo et al., 3d ed. (Bologna, 1973), 12; Nicaea (A.D. 325), c. 13: "De his qui ad exitum vitae veniunt, etiam nunc lex antiqua regularisque servabitur ita, ut, si quis egreditur e corpore, ultimo et necessario viatico minime privetur."

72. Watkins, *History of Penance*, 1.416, 481–82; Vogel, *Discipline pénitentielle*, 48–49, 54.

probably the usual practice: "He who asks for penance in sickness . . . may receive it. And if it is believed that he is about to die, he should be reconciled through the imposition of hands and the Eucharist should be placed in his mouth."[73] For some sinners, at least, the ritual guaranteed entry into paradise after death.[74]

It is generally agreed that the full public penance according to the antique model was seldom used in the centuries after 400. Thus penance would have been familiar more as a ritual for the dying than as a rite for the living. The evidence suggests that it was resorted to sometimes, as was baptism, when necessary. But both of these rituals were always unusual and involved special circumstances. The rites were performed, most probably, in an ad hoc manner in accordance with the urgency of the situation and were not considered to be the church's normal response to death and dying. In the normal case of a dying Christian, no preparation was necessary for communion as viaticum, and the deathbed ceremonies had a different character. This character is most evident in a ritual tradition that eventually came to be associated with the collections of Roman rituals known as *ordines romani*, and that in one form or another had its roots in the practice of the late antique Roman church.

The Earliest Latin Ritual for Death and Burial: The Old Roman *Ordo defunctorum*

In 1956 Michel Andrieu published an eleventh-century text of a ritual to accompany death and burial which he argued was purely Roman and of great antiquity.[75] Since that time, numerous other witnesses to the same tradition have been found and analyzed, by far the most comprehensive study being that of Damien Sicard.[76] Not only has Sicard reconstructed and painstakingly analyzed the

73. *Concilia Galliae a. 314–a. 506*, 170, c. 20: "Is qui paenitentiam in infirmitate petit . . . accipiat paenitentiam. Et si continuo creditur moriturus, reconcilietur per manus impositionem et infundatur ori eius eucharistia."

74. Vogel, *Discipline pénitentielle*, 51, cites a sepulchral inscription from Aix, dated to the year 492, which expresses this confidence: "Hic in pace quiescit adiutor qui post acceptam paenitentiam migrauit ad dominum."

75. "*Ordines Romani*," ed. Andrieu, 4.523–30, MS Vat. Ottob. lat. 312, fol. 151v: "Ordo qualiter agatur in obsequiis defunctorum" (Ordo XLIX). Cf. ibid., 1.316–17. On the Roman *ordines* in general, see Vogel, *Medieval Liturgy*, 135–224.

76. Sicard, *Liturgie*, 1–257; see also G. Haenni, "Un 'Ordo defunctorum' du xième siècle," EL 73 (1959): 431–34; Hieronymus Frank, "Die älteste erhaltene *ordo defunctorum* der römischen Liturgie und sein Fortleben in Totenagenden des frühen Mittelalters," ALW 7 (1962): 360–415.

component parts of the Roman tradition, he has also provided scholars with detailed indications of their transmission in ritual books from the eighth to the sixteenth century. Questions still remain, however. The reconstruction of the original ritual is hampered by the lack of manuscript sources before the end of the eighth century, and it has been suggested that the tradition in not Roman at all, but Frankish.[77] Although such a position finds support in the manuscript history, it flies in the face of the abundant evidence that something like Andrieu's Ordo XLIX conforms very closely to what we know of the attitudes and behavior of the late antique Roman church concerning death and burial. Thus, while disagreement over the "Roman" origins of particular elements of the rather late witnesses is possible, the general nature and structure of the Roman *ordo* as it probably emerged in the fourth and fifth centuries are clear. The ritual was built around a coherent set of actions—viaticum as the rite for the dying, the chanting of psalms, triumphal processions—and infused with a spirit of optimism concerning the salvation of Christians and the resurrection of the dead. It appears in a variety of forms in the manuscript witnesses of the eighth through the eleventh centuries, but most probably the old Roman *ordo* for death and burial included the features shown in Ritual 1.

Separation rites are conspicuously lacking in this ritual order.[78] The rite begins near the moment of death with the reception of communion as viaticum (1).[79] We have already seen that the necessity of the reception of the Eucharist before death for all Christians, even penitents, had been officially recognized at the Council of Nicaea. As this *ordo* clearly shows, the Roman tradition viewed the Eucharist as an aid to the dead at the future day of judgment, when it would be a *defensor et adiutor* at the last tribunal. The ritual connection between the viaticum given on the deathbed and the resurrection was rooted in the Christian understanding of the redemptive power of Christ. People who died to the accompani-

---

77. See Bernard Moreton's review of Sicard, *Liturgie,* in JTS 3 (1980): 231–37.
78. Pierre Boglioni, "Scène de la mort," 271–78, has demonstrated the lack of attention paid to separation rites and to the agony in the earliest layer of Christian hagiography. The saints had foreknowledge of their deaths; they were, in effect, already separated from the world. Cf. Février, "Mort chrétienne," 883–85.
79. "Mox ut eum viderint ad exitum appropinquare communicandus est de sacrificio sancto etiamsi comedisset ipsa die quia communio erit ei defensor et adiutor in resurrectione iustorum. Ipsa eum resuscitabit." This is among the most stable of the rubrics of the Roman *ordo,* appearing with only minor variants in six of the seven witnesses analyzed by Sicard and many related texts; Sicard, *Liturgie,* 35–39.

Ritual 1. Rubrics and psalmody of the old Roman *ordo defunctorum*

---

1. As soon as they see him approaching death he is to be given communion even if he has eaten that day, because the communion will be his defender and advocate at the resurrection of the just. It will resuscitate him. After the reception of communion, the Gospel accounts of the passion of the Lord are to be read to the sick person by priests or deacons until his soul departs from his body.

2. Immediately after the soul has left the body, the response *Subvenite sancti dei* is said, followed by the verse *Suscipiat te Christus* and a psalm (*In exitu Israel* [113] or *Dilexi quoniam* [114]) with the antiphon *Chorus angelorum.*

3. Afterward the body is washed and they place it on a bier. After it has been placed on the bier and before it is taken from the house, the priest says the antiphon *De terra formasti me* and a psalm (*Dominus regit me* [22], *Gaudete iusti* [32], or *Dominus regnavit* [92]).

4. The body is carried to the church and placed therein to the accompaniment of psalms and antiphons (e.g., the antiphon *Tu iussisti nasci me domine* and Psalm 41, *Quemadmodum*).

5. And when it has been placed in the church everyone should pray for its soul without intermission until the body has been buried. They should chant psalms, responses, and lessons from the book of Job. The vigil should be celebrated for him at the proper hour, but without Alleluia.

6. When the body is placed in the tomb they sing the antiphon *Aperite mihi portas iustitiae* and the psalm *Confitemini* [117].

SOURCE: Damien Sicard, *La liturgie de la mort dans l'église latine des origines à la réforme carolingienne* (Münster, 1988), 2–33 and the chart at the end of the book, giving the rubrics and psalmody of seven manuscripts containing versions of the Roman *ordo.* Some of the variants among the rubrics, psalms, verses, and antiphons are omitted to reveal the basic structure.

ment of the Roman death ritual lived their last moments listening to the story of Christ's own passion and death. They would understand their own suffering within the context of the death of Christ, and find assurance in the knowledge that by Christ's death their own would not be final, but would mark entry into a temporary state, the *refrigerium interim*, that would end with the final resurrection.[80]

The initial response to death (2) was hopeful. Drawing on the story of Lazarus and the rich man in Luke 16:19–31, the prescribed texts ritually recreate the circumstances of the poor man's ascent to paradise. They invoke the image of angels coming down to earth

---

80. On the theme of resurrection in the old Roman liturgy, see Ntedika, *Evocation de l'au-delà*, 241–44, 256–57; for the thoughts of the church fathers through Augustine, see McWilliam Dewart, *Death and Resurrection*. On the condition of souls between death and resurrection, see Alfred Stuiber, *Refrigerium interim: Die Vorstellungen vom Zwischenzustand und die frühchristliche Grabeskunst*, Theophania 11 (Bonn, 1957).

and taking Lazarus's soul to God—to the bosom of Abraham, to the
land of rest and peace.[81] "Aid him, saints of God; run to meet him,
angels of the Lord—you who receive his soul, you who offer him to
the sight of the most high. May Christ who created you receive you
and may the angels lead you to the bosom of Abraham. May a
chorus of angels receive you and may you have eternal rest with
Lazarus the poor man."[82] The recitation of Psalm 113 has the same
effect. It recalls the exodus of the Israelites from Egypt and describes the relationship between God and his people in the same
words used to characterize the viaticum: "The house of Israel has
placed its trust in the Lord who is its helper and protector [adiutor
et protector]. . . . Those who fear the Lord have placed their trust in
him who is their helper and protector."[83] The psalm expresses faith
and confidence in the relationship between God and his people. For
the attendants at a death it completed the images invoked in the
short texts that preceded it—images of successful transitions from
this world to the heavenly beyond. The other psalm sometimes
prescribed for this moment in the ritual, Dilexi quoniam (114),
invokes the alternate destination of the Christian dead—the place
of torment (tormentum)—when it gives thanks to God for salvation from the pains of death (dolores mortis) and the dangers of the
underworld (pericula inferni).

The body was then washed and placed on a bier (3).[84] Most manuscripts give no directions for accompanying psalmody, but the antiphon chanted before the mourners left the house echoes the ritual
action of reclothing the corpse: "My redeemer, you formed me
from the earth and dressed me in flesh; Lord resuscitate me on the
last day."[85] Similarly, two witnesses to the ordo follow that antiphon with Psalm 92, Dominus regnavit, which sings of God
dressed in beauty and strength ("decorem indutus est; indutus est
Dominus fortitudinem"). Thus began the singing that accom-

81. On the voyage of the soul to God as a central theme in the early saints' lives,
see Boglioni, "Scène de la mort," 281–86.
82. Sicard, Liturgie, 66–70: "R/Subvenite sancti dei; occurrite angeli domini;
suscipientes animam ejus, offerentes eam in conspectu domini. V/Suscipiat te
christus qui creavit te et in sinum abrahae angeli deducant te. Ant. Chorus angelorum te suscipiat et cum lazaro quendam paupere aeternam habeas requiem."
83. Psalm 113B.9, 11: "Domus Israel speravit in Domino; adjutor eorum et protector eorum est. . . . Qui timent Dominum speraverunt in Domino; adjutor eorum
et protector eorum est." So the Vulgate; the Septuagint has "auxilio et protector."
84. Sicard, Liturgie, 79–102, argues that the prose prayer Deus apud quem,
which appears in the Vatican Gelasian, was to be said between the initial response
to death and the washing of the body. This prayer is discussed further in chap. 2. For
more on the preparation of the corpse, see Rush, Death and Burial, 114–17.
85. Sicard, Liturgie, 119–22: "De terra formasti me et carnem induisti me redemptor meus domine, resuscita me in novissimo die."

panied the procession with the body to the church. The psalms recorded at this ritual moment express the utmost confidence in the saving power and goodness of God. Psalm 22 is that great prayer of trust in God, "The Lord is my shepherd." Psalm 32 speaks again of God as helper and protector (adjutor et protector).[86]

The procession to the church and the vigil (4–5) were also accompanied by psalms.[87] Several witnesses record the antiphon "You ordered me to be born, Lord; you promised that I would rise again. By your order the saints will come; you will not desert me because you are good."[88] Psalm 41, Quemadmodum, introduces the only note of sadness in the old ritual. It is a prayer of longing for God. The psalmist asks his soul, "Why are you sad; why do you disturb me?" But the dominant mood is quickly restored with the antiphon "I have heard a voice from heaven saying 'Blessed are the dead who die in the Lord,'" followed by Psalm 114.[89] After the attendants placed the body in the church, they began a continuous chant of psalms and responses or readings from the book of Job which lasted until the burial.[90] The mention of readings from Job is significant, for the

86. Psalm 32:29: "Anima nostra sustinet Dominum, quoniam adjutor et protector noster est."

87. The manuscript witnesses of the ordo vary on the number of psalms and antiphons that accompany the procession. Moreover, the ordo in Vatican MS Ottobonianus lat. 312 (Andrieu's Ordo XLIX) has a rubric, Dum ad sepulturam defertur, which seems out of place—it comes between two rubrics mentioning the church as the location of the ritual action (Et postea ponitur in ecclesia interim and Et cum in ecclesia positum fuerint omnes). The odd rubric is followed by a group of antiphons and psalms that include Psalm 50 (twice) and the antiphon "Vide domine humilitatem meam et laborem dimitte omnia peccata mea" followed by Psalm 122, a prayer of abject supplication, begging for God's mercy: "Miserere nostri Domine miserere nostri quia repleti sumus despectione." At one point Sicard asks if this portion of the ordo is truly Roman (Liturgie, 32); at another (203) he wonders if it might not be a Gallican addition. I think the latter suggestion is almost certain. On the one hand, the Roman ritual is otherwise so tightly constructed and so devoid of this kind of penitential attitude that the expression of such sentiments seems anomalous; and on the other, all available evidence links such penitential attitudes toward dying and death with the sensibilities of a later time and a different cultural milieu, as we shall see in chaps. 2 and 3. For more on the procession, see Rush, Death and Burial, 193–96; and Février, "Mort chrétienne," 898–902.

88. Sicard, Liturgie, 132–33: "Tu iussisti nasci me domine tu promisisti ut resurgerem iussu tuo venient sancti ne derelinquas me quia pius es."

89. Sicard, Liturgie, 130–31: "Ant. Audivi vocem de celo dicentem: beati mortui qui in domino moriuntur. Ps. Dilexi quoniam." See also ibid., 138–42.

90. Sicard, ibid., 174–202, argues that the oldest tradition did not entail an office of the dead or a mass that was specifically a mass of the dead rather than simply the mass of the day. See idem, "The Funeral Mass," in Reforming the Rites of Death, ed. Johannes Wagner, Concilium 32 (New York, 1968), 45–52; and Février, "Mort chrétienne," 902–7. The rubrics referring to a mass in some of the manuscripts of the Roman ordo are additions made under the influence of the Gallican milieux through which it passed; Sicard, Liturgie, 182.

antiphons *Tu iussisti nasci me* and *De terra formasti me* are both derived from the book of Job.[91] They preserve an Old Testament tradition of direct confrontation with God—of the creature's right to remind the Creator of the essential realities of their mutual relationship—which gives special force to the confidence in salvation expressed in the ritual as a whole.

In the old Roman *ordo*, burial was attended by the antiphon "Open to me the gates of justice and let me enter, for I will confess to the Lord. The Lord's just ones will enter by this gate."[92] The recurrent image of the gate (threshold) is particularly fitting at this stage of the ritual process, when the corpse is placed in the tomb, for it marks the transition from liminal to postliminal rites. The antiphon derives from the psalm it introduces, Psalm 117 (verses 19–20). The psalm as a whole is a great prayer of witness to the goodness of God. Though it speaks of confession, the confession is one of witness, not of penitence. It is an integral part of the ritual through its reiteration of themes struck earlier: "The Lord is my helper; I will not fear what man may do to me."[93] Its tone, so characteristic of the Roman attitude, is confident, affirmative, optimistic.

There is no missing the unity and coherence of this ritual tradition. Its various parts support one another in unambiguous relationships; resonances among the separate psalms and antiphons are the meat on the bones of its rubrics. Sicard has noted its main themes.[94] God is the giver of life, the recreator, the resurrector. He is attended by angels who carry the souls of the dead to join the community of souls already in repose. The dying person identifies with Christ through the reading of the Passion and, fortified for the final judgment with the body and blood of Christ, dies in the assurance of entry into the community of saints. The church organized the rite as a passage. It conducted its dead member symbolically from earth to heaven, praying in the name of the deceased, using the first person of the psalms. The funeral cortege was an *adventus*, a triumphal procession into perpetual light.[95]

---

91. Sicard, *Liturgie*, 124, 141.

92. Sicard, *Liturgie*, 225–26: "Aperite mihi portas iustitiae et ingressus in eas confitebor Domino. Haec porta domini iusti intrabunt in eam." This antiphon appears in nearly every record of chants to accompany transitional rites in medieval death rituals; ibid., 225.

93. Psalm 117.6: "Deus mihi adiutor; non timebo quid faciat mihi homo."

94. Sicard, *Liturgie*, 248–57.

95. Sabine MacCormack, *Art and Ceremony in Late Antiquity*, Transformation of the Classical Heritage 1 (Berkeley, 1981), 37–38, 121–27, has recently shown how

What holds the ritual together is its psalmody. As Johannes Quasten pointed out in his classic study of music in pagan and Christian antiquity, the Christian response to death necessarily demanded "a change in the songs about death".[96] Christian writers repeatedly emphasized the difference between the psalms of joy sung at their funerals and the sad dirges and lamentations that accompanied the burial of pagans.[97] The singing of psalms is often recorded in early sources as the proper accompaniment to Christian funeral ceremonies, and, as in the Roman *ordo*, the psalms chosen are songs of faith triumphant and confidence in salvation. The *Apostolic Constitutions* mentioned Psalm 114, *Dilexi quoniam*, in the context of burial rites, and St. John Chrysostom, urging his flock not to fall prey to the sadness of pagan funerals, reminded them of the joyfulness expressed in the psalms sung when a Christian died, referring to Psalm 114 as well as Psalm 22.[98] An apocryphal account of the death of the Virgin Mary from the fifth century features the psalm *In exitu Israel* (113), which the Roman *ordo* prescribed as the initial response to death.[99] Psalms 32 and 114 were also sung at the vigils of the martyrs, which may have been the model for the practice of holding vigils over the bodies of all dead Christians.[100] Indeed, the cult of the martyrs was a central factor in the development of the Roman Christian funeral ritual in the fourth and fifth centuries, for it was through the intercession of the martyrs that many late antique Christians sought a place among the blessed in heaven.[101]

The Roman *ordo defunctorum* is a rite of passage whose peculiar

---

the Roman imperial *adventus* in its Christian form relied on the same images that appear on Christian sarcophagi and in the liturgy, a phenomenon first discovered by Ernst Kantorowicz, "The 'King's Advent' and the Enigmatic Panels in the Doors of Santa Sabina," *Art Bulletin* 26 (1944): 207–31; repr. in his *Selected Studies* (Locust Valley, N.Y., 1965), 37–75.

96. Quasten, *Music and Worship*, 161.

97. Ibid., 161–63; cf. Rush, *Death and Burial*, 231–35; Rowell, *Liturgy of Christian Burial*, 22. There may have been some tendentiousness in their opinions, however, for Quasten's evidence of pagan customs cuts both ways. Though much pagan music was mournful, certain practices, such as the placing of a lyre or tambourine on a grave, could "express the conviction . . . that the deceased had attained a happy fate"; *Music and Worship*, 157.

98. Rowell, *Liturgy of Christian Burial*, 22; Rush, *Death and Burial*, 235.

99. Richard Rutherford, "Psalm 113 (114–115) and Christian Burial," in *Studia Patristica*, vol. 13, ed. E. A. Livingstone (Berlin, 1975), 391–95.

100. Quasten, *Music and Worship*, 169.

101. But cf. Février, "Mort chrétienne," 931, and "Vie et mort dans les 'Epigrammata Damasiana,'" 105–7.

nature derives from the antique understanding of a Christian death. The first rubric presents the dying person as a totality, body and soul, on the verge of dissolution into its constituent parts. The reception of the viaticum is expressly linked with that moment when the body and soul will once again be united, at the resurrection. At the moment of death, the body becomes separated out as an object different from the soul. Attention settles first on the soul in its passage to the other world. Then the focus turns to the body, its transition from the deathbed to the grave. But the treatment of the body mirrors the state of the soul. The body that is washed and reclothed, carried in procession, and incorporated in the earth is a symbol of the soul that is purified, transformed, and incorporated in the other world.[102] This symbolic mirroring implies a belief in an active afterlife for the soul, at least until its arrival among the blessed in the place of repose.[103] The use of Luke's story about Lazarus and the rich man in the responses to the death expresses this belief well enough. That same story, however, presents a vision of the alternative destination for the soul, for the rich man lies in torment in the depths of hell. Yet the ritual contains little reference to hell. A soul released to its accompaniment made it to heaven.[104] That was the purpose of the ritual; to die in the bosom of the church was a guarantee of safe passage to heaven. That is why we find little indication of a need for a period of purification or penitential supplication before incorporation into the ranks of the blessed. Like the Roman ritual attitude toward the sick, the attitude expressed in the *ordo defunctorum* is optimistic and confident. The relations between God and his people were familiar, and the community's petitions to its Lord express the expectation of a positive response.

102. Cf. Hertz, "Contribution," 46; and Huntington and Metcalf, *Celebrations of Death*, 67. The difference between the Christian ritual under discussion and those that Hertz studied is significant. The people of Borneo feared the corpse until its decomposition signaled the incorporation of the soul of the deceased into the other world.

103. For a provocative discussion of the belief in the presence of a "double" in the tomb among Christians in late antiquity, see Paul-Albert Février, "La tombe chrétienne et l'au-delà," in *Le temps chrétien de la fin de l'antiquité au moyen âge iiie–xiiie siècles*, Colloques internationaux du Centre National de la Recherche Scientifique 604 (Paris, 1984), 163–83.

104. If the ritual was constructed to counter a deep-seated fear that demons would inhibit the passage of the soul to the other world—both Février, "Mort chrétienne," 890–92, and MacCormack, *Art Ceremony*, 147, write that late antique Christians felt anxiety over the maleficent activities of demons at death and afterward—no hint of that fear appears in the prayers and psalms themselves.

The Legacy of Christian Antiquity

The ritual responses of the Latin church of Roman antiquity to
sickness, death, and dying have some common features. They are
practical, tolerant of human weakness, and confident that full
members of the community will abide with the saints in heaven
until the final resurrection. Rituals for the sick look toward the
expectation of the return of physical health, with an eye to the
spiritual condition of the sick, but without ascribing miraculous
powers to the prayers and gestures offered for them. Oil is regarded
as a medicament, religiously transformed by the episcopal blessing, but otherwise not so very different from other aids to healing
available in the late antique pharmacopoeia. Little attention is
paid to purificatory or transformative powers inherent in the oil or
to the connection between sin and sickness. At the most, sickness
is regarded as a reminder from God of the necessity to turn the
mind away from worldly pleasures and toward the eternal. This
attitude is nicely summed up in a fifth-century prayer after recovery from sickness which appears in a variety of related forms in the
so-called Verona Sacramentary (ca. 600): "You chastise us with
temporal inconveniences because you do not wish [us] to undergo
the loss of eternal things; and it is better, castigated by present
evils, to advance to the divine than in worldly prosperity to deviate
from the path to eternal beatitude."[105]

When death threatened, the church had one central goal, to provide the dying with the Eucharist—the symbol of full membership
in the community of the faithful. If the person was a catechumen,
he or she was baptized; if a penitent, reconciled. In both cases, the
rituals were necessary to allow for the reception of the viaticum.
As the old Roman *ordo defunctorum* makes clear, the death ritual
that emerged in the fourth and fifth centuries normally began with
the approach of death and the reception of the viaticum. Once
given, the viaticum assured the recipient of aid on the day of judgment. The funeral services were organized around psalms of confidence in salvation and joy at the passage of a Christian soul to the
next world. Commemorative rituals linked the needs of the living

105. Verona, no. 314: "Nos enim temporalibus flagellas incommodis, quia aeter-
narum rerum non uis subire dispendium, meliusque est praesentibus castigatos ad
diuina proficere, quam prosperitate mundana a beatitudinis sempiternae tramite
deuiare." Cf. nos. 314, 334, 465, 1060. On the Verona "Sacramentary," see Vogel,
Medieval Liturgy, 38–46.

poor with the dead, thus circumscribing the ideal limits of the Christian community. This was a ritual complex for a church triumphant, a church confident of its place in the world and sure of its relation with its God. So was the Latin church of the fourth and fifth centuries, when it emerged as the religious center of the Roman Empire. But it would not always be so. The empire was crumbling in the West and new people were looking to Christianity for guidance in an increasingly troubled world. The following centuries would see the formation of a scattering of more or less separate Christian communities in the West, all of whom struggled to make sense of sickness, death, and dying within their own understanding of the Christian message, some in conformity with Roman antiquity, others not. Only in the eighth and ninth centuries would they all be brought into contact; in the meantime, antique traditions were transmitted haphazardly. The new prayers, gestures, and rituals that emerged during this process were to alter significantly the Christian response to death and dying.

CHAPTER TWO

Rites for the Sick, the Dying, and
the Dead in the West, ca. 500–ca. 750:
Crosscurrents and Innovations

Merovingian Gaul

Both culturally and geographically, Merovingian Gaul stood with one foot in the Mediterranean south and the other in the barbarian north. Its history is to a great extent the history of the joining of those two worlds through the agency of the Christian religion.[1] Although the view that the conquests of Clovis all followed upon his conversion to Catholicism has been discredited, the new kingdom of the Franks was intimately bound up with the old structures of the orthodox church in Gaul and developed in the sixth century as a coalition of warrior-kings and Gallo-Roman bishops.[2] That coalition was weakened in the seventh century as Frankish aristocrats drained power and religious leadership from the royal courts to their rural estates, on which they settled troops of Irish monks. During the first phase, Christian cultural forms flowed from south to north; in the second, from north to south.[3] During both phases the Gallican church sought to soothe the ache of human mortality with ritual and symbol drawn from the past

1. See Patrick J. Geary, *Before France and Germany: The Creation and Transformation of the Merovingian World* (Oxford, 1988).
2. J. M. Wallace-Hadrill, *The Long-Haired Kings* (Toronto, 1982), 63–64; Geary, *Before France and Germany*, 123–35.
3. Geary, *Before France and Germany*, 178.

and shaped to meet the needs of a population in a process of almost constant cultural transformation.

The Contribution of Caesarius of Arles

The early sixth century was a time of transition for the Christian communities of the West. The disintegration of the Roman imperial government left the church hierarchy as the increasingly predominant administrative structure in the new barbarian kingdoms of the Franks, Burgundians, Ostrogoths, and Visigoths, whose wars for supremacy in the empire's western provinces created enormous social problems for the bishops in the *civitates*. One of the most successful responses to the changing times came from the church of southeastern Gaul, in the old province of Narbonensis Secunda, where a young monk from Lérins named Caesarius was elected bishop of Arles in the year 503.[4] As metropolitan over as many as twenty-five other bishops in Narbonensis II, the Viennoise, and the Maritime Alps, during his long episcopate (503–43) Caesarius oversaw what amounted to a reorganization of the church in southern Gaul and northeastern Spain. Caesarius spent his first years as bishop under the overlordship of the Visigothic king of Toulouse, Alaric II, whose hope of unifying the mixed Gothic and Roman population of his territories resulted in the famous compilation known as the Breviary of Alaric, or the *Lex Romana-Visigothorum*, issued in 506. In the same year Caesarius held a council at Agde, and he asked Alaric if he might hold another in 507 at Toulouse to organize the church of the Visigothic kingdom. The victory of the Franks under Clovis at the battle of Vouillé interfered with those plans. The Goths were forced into Spain and Caesarius's own territories fell under the protection of the Ostrogothic kings of Italy. Nevertheless, Caesarius worked steadily during the following years. In 514 Pope Symmachus appointed him apostolic vicar in Gaul and over the next twenty years the bishop presided over five more councils and inspired a number of others. Under attack from the armies

4. On Caesarius, see A. Malnory, *Saint Césaire: Evêque d'Arles, 503–543* (Paris, 1894; repr. 1978); Carl Franklin Arnold, *Caesarius von Arelate und die gallische Kirche seiner Zeit* (Leipzig, 1894; repr. 1972); G. de Plinval, "Césaire d'Arles (Saint)," DHGE 12.186–96; and William M. Daly, "Caesarius of Arles, a Precursor of Medieval Christendom," *Traditio* 26 (1970): 1–28, who assigns a pivotal role to Caesarius in the definition of a new Christian society in the West independent of Rome. See also Vogel, *Discipline pénitentielle*, 79–85; and Henry G. J. Beck, *The Pastoral Care of Souls in South-East France during the Sixth Century*, Analecta Gregoriana 51 (Rome, 1950).

of Rome in 536, the Ostrogoths turned Provence over to the Franks, and Caesarius's final years were spent under the rule of the Merovingian kings.

Although the changing political winds of the early sixth century brought social disruption and hardship, they actually contributed to the wide dispersion of Caesarius's influence. Recent research on the history of the liturgy has shown the importance of the links forged between southern Gaul and the Iberian peninsula during the episcopate of Caesarius. Rather than separating the two areas, the emigration of the Visigoths over the Pyrenees simply shifted one of the axes of Caesarius's work from Toulouse to Tarragona, by way of Narbonne, which remained in Visigothic hands.[5] The decrees of the many councils presided over or influenced by Caesarius became the foundation of both Merovingian and Visigothic conciliar history.[6] And the bishop's voluminous sermons, transmitted in homilaries, left an indelible mark on the churches of both Visigothic Spain and Merovingian Gaul.[7]

The surviving records of Caesarius's episcopate include significant information on the ritual practices that we have been considering. The bishop discussed the ritual anointing of the sick a number of times in his sermons, and considerably altered its focus and meaning. Others of his sermons and some of the conciliar decrees of his time illuminate changing practices of granting penance to the dying in the early sixth century. Finally, a short prayer service said over a dead body and at burial, which Caesarius may have written for the nuns of his sister's convent, provides a glimpse

5. See Miquel Gros, "Le pontifical de Narbonne," in *Liturgie et musique (ixe–xive s.)*, Cahiers de Fanjeaux 17 (Toulouse, 1982), 101–3; idem, "Los ritos de la Tarraconense y Narbona," in José Janini, *Manuscritos litúrgicos de las bibliotecas de España*, vol. 2, *Aragón, Cataluña y Valencia*, Publicaciones de la Facultad de Teología del Norte de España, Sede de Burgos, 38 (Burgos, 1980), 7–9; Roger E. Reynolds, "Narbonne Rite," DMA 9.62–63; and Anscari M. Mundó, "Sur quelques manuscrits liturgiques languedociens de l'époque carolingienne," in *Liturgie et musique*, 81–83.

6. Caesarius presided over councils at Agde (506), Arles (524), Carpentras (527), Orange (529), Vaison (529), and Marseilles (533); see Malnory, *Saint Césaire*, 62–90, 129–58; and *Concilia Galliae*, CCL 148, 148A (Turnhout, 1963). More than one scholar has seen this work as fundamental to the development of the church in Merovingian Gaul; see Daly, "Caesarius," 1. Gros sees the direct influence of Caesarius in the Spanish councils at Tarragona (516) and Gerona (517); "Ritos," 7–9. Mundó includes the councils of Agde, Tarragona, and Gerona among those fundamental to the formation of the Visigothic liturgy; "Quelques manuscrits," 81–82.

7. On the dissemination and importance of Caesarius's sermons, see Malnory, *Saint Césaire*, 241–44; Arnold, *Caesarius von Arelate*, 166; Daly, "Caesarius," 8–9; and Gros, "Pontifical de Narbonne," 103.

of early Gallican ritual action, attitudes, and beliefs surrounding death and the dead.

Anointing the Sick

In his admonitions to the Christian communities of southeastern Gaul delivered over a lifetime of active preaching, Caesarius redefined the practice of ritually anointing the sick with oil.[8] He was the first to use the text of St. James as the basis for a specifically clerical ritual of anointing. A century earlier Pope Innocent I had interpreted the scriptural text in accordance with common practice, which permitted any Christian to anoint the sick with blessed oil; now Caesarius explicitly linked anointing with the reception of communion and urged that the act take place in a church.[9] The reasons had to do with the nature of medical practice among the people for whom he felt responsible. Finding himself in competition with traditions of folk-magical medicine, Caesarius counseled his flock to take advantage of the double rewards of ritual unction in the church—both forgiveness of sins and healing—rather than risk grave sin at the hands of diviners and folk healers. It was not that Caesarius opposed medicine as such, just such practices as divination and the use of curative incantations, ligatures, suspensions, and phylacteries, which he regarded as remnants of paganism and which were becoming increasingly more prevalent in medical practice.[10] In one sermon he declared, "If only the sick would seek health from the pure art of doctors; but they say to themselves 'Let us consult that soothsayer, fortuneteller, diviner, or herbalist.'"[11] Yet even priests sometimes prescribed such cures.[12] Thus Caesarius's insistence that anointing

8. This aspect of Caesarius's work was first noted by Chavasse; *Etude*, 99–117; cf. Beck, *Pastoral Care of Souls*, 243–48.

9. Chavasse, *Etude*, 111–12.

10. On the changing nature of medicine in Caesarius's time, see Lynn Thorndike, *A History of Magic and Experimental Science* 1 (New York, 1923), 566–93. On the hospital that Caesarius built in Arles, see Arnold, *Caesarius von Arelate*, 395.

11. *Sancti Caesarii Arelatensis sermones*, ed. G. Morin, CCL 103, 104 (Turnhout, 1963), 1.232, sermon 52, c. 5: "Et atque utinam ipsam sanitatem vel de simplici medicorum arte conquirerent. Sed dicunt sibi: Illum ariolum vel divinum, illum sortilegum, illam erbariam consulamus."

12. Ibid., 1.225, sermon 50, c. 1: "Et aliquotiens ligaturas ipsas a clericis ac religiosis accipiunt; sed illi non sunt religiosi vel clerici, sed adiutores diaboli." Galen had accepted the use of organic or mineral substances in suspensions but not the efficacy of chants, inscriptions, or images. Medical writers such as Marcellus of Bordeaux in the fifth century and Alexander of Tralles in the sixth, however, referred regularly to such methods: see Thorndike, *History of Magic*, 1.173–74, 580–82.

and communion were the only acceptable ritual responses to sickness worked to control the activities of both priests and laity. Those who sought unacceptable alternatives were lapsing into paganism and would suffer the consequences attendant upon their behavior.[13] Certainly God might heal the sick through rites of anointing, but that was not their main purpose. They were a means of purification and salvation. Even if no cure followed, death brought about through resistance to the temptations of the devil (in this case phylacteries, ligatures, and suspensions) was a form of martyrdom, and thus a sure road to heavenly reward.[14] Thus, while promoting clerical participation in ritual healing, Caesarius subtly altered the meaning of the anointing of the sick. No longer directed solely at the restoration of the health of the body, it had become a ritual alternative to pagan magic and a means to spiritual health and eternal life.

Deathbed Penance

As we have seen, the severity of the ancient discipline of public penance had led to the decline of petitions for penance by the sixth century, so that, in Gaul as elsewhere, rites of penance were generally performed only for the dying.[15] Caesarius preached often on the subject, pointing out the dangers of postponing penance until the approach of death. His remarks are a response to the frequency of the practice, and though he might eschew judgment of the efficacy of deathbed penance, he did not deny it to anyone.[16] As in Rome, communion as viaticum was the normal rite for the dying, and a decree from the council of Agde in 506 reiterated the orthodox position that no one was to be denied viaticum at death.[17] As

13. *Caesarii sermones*, 1.225, sermon 50: "Qui enim filacteria facit, et qui rogant ut fiant, et quicumque consentiunt, toti pagani efficiuntur; et, nisi dignam egerint paenitentiam, non possunt evadere poenam."

14. Ibid., 2.750, sermon 184, c. 4: "Solet fieri, fratres, ut ad aliquem aegrotantem veniat persecutor ex parte diaboli, et dicat: Si illum praecantatorem adhibuisses, iam sanus esses; si characteres illos tibi voluisses adpendere, iam poteras sanitatem recipere. Huic persecutori si consenseris, diabolo sacrificasti; si contempseris, martyrii gloriam acquisisti."

15. Vogel, *Discipline pénitentielle*, 117–18, 121; Arnold, *Caesarius von Arelate*, 189–92; and Beck, *Pastoral Care*, 199–200.

16. *Caesarii sermones*, 1.263–74, sermons 60–63; Vogel, *Discipline pénitentielle*, 118–21; Beck, *Pastoral Care*, 203–5.

17. Beck, *Pastoral Care*, 254–55; *Concilia Galliae a. 314–a. 506*, ed. C. Munier, 201, Council of Agde, c. 15: "Viaticum tamen omnibus in morte positis non negandum."

to those penitents whose terms of penance were not yet fulfilled at death, Caesarius ruled that communion as viaticum would act as their formal reconciliation with the church.[18] Under such circumstances, the two ritual acts could be conceived as one. A canon from the Council of Gerona (517), for example, explicitly equates the rite of deathbed penance and the reception of the viaticum.[19] Since the model of the rite was the full ritual of public penance— enrollment as a penitent, reconciliation, and communion—communion following reconciliation would naturally be regarded as the viaticum of the dying. Thus it is not surprising that penance received when death seemed imminent would come to share in the title and meaning of the viaticum. In this manner, a precedent was set for rituals in preparation for death whose emphasis was on the purification and symbolic transformation of the dying.[20]

Death and Burial

A short prayer service over a dead body and for burial appears in an appendix to a copy of the rule of life written by Bishop Caesarius for the nuns of his sister's convent.[21] Although the manuscript in which it appears is from the ninth century, there is no reason not to regard the ritual as a work of the sixth-century Gallican church, if not of Caesarius himself.[22] The prayers of this ritual are basic to all later Gallican and Frankish burial services, which developed within and around its basic structural elements. This simple ritual comprises six prayers arranged in two moments: an initial response after death and a graveside service (Ritual 2). In the manuscript it is given a short title and two rubrics to define the ritual action.[23]

18. Vogel, *Discipline pénitentielle*, 127.
19. *Concilios visigóticos*, ed. Vives, 41, Gerona, c. 9: "Is vero qui aegritudinis langorem depressus poenitentiae benedictionem, quod viaticum deputamus, per communionem acceperit, et postmodum revalescens caput poenitentiae in ecclesia publice non subdiderit, se prohibitis vitiis non detinetur obnoxius, admittatur ad clerum." Cf. ibid., 53, Council of Barcelona, cc. 8–9.
20. Arnold notes that Caesarius used penitents to help with the burial of the dead and at funerals; *Caesarius of Arelate*, 195.
21. *Sancti Caesarii Arelatensis opera omnia*, ed. G. Morin, vol. 2, *Opera varia* (Maretioli, 1942), 127–28. See also Sicard, *Liturgie*, 260–79; and, on the rule, Malnory, *Saint Césaire*, 267–72, and Arnold, *Caesarius von Arelate*, 407–17.
22. Sicard, *Liturgie*, 260.
23. *Caesarii opera*, 2.127–28: "Incipiunt orationes super defunctae corpus"; "Hoc est quando migrat soror de corpore"; "Supra sepulchrum quando sepelitur." One should not make too much out of such sparse rubrics, but the reference to the departure of the person and not to the soul of the dead sister is unusual in either prayers or rubrics concerning the dead.

Ritual 2. Prayer service over the dead and at the grave
for Caesarius's sister's community

Prayers over the body of a dead sister

This is [what to say] when the sister departs from her body:
Pio recordationis affectu
Te domine

Over the grave when she is buried:
Debitum humani corporis
Omnipotens aeterne deus
Praesta domine
Conmendamus tibi domine

SOURCE: *Sancti Caesarii Arelatensis opera omnia,* ed. G. Morin
(Marietoli, 1942), 2.127–28.

The first of the two prayers in response to a death, *Pio recordationis affectu,* bids all in attendance to commemorate the soul of
their dead sister and to beg God to forgive her sins and grant her
rest and peace.

In the pious activity of remembrance, most dear brethren, let us
commemorate our dear sister N., whom the Lord has called from the
temptations of this world, begging the mercy of our God, so that he
himself may deign to grant her a quiet and pleasant dwelling; that he
may remit all the offenses of momentary thoughtlessness; that having been granted the grace of full indulgence for whatsoever her own
wandering in this world brought about, he may in his ineffable piety
and goodness compensate her in full; through our Lord Jesus Christ
his son.[24]

While admitting to the certainty of worldly error, this prayer shares
some of the calm confidence of the Roman *ordo defunctorum* that
God will grant salvation to his people. Taking the characteristic
Gallican form of a "bidding" or "preface," gathering together the
community to the task of supplicating God, this form of prayer
emphasizes communal participation and shared experience.[25] The

24. *Caesarii opera,* 2.127: "Pio recordationis affectu, fratres carissimi, memora-
tionem faciamus carae nostrae ill. quam dominus de temptationibus huius saeculi
adsumpsit. obsecrantes misericordiam dei nostri. ut ipse ei tribuere dignetur
placitam et quietam mansionem. remittat omnes lubricae temeritatis offensas. ut
concessa venia plenae indulgentiae quicquid in hoc saeculo proprius error adtulit,
totum ineffabili pietate ac benignitate sua conpenset: per dominum nostrum Iesum
Christum filium suum."
25. Joseph A. Jungmann, *The Mass of the Roman Rite: Its Origin and Develop-*

second prayer, *Te domine*, sums up the antique inheritance of Christian belief about the afterlife.

> To you, Lord, we pray for the soul of your servant, whom you have ordered to be brought to you from the abysses of this world, that you will see fit to grant her a place of refreshment and quiet, permit her to cross over the gates of hell and the paths of darkness and remain in the mansions of the saints and in the blessed light as you once promised to Abraham and his descendants; let her spirit suffer no injury, but when that great day of resurrection and regeneration comes, deign to raise her together with your saints and elected ones, erase her crimes and sins down to the last penny, and let her obtain with you the life of immortality and the eternal kingdom.[26]

In this representation, death is a summons from God and the journey of the soul a *migratio ad dominum*. The soul's destination is a realm of light that it reaches after crossing a region of darkness and shadows, and the final resurrection is more important than the interim period, which appears as a quiet interlude of light and peace in the mansions of paradise.[27]

The Caesarian ritual entered a second phase at the graveside. As in the Roman *ordo defunctorum*, the burial prayers draw attention to the relationship of the body and soul. The first prayer, *Debitum humani corporis*, speaks of the separate fates of the body and the soul, the first laid in the earth until the resurrection and the second called to congregate with the saints and the faithful in heaven.[28] The second notes the role of God in joining and separating the two parts: "Omnipotent eternal God who deigns to breathe a soul

---

ment *(Missarum Sollemnia)*, trans. Francis A. Brunner, 2 vols. (New York, 1951–55), 1.366–67.

26. *Caesarii opera*, 2.127: "Te domine . . . deprecamur pro spiritu famulae tuae ill. quam de voraginibus huius saeculi ad te arcersire praecepisti. ut digneris domine dare ei locum refrigerii et quietis. Liceat ei transire portas infernorum et vias tenebrarum. maneatque in mansionibus sanctorum. et in luce sancta. quam olim Abrahae promisisti et semini eius. nullam laesionem sustineat spiritus eius. sed cum magnus dies ille resurrectionis ac regenerationis advenerit. resuscitare eam digneris domine una cum sanctis et electis tuis. deleas ei delicta atque peccata. usque ad novissimum quadrantem. tecumque immortalitatis vitam et regnum consequatur aeternum."

27. See Bernard Botte, "Les plus anciennes formules de prière pour les morts," in *Maladie et la mort*, 83–99.

28. *Caesarii opera*, 2.128: "Debitum . . . conplentes. deum . . . deprecemur. ut hoc corpusculum a nobis in infirmitate sepultum. in virtute et ordine sanctorum resuscitet. et eius spiritum sanctis ac fidelibus iubeat adgregari."

into a human body from yourself, while by your decree dust returns to dust, may you order your image to join in health with the
saints and elect together with the angels and archangels."[29] The
ritual ends with two short prayers. The first, *Praesta domine*, asks
Jesus to grant the dead sister remission of sins and solace and rest
among the saints.[30] The final prayer, *Conmendamus tibi*, com-
mends to God the soul, which, having migrated from this world of
uncertain motion and change, yearns for eternal life and joy in
heaven.[31] These prayers breathe the spirit of late antique beliefs
and attitudes toward death and the afterlife. Though they do not
reproduce the psalmodic structure of the Roman *ordo defunctorum*, they nonetheless maintain much of that Roman trust in the
ultimate salvation of Christian souls summoned from this world
to God.

Developments in Gaul after Caesarius
Ritual Healing

Our picture of religious life in late sixth-century Gaul is dominated by the personality of Bishop Gregory of Tours. Like Caesarius, Gregory recommended spiritual healing in opposition to
the pagan practices of diviners, seers, and folk healers. But unlike
the bishop of Arles, Gregory had little faith in the traditions of
antique medical science and never mentioned the gentle rituals of
anointing and communion urged by Caesarius.[32] He was more at
home with the magical and the dramatic. As a child, Gregory once
treated his father for an attack of gout by recourse to a practice not
unlike those that Caesarius had criticized. A figure in a vision
directed him to fashion a small block of wood, write the biblical

29. Ibid.: "Omnipotens aeterne deus. qui humano corpori a te ipso animam inspirare dignatus es. dum te iubente pulvis pulveri redditur tu sane imaginem tuam
sanctis et electis una cum angelis et archangelis iubeas sociari."
30. Ibid.: "Praesta domine Iesu Christe defunctae famulae tuae ill. remissionem
ac solatium. ut quae hodie destitutam se terrenis opibus cernit. nunc admirabilem
splendorem laeta sanctorum consortio et requie glorietur."
31. Ibid.: "Conmendamus tibi domine animam sororis nostrae. . . . Migranti in
tuo nomine de hac mobilitate incerta sempiternam illam vitam atque laetitiam in
caelestibus praesta domine."
32. Loren C. MacKinney, *Early Medieval Medicine: With Special Reference to
France and Chartres* (Baltimore, 1937; repr. New York, 1979), 24–25, 61–68. But see
now the reassessment of Gregory's attitude toward medicine in Jerome Kroll and
Bernard Bachrach, "Sin and the Etiology of Disease in Pre-Crusade Europe," *Journal
of the History of Medicine and the Allied Sciences* 41 (1986): 405–6.

name Joshua on it, and place it under his father's pillow. When Gregory did so, the old man was cured.[33] As an adult, Gregory was an enthusiastic booster for the holy power of the saints, a power that reached from beyond the grave to cure the infirmities of the sick, often in sudden miracles.[34] To Gregory the cure of illness or injury by direct divine intervention was "celestial medicine" (*caelestis medicina*), and he cautioned his readers not to vitiate its effects by recourse to "earthly remedies" (*terrena medicamenta*).[35]

With the passing of Gregory and the coming of Irish monks to Gaul, a different mood came slowly to prevail—a mood expressed by a subtle shift in the balance set up by Caesarius. Prayers and ritual acts increasingly emphasized the cure of the soul over that of the body. This change may have to do with the fact that the use of oil for anointing the sick continued to be discussed primarily as an alternative to pagan practices. In the middle of the seventh century, Bishop Eligius of Noyon deliberately mined the writings of Caesarius in urging his flock to eschew the magical methods of diviners and folk healers for the benefits of communion and anointing with oil at the hands of priests.[36] The change may also have to do with Columbanus's rejection of medical (and all other nonscriptural) learning in favor of a life of penitential asceticism.[37] It almost certainly had to do with a change in spirituality among the Frankish aristocracy, who, deeply affected by the asceticism of the Irish monks, turned toward a more penitential lifestyle. When the Merovingian queen Balthildis (d. ca. 680) fell sick, for example, she chose between the skill of her doctors and a simple faith in God—the "celestial doctor" (*caelestis medicus*)—letting the illness take its course and rejoicing

33. *Gregorii episcopi Turonensis liber in gloria confessorum,* chap. 39, ed. Bruno Krusch, MGH, SRM 1, pt. 2 (Hanover, 1885), 772.

34. Peter Brown, "Relics and Social Status in the Age of Gregory of Tours," in his *Society and the Holy in Late Antiquity* (Berkeley and Los Angeles, 1982), 222–50; and idem, *Cult of the Saints,* 106–27.

35. *Gregorii episcopi Turonensis libri historiarum decem,* bk. 5, chap. 6, ed. Bruno Krusch and Wilhelm Levison, 2d ed., MGH, SRM 1, pt. 1 (Hanover, 1951), 203: "Hic tantum, quid neglegentibus evenerit, qui post virtutem caelestem terrena medicamenta quaesierunt. . . . Ideo doceat unumquemque christianum haec causa, ut, quando caelestem accipere meruerit medicinam, terrena non requirat studia." Cf. ibid., bk. 2, chap. 1, p. 37: "Quadam tamen die dum quidam infirmus medicinam a beato Martino expeteret."

36. *Vita Eligii episcopi Noviomagensis,* ed. Bruno Krusch, MGH, SRM 4 (Hanover, 1902), 707; Chavasse, *Etude,* 118–23.

37. Pierre Riché, *Education and Culture in the Barbarian West, Sixth through Eighth Centuries,* trans. John J. Contreni (Columbia, S.C., 1976), 325.

in the opportunity offered by her suffering to prepare for her death, which followed shortly.[38]

There are no extant rituals of blessing or anointing the sick from Merovingian Gaul, but certain items in Gallican ritual books, several of which survive from the late seventh and early eighth centuries, reveal these same tendencies, as do changes made in Roman materials after they were brought north.[39] Though the desire for physical healing never entirely disappears, the fragments of the early Gallican liturgy that concern the sick express a more spiritualized understanding of the efficacy of the oil for the sick and of the meaning of sickness itself in the life of a Christian.

The *Missale Gothicum*, written between 690 and 710 in Burgundy, includes two prayers for the sick.[40] The first is a bidding calling on the people to entreat God to grant the gift of his celestial medicine to the ill members of the congregation. "Let us beg the God of universal salvation and Lord of universal power for our brothers and sisters who have been struck according to the flesh by diverse types of sickness, that the Lord may grant them the heavenly gift of his medicine."[41] The second addresses God directly: "Lord, for whom it is easy to raise the dead, restore the sick to their previous health, lest they who beg the cure of your celestial mercy lack the remedies of earthly medicine."[42] These prayers seem to seek the return of health in terms of the "celestial medicine" familiar to Gregory of Tours. But there are differences. The help they seek is to come directly from God and not from the saints, an indication that the prayers have their roots in the old Roman liturgy. But when references to *medicina caelestis* appear in Roman liturgical books,

38. *Vita sanctae Balthildis*, chap. 12, ed. Bruno Krusch, MGH, SRM 2 (Hanover, 1888), 497–98: "Coepitque ipsa domna Balthildis corpore infirmari . . . et nisi medicorum studia subvenissent, pene deficere. Sed magis ipsa ad caelestem medicum semper fidem habebat de salute sua. Ipsa vero . . . non cessabat Deo gratias agere de sua castigatione." On Balthildis, see Geary, *Before France and Germany*, 186–90.

39. On the Gallican ritual books, see Vogel, *Medieval Liturgy*, 108, 275–77; on the Gallican liturgy in general, see James W. McKinnon, "Gallican Rite," DMA 5.344–45, and William S. Porter, *The Gallican Rite*, Studies in Eucharistic Faith and Practice 4 (London, 1958).

40. Vatican MS Reg. lat. 317; CLLA 210.

41. Gothicum, no. 240: "Uniuersae salutis deum et uniuersae uirtutis dominum dipraecimor pro fratribus et sororibus nostris, qui secundum carnem diuersis aegretudinum generibus insultantur, ut his dominus caeleste medicinae suae munus indulgeat."

42. Ibid., no. 241: "Domine, cui uiuificare mortuos facile est, restitue aegrotantibus pristinae sanitati, ne terreni medicaminis remedia desiderent, quicumque medillam caelestis misericordiae tuae dipraecantur."

they do so always in contexts of spiritual rather than physical health.[43] The same is true of the word for *remedy* in the second prayer (*medella,* here *medilla*). In Roman liturgical usage it refers to a remedy for the soul, not for the body.[44] A Roman prayer that represents the paschal ceremonies as God's *caelestia remedia,* originally meant for the Tuesday of Easter week, appears in the Holy Thursday mass in the *Missale Gothicum*—that is, the mass in which the oil for the sick was to be blessed.[45] Such peculiarities in this most Gallican of massbooks present a different emphasis than was apparent in the Roman prayers for the sick and in the writings of Gregory of Tours. The Gallican prayers make no mention of returning to an active life in the church community. By subtle shifts in the meaning and use of old terms, they suggest that what was sought was primarily a form of spiritual health—a health of the soul, not of the body.

Other sources support this interpretation. The old Roman formula for blessing the oil used to anoint the sick probably arrived in Gaul via a Roman sacramentary that crossed the Alps before the year 700.[46] When it did, it was altered to emphasize the spiritual powers of the oil. Where the original Roman formula mentioned only the healing of the body, the Gallican speaks of the body and mind (*corporis et mentis*) and of the body, soul, and spirit (*corporis animae et spiritus*).[47] Whatever may have been meant by the individual terms, the Gallican additions extended the power of the oil beyond physical healing to encompass a restoration of the purity of the whole person, body and soul. A similar redefinition is apparent in an exorcism and two benedictions for oil preserved in the early eighth-century Bobbio Missal. The exorcism asks that "those who are anointed with this thing created of oil . . . be found worthy to gain eternal life."[48] The benediction that follows strikes the same chord: "Lord of glory . . . bless and sanctify this thing created of oil . . . so that whosoever's body or members have been soothed and bathed with it shall be found worthy to obtain, with celestial

43. See, e.g., Gelasian, no. 1240, which refers to the spiritual benefits derived from the offering of the mass: "Caelestem nobis praebeant haec mysteria, quaesumus, domine, medicinam et uicia nostri cordis expurgent."
44. Albert Blaise, *Le vocabulaire latin des principaux thèmes liturgiques* (Turnhout, 1966), 399–400.
45. Cf. Gelasian, no. 474, and Gothicum, no. 297.
46. Chavasse, *Sacramentaire gélasien,* 689.
47. Chavasse, *Etude,* 40–51; and see above, chap. 1, n. 48.
48. Bobbio, no. 574: "qui ex hac creatura. olii contingitur . . . uitam eterna percipere meriantur."

health, the grace of salvation and the forgiveness of sins."[49] These prayers seem intentionally to play with the ambiguities inherent in the Latin terms for health and salvation (*sanitas* and *salus*). In so doing, they focus their entreaties more on the wounds of the soul than on those of the body, and the goal that is sought is eternal rather than temporal life.

Meager as they are, these Gallican sources hint at a changing understanding of the proper ritual response to sickness. The liturgical sensibility expressed in the Roman rites and prayers for the sick was directed wholly toward the restoration of physical health. Its expression in the sources, even those not completely or purely "Roman," is always consonant with that sensibility. Caesarius of Arles made ritual anointing a means of restoring health and forgiving sins—a ritual alternative to pagan magical medicine. The Gallican materials of the late seventh and early eighth centuries, whether indigenous or built on Roman foundations, expand on the model of Caesarius. They shift attention more exclusively toward the spiritual health of the sick, for the sake not just of this life but of the life to come.[50]

Deathbed Penance

A similar shift in meaning can be dimly discerned in the fragmentary remains concerning rituals of deathbed penance from the same time and place. Merovingian conciliar decrees up to the year 695 do not address the issue of deathbed penance; nor does any trace of the practice appear in the Gallican liturgical books.[51] Yet references in saints' lives and other narrative sources from the sixth century reveal that it continued to be sought by people in danger of death. In the violent and bloody world of early Merovingian Gaul it was many people's only hope of salvation: fearing

49. Bobbio, no. 575: "Rex gloriae . . . benedic hanc creatura olei et sanctifica eam . . . ut cuiuscumque corpus. uel membra ex eo fuerit lenitum. uel perfusum salutaris graciam et peccatorum ueniam. et sanitate celeste consequi meriantur." The Latin is very irregular; *salutaris graciam* should be either *salutarem graciam* (healthful grace) or *salutis graciam* (grace of salvation).

50. A final benediction in the Bobbio Missal (no. 576), an addition to the original manuscript and written in even worse Latin that the rest, while mentioning the restoration of bodily health, explicitly links the anointing with purgation and the journey to God: "sumant sibi sanetatem corpores et anime tutelam salutes intellectum et sensom Aiuro te criaturi oliae . . . ut sis sanctefecacio et purgacio hominum quia ex te ongendi fuerent uel sumti quos deus ad suam graciam uocare dinatus est." Cf. Chavasse, *Etude*, 79.

51. *Concilia Galliae a. 511–a. 695*, ed. de Clercq; Vogel, *Discipline pénitentielle*, 164–66.

to face the judgment of God for their crimes, they desperately turned to the church for help. Gregory of Tours described instances in which laymen and clerics demanded or received penance before death, as well as a case in which a timely confession resulted in the cure of a mortally ill archdeacon.[52] The frequency of such incidents appears to have fallen off in the seventh century, however, as the Franks, under the tutelage of the Irish, came to live lives of more constant penitential activity. José Janini has argued that refugees from Spain carried a rite of deathbed penance into Francia after the Muslim invasion in 711.[53] Clearly such a ritual order was lacking, since neither the Roman nor the Gallican books contained organized rites for deathbed penance. Nonetheless, the Frankish church seems not to have felt the need to organize rites of deathbed penance along Visigothic lines. Instead, ritual activity around deathbeds began to draw on themes and symbols of penance as extensions of life practices that were in general directed toward purification of the soul and preparation for the afterlife.

In the second book of his *Lives of Columbanus and His Disciples*, Jonas of Bobbio recorded several stories about the deaths of holy men and women in the seventh century. In his telling, penitential themes and gestures abound, often mixed with references to the purificatory effects of sickness. Prompted by a nocturnal vision, Columbanus's companion Eustasius chose thirty days of heavy suffering over forty days of lighter pains to purge himself in preparation for death. As a result, his soul passed immediately into heaven. Sisetrudis, a nun of Faremoutiers, also received a revelation about her approaching death. After she had done penance for thirty-seven days, two heavenly youths appeared and took her away to join the heavenly choir. Nevertheless, she was sent back to fulfill an ordained period of forty days and to provide an example for the other nuns. Ercantrudis, a novice at Faremoutiers, suffered horribly from sickness, but "the more pains brought upon her afflicted body, the more the hope of delights to come and rejoicing in eternal life gladdened her soul." Another young woman, nearing her death, informed her mother, who had been tempted to leave the convent, that she would see if the heavenly court would accept her intercession. The mother did penance for forty days. At the end of that time her visions of terrible demons gave way to calm and she died

52. See Vogel, *Discipline pénitentielle*, 152–53, 164–65, 158.
53. José Janini, "Las oraciones visigóticas de los formularios penitenciales de Reginensis 316," *Hispania Sacra* 37 (1985): 191–204.

confident that her daughter's intercession had led to her forgiveness. Jonas comments: "So you see, one who was not strong enough to evade ruin in this life through her own merits won salvation through the intervention of her daughter and a short term of penitential discipline."[54]

From Death to Burial

The evidence from the later sixth century to the middle of the eighth for the development of rituals for the period between death and burial is scattered and difficult to interpret. The old Roman *ordo defunctorum* may have been in use in Rome, but if so it left little trace on the emerging Roman sacramentaries, which began to have an impact on the Frankish church when they arrived in Gaul around the turn of the eighth century. The Gregorian sacramentary contains no death ritual, though at some point in the seventh century three prayers *ad agenda mortuorum* became attached to it.[55] The other Roman sacramentary, known as the Gelasian, which took shape in the seventh century in Rome, and whose original content has been reconstructed from the Frankish Vatican Gelasian (written around 750), also seems to have contained little or no material on death and dying.[56] Antoine Chavasse and Damien Sicard believe that it contained one prose prayer, the *Deus apud quem*, that was based on the psalmody of the Roman *ordo* and was meant to be spoken as part of it.[57] This judgment has been questioned more than once, and the prayer's origin is just as likely to be found in the liturgical workshops of Visigothic Spain or Burgundy.[58] Whatever the case may be, the prayer expresses ideas that were common in the Latin church in the seventh and eighth centuries and that in one form or another survived throughout the Middle Ages:

54. Jonas of Bobbio, *Vitae Columbani abbatis discipulorumque eius*, ed. Bruno Krusch, MGH, SRM 4 (Hanover, 1902), 129–31; 133: "in quantum corpus angebant poene illate, tantum animam laetificabat spes gaudiorum et exultatio vitae aeternae"; 135: "Quippe datur intellegi, ut qui suis meritis non valuit saeculi evadere ruinas, interventu filiae meruit paenitendo in parvo spatio per poenas inlatas salvari."

55. Hadrianum, nos. 1015–17; these prayers are discussed in chap. 4.

56. The prayers for death and burial in the Vatican Gelasian are Frankish additions; see Deshusses, "Sacramentaires," 26–28; Vogel, *Medieval Liturgy*, 66–67.

57. Chavasse, *Sacramentaire gélasien*, 58–61; Sicard, *Liturgie*, 79–102.

58. See Bernard Moreton, review of Sicard, *Liturgie*, in JTS 31 (1980): 233–34; and José Janini, "'In sinu amici tui Abrahae': Origen de la recomendación del alma, del Reginensis," *Miscel.lània litúrgica catalana* 3 (Barcelona, 1984): 79–90.

God in whom all mortal things live, to whom our bodies do not perish by dying but are changed into something better, as suppliants we entreat you to order the soul of your servant N. to be gathered up through the hands of the blessed angels, led into the bosom of your friend Abraham the patriarch, and resuscitated on the last day of the great judgment. Through the indulgence of your piety, wash away whatever, under the sway of the devil, it may have done in this world contrary to you.[59]

Added to the ancient request for reception of the soul into the interim condition that would last until the end of mortal time is a reference to cleansing and forgiveness, echoing the heightened concern for the purification of the soul evident in the prayers and rites for the sick and the dying.[60]

This penitential attitude also played a role in changing burial practices among the Frankish aristocracy in the late seventh and early eighth centuries. The Franks had taken from the Romans the custom of burial with articles of personal apparel and domestic use, to which they added the weapons and treasure that were the signs of their status in life. Thus the typical Frankish "row grave" cemeteries usually centered on the graves of a wealthy warrior and his family, richly attired and buried with weapons.[61] The Gallo-Roman church saw nothing untoward in this style of burial—the Christian Frankish kings were buried thus in church graves and the practice survived throughout the seventh century.[62] Change came

59. Gelasian, no. 1627: "Deus, apud quem omnia moriencia uiuunt, cui non periunt moriendo corpora nostra sed mutantur in melius, te supplices deprecamur, ut suscipi iubeas animam famuli tui *illius* per manus sanctorum angelorum deducendam in sinu amici tui patriarchae Abrahae, resuscitandam in die nouissimo magne iudicii; et si quid de regione mortali tibi contrarium contraxit fallente diabulo, tua pietate ablue indulgendo." For variants, see Sicard, *Liturgie*, 89–92.
60. Cf. the language of the *Hanc igitur* prayer from the first of the masses *super defunctos* in the so-called Verona sacramentary (Verona, no. 1140), "quidquid terrena conuersatione contraxit, his sacrificiis emundetur," with the reconciliation prayer from the Spanish deathbed penance rite (Liber ordinum, 92): "Renoua in eum, piissime Pater, quicquid diabolica fraude uiolatum est"; the first prayer from the ritual of Caesarius of Arles, *Pio recordationis*, Gelasian, 1607: "concessa uenia plenae indulgenciae, quicquid in hoc saeculo proprius error adtulit"; and the *Deus, apud quem* (n. 59). The exact provenance of these prayers is less important than the light they shed on the links between the language of prayers of penitence and those said for the soul after death in the ritual life of the sixth and seventh centuries.
61. Geary, *Before France and Germany*, 74–75, 167–69; Edward James, *The Franks* (Oxford, 1988), 137–61; see also Young, "Paganisme, christianisation et rites funéraires mérovingiennes."
62. Donald Bullough, "Burial, Community, and Belief in the Early Medieval West," in *Ideal and Reality in Frankish and Anglo-Saxon Society,* ed. Patrick Wormald (Oxford, 1983), 186–87.

about because the penetration of Irish monasticism reoriented power and spirituality in Gaul. When the Frankish aristocracy founded Irish monasteries on their rural estates, the monastic churches became the loci of family mausoleums.[63] The close connections between the aristocracy and monasticism led then to a retreat from ostentatious burial. Bailey Young has traced the first such retreat to St. Gertrude (d. 659), the daughter of the Frankish mayor Pippin I, one of the founders of the Carolingian house.[64] Before her death, as an act of penitential piety, Gertrude asked that she be buried in nothing more than a simple linen shroud.[65] Her example was followed; by the mid-eighth century, grave goods had disappeared from the tombs of the Franks.

But let us return to the deathbed rituals themselves. The Bobbio Missal preserves a group of five prayers *ad defunctum*—three new prayers sandwiched between the two from the service appended to Caesarius's rule for nuns—which were said immediately after death and before the graveside prayers. Thus the Bobbio prayers represent an elaboration of the immediate liturgical response to death which began the older ritual. The first two of the three new prayers reiterate ideas from the Caesarian prayers *Pio recordationis* and *Te Domine*. They beg God to receive the soul now in transit and allow it to evade the fires of hell.[66] The third prayer is a bidding recalling to the attendants their common condition as descendants of Adam and thus bringing the community of witnesses into a state of identification with the dead person and deeper participation in the ritual action.[67]

All the prayers in the ritual of Caesarius and the Bobbio Missal

63. Geary, *Before France and Germany*, 169–75.

64. Bailey K. Young, "Exemple aristocratique et mode funéraire dans la Gaule mérovingienne," AESC 41 (1986): 370–407.

65. *Vita Sanctae Geretrudis*, c. 7, ed. Bruno Krusch, MGH, SRM 2 (Hanover, 1888), 461–62.

66. Bobbio, nos. 536: "Tu nobis domine auxilium prestare digneris. tu per misericordiae largiaris animam quoque famulo tuo *ill.* a uinculis corporalibus. liberato in pace sanctorum tuorum recipias. et gehenne ignis. euadat," and 537: "Deus qui iustis supplicacionibus semper presto adest (*sic*). qui pia uota dignaris intuere da animam famulo tuo *ill.* cuius transetus. hodie. officia prestamus; cum sanctis adque elictis tuis beati muneris. porcionem." Cf. Sicard, *Liturgie*, 280–85. *Transetus* in the second prayer is a rare usage of this term to refer to death in the early liturgical sources.

67. Bobbio, no. 538: "Antique memores. cyrographum. fratres dilectissimi. quo primo homenis. peccato et corrupcione addicta est. humana condicio sub cuius lege id. sibi unusquisque formidat. quod alia inuistigauit. uideatque omnipotentis dei. misericordia. deprecimur. pro anima kari nostri *ill.* cuius hodiae deposicionem celebramus. ut. eam in aeternam requiem suscipiat. et beate resurreccionis repre-sentit."

appear within the extensive service over the dead body and during burial in the Vatican Gelasian. Sicard has seen in the remaining Gelasian prayers a third Gallican ritual that circulated in the late seventh and early eighth centuries, but I find the evidence inconclusive.[68] What seems certain to me is that the ritual in the Vatican Gelasian incorporates the continued development of prayers for the various moments in the ritual process.

The recognition that the prayers in the Bobbio Missal developed the initial response to death expressed in the first two prayers of the Caesarian ritual for nuns is evident in their placement in the expanded ritual in the Vatican Gelasian, where they figure among the prayers *post obitum* and before the body was taken out for burial.[69] Along with them are two other prayers. The first, *Diri uulneris*, appears to be a Gallican composition. It reiterates the supplications of the opening prayer, *Pio recordationis*, imploring God to receive the soul, cleanse it of the stains contracted in the world, and order it to join with the saints in praise of its creator when it is reunited with its body at the end of time.[70] The second, beginning *Suscipe, domine*, is a prose rendering of the vocabulary and ideas of the psalmodic response to death in the Roman ritual. It begins: "Receive, Lord, the soul of your servant returning to you, departing from the lands of Egypt. Send forth your holy angels to meet him and show him the way of justice. Open to him the gates of justice and repel from him the princes of darkness."[71]

A second form of the prayer *Suscipe* seems to have been meant to accompany the laying out and washing of the corpse. Its imagery links the ritual washing and reclothing of the body on earth with a

68. Sicard, *Liturgie,* 304–32. I find unconvincing Sicard's reasoning (305) based on the phrase "Obsequiis autem rite celebratis, membris ex feretro depositis, tumulo ex more conposito, post Israhelis exitu ex Aegypto" in the last prayer before the commendation in the Vatican Gelasian (Gelasian, no. 1625). The ablatives more likely refer only to the burial phase of the ritual rather than to the whole. See the critical remarks of Moreton in JTS 31 (1980): 232, 234.

69. Bobbio, no. 536 = Gelasian, no. 1609; Bobbio 538 = Gelasian 1613; Bobbio 537 = Gelasian 1614.

70. Gelasian, no. 1608; cf. Sicard, *Liturgie,* 305–8.

71. Gelasian, no. 1610: "Suscipe, domine, animam serui tui *ille* ad te reuertentem de Aegypti partibus proficiscentem ad te. Emitte angelos tuos sanctos in obuiam illius et uiam iusticiae demonstra ei. Aperi ei portas iusticiae et repelle ab ea principes tenebrarum." Cf. Liber ordinum, 110. Note the parallels between these images and those of the psalmody in the Roman *ordo defunctorum:* the reception by angels, the return from Egypt, the opening of the gates of justice. Sicard did not comment on these parallels in his study; see *Liturgie,* 308–19. As before, questions of provenance, which may one day be settled, are less important than the fact that, especially in Visigothic Spain and Francia, older materials were being reworked to fill out the ritual structure.

parallel ceremony in heaven: "Receive, Lord, the soul of your servant . . . clothe it in heavenly vestments and wash it in the holy font of eternal life."[72] The last *Suscipe* prayer is more difficult to place, but it may have accompanied the burial, as it pays the same attention to the relationship of the body and soul that appeared in the Caesarian ritual at this point and looks forward to the reunification of the two at the end of time. "Receive, Lord, your servant N. in his eternal home and grant him peace and the kingdom, that is, the celestial Jerusalem . . . grant him a place in the first resurrection; let him rise with those who rise, and receive his body with all those who will receive their bodies on the day of the resurrection; let him come with the blessed who will come to the right hand of the father, and let him possess eternal life with all those who will possess it."[73] The Visigothic origin of this prayer and the preceding one is evident in the use of rhymed couplets, a textual signature of Visigothic Spanish compositions, as Jean Deshusses has shown.[74] Their appearance in a fragment of an eighth-century Irish sacramentary points to the sharing of images and ideas among Spain, Gaul, and Ireland during this period. Their eschatological terminology, especially in regard to the *prima resurrectio*, appears in contemporary Gallican prayers for the dead. This "first resurrection" referred to the millennial period after the second coming, when Christ would reign on earth with the elect. It is often referred to in the prayers *post nomina* of the *Missale Gothicum* as well as in a prayer *pro spiritibus pausancium* in the same sacramentary.[75]

72. Gelasian, no. 1611: "Suscipe, domine, animam serui tui . . . uestem caelestem indue eam et laua eam sanctum fontem uitae aeternae." Cf. Liber ordinum, 110–11; echoes here of the baptismal liturgy may be heard as well in the Visigothic rite of deathbed penance, discussed below. They suggest that it was Spanish liturgists who modeled rites for the dying and the dead on the ritual of baptism, with its overtones of penance and spiritual transformation and its tight structure as a rite of passage.

73. Gelasian, no. 1612: "Suscipe, domine, seruum tuum *illum* in aeternum habitaculum et da ei requiem et regnum id es Hierusalem caelestem . . . et habeat partem in prima resurrectione, et inter surgentes resurgat, et inter suscipientes corpora in die resurrectionis corpus suscipiat, et cum benedictis ad dexteram dei patris uenientibus ueniat, et inter possidentes uitam aeternam possideat."

74. Jean Deshusses, "Le 'Supplément' au sacramentaire grégorien: Alcuin ou Saint Benoît d'Aniane?" ALW 9 (1965): 52–58.

75. Gothicum, nos. 207, 479, 534, 248; Sicard, *Liturgie*, 292–95. Cf. Bernard Botte, "Prima resurrectio, un vestige de millénarisme dans les liturgies occidentales," *Recherches de théologie ancienne et médiévale* 15 (1948): 5–17; Ntedika, *Evocation de l'au-delà*, 227–31. Ntedika argues that the theme of the *prima resurrectio* appeared in the liturgy at the end of the fourth century and the beginning of the fifth, a period of millennial feeling. And see below n. 121.

New prayers at the graveside also date from this period. They reiterate many of the familiar themes while stressing the separation of body and soul at death and their reunification at the resurrection: "Let us pray, dearest friends, for the soul of our dear one N., which the lord found worthy to liberate from the snares of this world, whose body is borne today to burial"; "Now that we have celebrated these ritual obsequies, deposited the body from the bier in the grave, which has been made according to custom, and after [we have sung of] the passage of the Israelites from Egypt, let us beseech the clemency of God the father for the soul of our dear one."[76] The custom of ending the burial service with a prayer of commendation, first seen in the ritual of Caesarius of Arles, became through its incorporation in the Vatican Gelasian a standard feature of Frankish rituals.[77]

The Mass as a Rite of Incorporation

The mass had been offered since antiquity in the name of the dead members of church communities, but from the end of the sixth century in the West it came to play an increasingly important role in commemoration of the dead and in posthumous rituals of expiation. Commemoration in this form was directed at the incorporation of the souls of the dead in the community of the blessed in the other world and was a response to a growing sense among Christians that their immediate destination after death was not the bosom of Abraham but some state of purgation, suspended between heaven and hell, between the living and those at rest in God. The offering of the mass, the celebration of the Christian meal, came to symbolize, even to trigger, an end to interim suffering of souls and the completion of their passage into heaven. The first person to articulate this attitude was Pope Gregory I (590–604).[78] The discussions at the end of Gregory's *Dialogues* leave the reader (or listener) to ponder on the mass as the one thing that can "possi-

---

76. Gelasian, nos. 1620: "Oremus, fratres karissimi, pro anima cari nostri *illius*, quem dominus de laqueo huius saeculi liberare dignatus est, cuius corpusculum hodie sepulturae traditur," and 1625: "Obsequiis autem rite celebratis, membris ex feretro depositis, tumulo ex more conposito, post Israhelis exitu ex Aegypto [i.e, Ps. 113] deprecemur clemenciam dei patris pro anima cari nostri *illius*."
77. Gelasian, no. 1626; cf. Sicard, *Liturgie*, 275–79.
78. Cyril Vogel, "Deux conséquences de l'eschatologie grégorienne: La multiplication des messes privées et les moines-prêtres," in *Grégoire le Grand*, Colloques internationaux du Centre National de la Recherche Scientifique, ed. Jacques Fontaine, Robert Gillet, and Stan Pellistrandi (Paris, 1986), 267–76.

bly benefit the soul after death."[79] Gregory's ideas fell on fertile ground among northern Christian communities over the next two centuries. The Irish compilation of canon law known as the *Collectio Hibernensis* (ca. 700) cities the *Dialogues* in support of the use of the mass to release souls from suffering in the afterlife and gives directions for the commutation of penances after death.[80] Irish practice in this matter had a great effect on the Frankish church in the eighth century, both directly and indirectly, through the Anglo-Saxons.[81]

The new approach to commemoration can be seen in the ritual books of the period. Between the beginning of the seventh century and the first quarter of the eighth, the formulas of the Roman masses for the dead in the private collection of mass prayers known as the Verona "sacramentary" (ca. 600) were reused in the creation of a series of commemorative masses for the dead which eventually became incorporated in the Gelasian sacramentary.[82] Chavasse has identified the Roman origins for most of these masses, assigning some of them to monastic milieux.[83] For the most part, the masses remained unaltered when they arrived in Francia, but the changes that were made are significant. A commemorative mass in the Vatican Gelasian, for example, was originally intended for the seventh and thirtieth days after a burial.[84] Chavasse has shown how, under the influence of the penitential collections circulating in the early eighth century under the name of Theodore of Tarsus, archbishop of Canterbury (669–90), a scribe altered that mass to make it suitable as a funeral mass for clergy and a commemorative mass for the laity as well.[85] Arnold Angenendt, in commenting on this change, has argued that the stipulations under which religious could have a mass on the day of their death, "good" members of the laity on the third day afterward, and penitents only after their

79. Grégoire le Grand, *Dialogues*, bk. 4, cc. 57–62, ed. Adalbert de Vogüé, 3 vols., Sources Chrétiennes 252, 260, 265 (Paris, 1978–80), 3.184–207; 4.57 begins with the question: "Quidnam ergo esse poterit, quod mortuorum ualeat animabus prodesse?"

80. *Die Irische Kanonensammlung*, ed. H. Wasserschleben, 2d ed. (Leipzig, 1885), 43, bk. 15, c. 3, *De sacrificiando pro mortuis;* and 44, c. 7, *De estimatione animae redemptae.*

81. Kathleen Hughes, "Some Aspects of Irish Influence on Early English Private Prayer," *Studia Celtica* 5 (1970): 48–61.

82. Gelasian, nos. 1628–95; Verona, nos. 1138–60.

83. Chavasse, *Sacramentaire gélasien,* 61–71.

84. Gelasian, nos. 1690–95.

85. Chavasse, *Sacramentaire gélasien,* 68–71.

relatives had fasted and offered oblations for seven or thirty days signal a change in thinking about memorial services. No longer simply opportunities to commemorate the deceased, they now marked periods of time in a process of purification. The slow penetration of new penitential practices from Ireland and England had carried with it the sense that every sin had its penance, and wrongs not atoned for in life would have to be expiated after death. Since the dead could not help themselves, they needed the help of their surviving kin, either natural or spiritual.[86]

This help was mediated by the clergy through a new form of the mass, the *missa specialis* or votive mass. What distinguishes these eighth-century votive masses from the ancient tradition of offering the mass in the name of the living or the dead is the presence of a contractual relation between the persons who requested such a mass and the priest or community who sang it. The wording of the prayers implies an exchange of alms between the officiant and the persons who requested a special mass as well as the presence on the altar, in written form, of the names of the persons, living or dead, for whom the mass was sung. The practice as a whole was predicated on the assumption that the mass was a gift to God, which he would reciprocate.[87] The earliest examples of these votive masses are in the Bobbio Missal—masses for priests to sing for their own sins, miscellaneous masses, and a mass for the living and the dead.[88] Their immediate origin, however, lies in the dovetailing of the social practice of gift giving in early medieval society and the import of Pope Gregory's answer to a query about aid to souls in the afterlife: "If their sins are not indissoluble after death, the holy offering of the saving sacrifice may bring aid to many souls even then."[89]

86. Arnold Angenendt, "Theologie und Liturgie der mittelalterlichen Toten-Memoria," in *Memoria*, ed. Karl Schmid and Joachim Wollasch (Munich, 1984), 171–72, 131–64; and cf. the story told by Jonas of Bobbio about a daughter's intercession for her mother in n. 54 above.

87. Arnold Angenendt, "Missa Specialis: Zugleich ein Beitrag zur Entstehung der Privat-Messen," FS 17 (1983): 153–221. See also Vogel, "Deux conséquences de l'eschatologie grégorienne," 270–71.

88. Bobbio, nos. 405–40; Angenendt has found echoes of the Penitential of Columbanus in the wording of the prayer *post nomina*—after the reading of the names—in the priest's mass; "Missa Specialis," 184.

89. Grégoire le Grand, *Dialogues*, 4.57.2, ed. de Vogüé, 3.184: "Si culpae post mortem insolubiles non sunt, multum solet animas etiam post mortem sacra oblatio hostiae salutaris adiuuare." On gift giving in early medieval society, see Geary, *Before France and Germany*, 50; Georges Duby, *The Early Growth of the European Economy: Warriors and Peasants from the Seventh to the Twelfth Century*, trans. Howard B. Clarke (Ithaca, N.Y., 1974), 48–56, 68–69; and for a classic

I have more than once mentioned the crosscurrents that were flowing through Gaul, especially from the Christian communities of Italy, Spain, and Ireland from the sixth century to the middle of the eighth. Certain rituals that emerged concurrently in Visigothic Spain and in Ireland affected both the changes we have seen and others that would later emerge from the reform of church and society under the Carolingians.

Visigothic Spain

At the end of the sixth century, the Visigothic king Reccared converted to Catholic Christianity from the Arian faith of his predecessors, thus setting the Visigothic (or old Spanish, or Mozarabic) church on a new course and ushering in a century of vibrant activity on all levels of ecclesiastical organization.[90] The manuscripts that preserve the rituals of the early medieval Spanish church, the *Libri ordinum*, are late, one from the tenth century and two from the eleventh, but most of the material in them originated in the sixth and seventh centuries.[91] They preserve *ordines* that reveal the pecu-

anthropological discussion of its centrality in cultures with limited resources, see Marcel Mauss, *The Gift: Forms and Functions of Exchange in Archaic Societies,* trans. Ian Cunnison (New York, 1967).

90. On the Visigothic church, see José Orlandis and Domingo Ramos-Lisson, *Die Synoden auf der Iberischen Halbinsel bis zum Einbruch des Islam (711)* (Paderborn, 1981); and the articles and bibliography in *Visigothic Spain: New Approaches,* ed. Edward James (Oxford, 1980).

91. On the *Libri ordinum* and the historical development of the old Spanish liturgy, see J. M. Pinell, "Liturgia (Hispánica)," *Diccionario de historia eclesiástica de España* (Madrid, 1972), 2.1303–20; Janini, *Manuscritos litúrgicos,* vol. 1, *Castilla y Navarra* (Burgos, 1977), 8–29; T. C. Akely, *Christian Initiation in Spain c. 300–1100* (London, 1967), 109, 111–13. There is much disagreement on the extent to which the *Libri ordinum* reflect the ritual life of the Spanish church in the seventh century, before the Muslim invasion. Férotin, *Liber ordinum,* p. ix; H. B. Porter, "The Origin of the Medieval Rite for Anointing the Sick or Dying," JTS, n.s. 7 (1956): 217; and Ntedika, *Evocation de l'au-delà,* 35–36, all argue for the fidelity of the late manuscripts to early practice. Sicard, *Liturgie,* and Deshusses, "Sacramentaires," tend to ignore the issue. As for me, I see good reason to judge each ritual or prayer on a separate basis. In the case of the rite of anointing the sick, the antiquity of the form in the *Libri ordinum* is proven by the use made of it by Benedict of Aniane in the ninth century (as we shall see in chap. 4); in the case of the deathbed penance rite, its antiquity is assured by the abundant references to the practice in narrative and conciliar sources. The rites for death and burial are more problematic. The long ritual in the *Libri ordinum* (Liber ordinum, 107–35; Liber ordinum sacerdotal, 62–71) unquestionably has its origins in the early period—narrative and conciliar sources establish the antiquity of the central place held by the singing of psalms in the ritual, and some of its prayers appear in eighth- and ninth-century

liarities of the ritual care of the sick and dying in the late sixth- and seventh-century Spain.

Anointing the Sick in the *Libri ordinum*

The legacy of Caesarius of Arles on the ritual treatment of the sick was adapted differently in Visigothic Spain than in Merovingian Gaul. Caesarius had repeatedly stressed the twofold nature of the anointing of the sick: the forgiveness of sins and the return of health. The bishop's concern was that the magical medicine of ligatures and suspensions might bring a physical cure, but at the expense of the soul's good health. Caesarius hoped to encourage the people to seek both forms of health within the ritual structures of the Catholic church. The balance drawn by Caesarius between the two sides of this *duplicia bona*, however, was not long maintained in Spain. The remains of blessings, prayers, and rituals for the sick in use there between 550 and 750 reveal that their action and symbolism tended more toward the old Roman emphasis on physical healing.[92]

Blessing and Exorcising the Oil for the Sick

There are two types of Spanish *Libri ordinum*, episcopal and priestly; both record various benedictions and exorcisms of the oil for the sick, offices of vespers and matins for the sick, and a rite for anointing a sick person at home. Unlike the Roman bishops, who performed the blessing on Holy Thursday and used simple olive oil, Visigothic bishops used chrism (a mixture of oil and perfume) and performed the blessing at the end of the mass on the feast of the Byzantine doctor-saints Cosmas and Damian.[93] Neither the bish-

---

northern manuscripts—but the uncertainty about the precise nature of the rites before the ninth century has placed it outside of my analysis here.

92. Cf. the suggestive conclusion to Annette Niederhellmann's study of doctors and medicine in the barbarian law codes, *Arzt und Heilkunde*, 298–305; Niederhellmann found significant differences in attitudes toward doctors, illness, and magic expressed in the laws of Visigoths, Burgundians, and Lombards on the one hand and those of the Franks, Bavarians, and Allemans on the other.

93. Liber ordinum, 69–71; because it was an episcopal ceremony, the blessing does not appear in the *Liber ordinum sacerdotal*, which was a ritual book for priests. Férotin's edition was based on the episcopal *Libri ordinum* in MSS Madrid, Real Academia de la Historia, Aemilianensis, 56, and Silos, Biblioteca del Monasterio, 4; the priest's ritual in MS Silos, 3, which Férotin published in the notes to his edition, is now available in Janini's separate edition (Liber ordinum sacerdotal).

op's prayer that precedes the blessing nor the blessing itself ignores the state of the soul, yet it is clear that the ritual action was to be directed primarily toward the health of the body. Here are portions of both.

> God . . . through the power of your blessing, with all pestilence driven out and all weakness removed, let faith obtain the fruit of its petition, the soul the confidence of salvation, the flesh the grace of health. . . . Omnipotent God, bless and sanctify this ointment . . . which confers good health to all. Season this ointment, Lord, with the aromas of sanctity, whence all the sick receive the cure of health, so that all who are anointed with it may receive forgiveness of sins, the grace of your piety, and the medicine of health.[94]

The prayers said by priests have a similar tone. As the oil for the sick was not prepared in the context of a mass, the priest would have spoken the words when the need arose. The *Liber ordinum sacerdotal* records an exorcism and a benediction of the oil for that purpose. The exorcism was taken from the baptismal liturgy and adapted for use with the oil for the sick by the addition of a phrase concerning the health of the body and the soul.[95] The prayer of benediction, on the other hand, refers only to physical healing, and lists generically the ailments that will, it is hoped, be cured through its agency. It starts with the text of the letter of James on anointing:

> Lord Jesus Christ, who spoke through your apostle [James 5:14–15] . . . Sanctify this oil in that manner, by which nothing is impossible to you, in that power which can not only cure the sick but bring the dead back to life. . . . Let this healing unction counteract through you all sicknesses from all causes internal and external. Amen. Let no sickness and no pestilence affect them within or without, but let all deadly poison expire. Amen. May it cleanse, cast out, purge and con-

---

94. Liber ordinum, 70–71: "*Oratio:* Deus. . . . Per uim benedictionis tue omni repulsa peste, omnique ablato languore, obtineat fides fructum petitionis, anima confidentiam salutis, caro gratiam sanitatis. . . . *Benedictio eiusdem:* Omnipotens Deus, benedic et sanctifica hoc unguentum . . . qui [sic] ualitudinem sanitatis conferat uniuersis. Condi unguentum hoc, Dominc, aromatibus sanctitatis: unde omnes languidi medallam percipiant sanitatis; ut omnes qui ex hoc fuerint peruncti, ueniam delictis, gratiam tue pietatis et medicinam percipiant sanitatis."
95. Liber ordinum sacerdotal, no. 138: "Exorcidio te, inmunde spiritus . . . ut sit omnibus qui fuerint ex eo peruncti in preparationem consequende salutis animarum et corporum, adobtionem spiritalium et filiorum dei et remissionem omnium peccatorum. Amen." Cf. Chavasse, *Etude*, 80.

quer because it will be blessed in your name, in whom all creatures are saved. Amen.[96]

Ritual Anointing

The emphasis on healing is most explicit in the rite of visitation and anointing the sick preserved in both the priestly and the episcopal *Libri ordinum*.[97] These books bear the earliest witness to a full ritual answer to Caesarius's call to make anointing the religious response to sickness. The rite had the characteristic Spanish pattern of "administration, psalmody, principal prayer, blessing."[98] The priest entered the room and immediately blessed the sick person while making the sign of the cross on his head with oil. There followed a series of antiphons and responses built around biblical texts and images of healing; for example: "Heal me, Lord, my bones are in torment, my soul is in utter torment. Return, O Lord, and rescue my soul. . . . The Lord said to his disciples, 'Receive the Holy Spirit, in my name cast out demons and place your hands on the sick and they will be well.'"[99] The bidding that follows the antiphons is a simple plea for a cure: "Let us pray to God omnipotent, that he will propitiously deign to cure and heal the wounds of his servant."[100] That bidding is followed in turn by a long prayer addressed to "Jesus, our savior, who is the true health and medicine." The language of this prayer is striking for its juxtaposition of illness and vice: "Extinguish in him, Lord, the heat of

96. Liber ordinum sacerdotal, no. 139: "Domine Ihesu Christe, qui per apostolum tuum dixisti . . . Sanctifica oleum more illo, quo tibi inpossible nicil est, uirtute illa, que non solum curare morbos, sed etiam suscitare mortuos potest. . . . Omnibus ergo per te morbis omnibusque causis internis externisque hec unctio salutaris occurrat. Amen. Nulla morbus eis nullaque pestis interior exteriorque efficiat, sed omne uirus letale expiret. Amen. Subexpurget, excludat, euacuet, et uincat, quia in nomine tuo benedicetur, in quo omnis creatura salbatur. Amen." Cf. Chavasse, *Etude*, 70–74.

97. Liber ordinum, 71–73; Liber ordinum sacerdotal, 58–60, nos. 36–48. This ritual is wrongly identified as a rite of "extreme unction" in Justo Fernández Alonso, *La cura pastoral en la España romanovisigoda* (Rome, 1955), 577–78, a book that must be used with caution.

98. Porter, "Origin," 217.

99. Liber ordinum, 71–72; Liber ordinum sacerdotal, 59: "Sana me, domine, turbata sunt ossa mea et anima mea turbata est ualde. Tu, Domine, conuertere, et eripe animam meam [Ps. 6:3–4]. . . . Dominus locutus est discipulis suis: Accipite Spiritum Sanctum: in nomine meo demonia eicite, et super infirmos imponite manus uestras et bene habebunt [Mark 16:17–18]."

100. Liber ordinum, 72: "Oremus Dei omnipotentis, ut uulnera famuli sui propitius curare ac sanare dignetur." The text in Liber ordinum sacerdotal, 59, differs somewhat: "Oremus dei omnipotentis. Ut uulnera famulorum suorum Ill. per angelum suum sanctum sanare et confortare dignetur."

lusts and fevers, destroy the torture of vices and the sting of pains, dissolve the torment of cupidity and sickness, suppress the swelling of pride and tumors, empty out the rottenness of vanity and ulcers, calm the inside of the entrails and the heart . . . remove the scars of conscience and wounds . . . put in order the works of the flesh and the material of the blood and grant him forgiveness of his sins."[101] This highly rhetorical language may indicate that its author drew a causal connection between specific sins and infirmities or simply that the moral condition of the patient was as important as the physical. The ritual ends with expressions of hope that God will grant the sick person health of the heart and of the body through the agency of an angel of health and peace.[102]

The attitude toward the sick expressed in this simple ritual matches that expressed in the benedictions and exorcisms of the oil. It maintains the Roman emphasis on physical healing while providing a ritual context in line with the goals of Caesarius of Arles. The prayers and the ritual action look toward the return of health and the continued participation of the sick person in the community of the faithful here on earth.

Deathbed Penance as a Rite of Passage

As we have seen, the penitential practices of the Western church were in a state of transition in the time of Caesarius of Arles. The ancient ritual of public penance was not repeatable, and penitents, even after reconciliation, could no longer engage in the full range of activities open to nonpenitents. The Spanish council of Barcelona (540), for example, decreed that male penitents were to be tonsured, to wear the clothing of monks, and to spend the rest of their lives in fasting and prayer.[103] Unwilling to bear such severe consequences,

101. Liber ordinum, 72: "Ihesu saluator noster, qui es uera salus et medicina . . . extingue in eum, Domine, libidinum et febrium estus, dolorum stimulos ac uitiorum obtere cruciatus. Egritudinum et cupiditatum tormenta dissolue. Superbie inflationem tumoresque compesce. Vlcerum uanitatumque putredines euacua. Viscerum interna cordiumque tranquilla. . . . Conscientiarum atque plagarum abducito cicatrices. . . . Opera carnis ac sanguinis materiamque conpone, ac delictorum illi ueniam propitiatus adtribue."

102. Ibid., 73; Liber ordinum sacerdotal, 60: "Atque ita tibi Dominus cordis et corporis medallam adtribuat. . . . In nomine sancte et indiuidue Trinitatis uisitet uos angelus salutis et pacis."

103. Concilios visigóticos, ed. Vives, 53, c. 6: "Poenitentes uiri tonso capite et religioso habitu utentes ieiuniis et obsecrationibus vitae tempus peragant." This requirement could have disastrous results. In the late seventh century, the Suebian king Wamba was given the rite of penance while under the effects of a drug that a rival, Ervig, had managed to slip to him. When he recovered, he was no longer able

most Spanish Christians, like their Frankish contemporaries, turned to the rite of penance only when death seemed imminent.[104] The Spanish church, however, may have been alone in responding to this change in practice by creating a ritual of penance for the dying, which is now preserved in the various manuscripts of the *Libri ordinum*.[105] A condensed form of the full ritual of public penance, the deathbed ritual carried the same consequences as its model, and recipients had to accept those consequences if they recovered.[106] But the severity of its consequences was matched by its transformative power. Public penance, like baptism, holy orders, and monastic profession, was in one sense a rite of preparation for death, since it symbolized a passage from involvement in this world to a condition closer to the next. Deathbed penance, as a compressed form of public penance, shared in its symbolic power; it brought the full ritual lexicon of Christian rites of passage to bear on the period immediately preceding physical death. People who underwent the full ritual had moved beyond the borders of this world. If death followed, the ritual had prepared them for a successful transition to the other world. If death were postponed, they still were not of this world but of the next.[107] Ritual 3 gives the rubrics of the Spanish ritual and the incipits of its prayers and psalmody, as they appear in the *Libri ordinum*.

The three parts of this ceremony correspond to the three basic phases of any rite of passage. The first is a rite of separation involving tonsure, communion, the laying on of sackcloth, and signing with ashes.[108] The act of tonsure permanently separated the recipient from ordinary laymen, placing him among the ranks of the clergy. The reception of communion then recognized this new state. The ritual laying on of sackcloth and the signing with ashes

---

to be king, for he was *velut mortuus huic mundo.* Wamba entered a monastery and Ervig became king! Orlandis and Ramos-Lisson, *Synoden,* 245.

104. J. N. Hillgarth, "Popular Religion in Visigothic Spain," in *Visigothic Spain,* ed. James, 28.

105. Liber ordinum, 87–92. See also Lozano Sebastián, "Legislación canónica," and Janini, "Oraciones visigóticas."

106. *Concilios visigóticos,* ed. Vives, 53, Barcelona, c. 8: "De his qui in infirmitatibus poscunt poenitentiam et a sacerdote accipiant, si postea convaluerint, vitam poenitentiam peragant."

107. The seriousness of the rite is also reflected in the hesitancy to perform it for a young person for whom a life of permanent liminality might be too strenuous in the event of recovery. Thus in some manuscripts a prayer of "viaticum" for a young person in danger of death takes the place of deathbed penance; Liber ordinum, 86–87: "Oratio uiatica super infirmum iuuenem."

108. On rites of separation, see van Gennep, *Rites of Passage,* 11, 21, 105, 106.

Ritual 3. Spanish rite of deathbed penance, seventh century

1. If a sick person should wish to receive penance, a priest, upon going in, should first of all tonsure him. Next he should give him communion. He then covers him in sackcloth, makes the sign of the cross with ashes, and says the following.

Antiphon	Deus, qui das locum penitentie
Verse	Tu es Deus, et in te est Deus et non alius
Bidding	Oremus ut huic famulo suo remissionem peccatorum

2. Then the priest says this prayer without the Lord's Prayer.

Prayer	Iungentes nostros cum fletibus fletus

3. After this prayer he sings the following antiphon and Psalm 50 up to the verse *Ne Proycias me.*

Antiphon	Memento mei, Domine, dum ueneris in regnum tuum
Psalm	[Ps. 50:3–13]
Antiphon	Memento mei, Domine, dum ueneris in regnum tuum

4. If the moment of death seems imminent, the aforementioned antiphon is recited, if not, the antiphon *Auerte faciem tuam a peccatis meis, Domine. Miserere mei Deus.*
5. Then these three prayers:

Prayer	Exaudi, Domine, supplicum preces
Prayer	Omnipotens et misericors Domine, miserere
Prayer	Precamur, Domine, tue clementie Maiestatem
Benediction	Propitietur Dominus cunctis iniquitatibus tuis
	Redimat te interitu uitam tuam
	Atque ita tibi Dominus cordis et corporis
	Qui solus in Trinitate

6. After the recitation of the Lord's Prayer, the sackcloth is removed, and if he seems not about to die, communion is postponed. If death is imminent, however, after he is changed into clean clothes, the remainder of Psalm 50 is sung, with this antiphon.

Antiphon	Parce, Domine, quia spreui precepta tua, qui das post peccata indulgentiam
Psalm	[Ps. 50:14–21]
Prayer	Deus misericors, Deus clemens, qui multitudinem
Benediction	Omnipotens Dominus, qui fidelissimum
	Quique nostram in se suscepit infirmitatem
	Sicque omnes in commune

7. When the benediction is completed, the priest gives him communion and says this prayer.

Prayer	Propitiare, Domine, supplicationibus nostris

SOURCE: *Le liber ordinum en usage dans l'église wisigothique et mozarabe d'Espagne du cinquième au onzième siècle,* ed. Mario Férotin (Paris, 1904), 87–92.

first emerged in the penitential discipline of the Spanish church to mark off penitents from the larger community.[109] They served a similar function here, both separating the recipient from his fellows through symbols of penitence and, through the sign of the cross, maintaining a link with the Christian community into which he desired readmittance.

The prayers, psalms, and antiphons begging God for absolution (2–5) form a ritual of transition, in which the penitent was suspended between his former and future states, neither of the community nor out of it.[110] Dependent on the mercy of God and on the intercessory prayers of the people attending him, the dying man played a passive part in the following proceedings. First, the priest bade the attendants (Oremus ut) to pray that God would award the penitent "the fruit of penance and the remedy of eternal life." Then he asked all present to supplicate God with him: "Joining your tears with ours, dear brothers, together let us beg the merciful God, that he, who allows no one to perish, will deign to receive in this submissiveness this his servant, whom the desire for satisfaction has aroused to the remedy of penitence."[111] The juxtaposition of the verses of Psalm 50 with the words of the "good thief" who died with Jesus on the cross (Memento mei), "Remember me, Lord, when you enter your kingdom," recall the one episode in the New Testament concerning immediate entry into paradise after death.[112] The repetition of these words anticipated Jesus' response to the thief: "This day you will be with me in paradise."[113] The thief, like the dying man, was a penitent. His forgiveness was immediate, and so was his

109. Isidore of Seville, De ecclesiasticis officiis, 2.17 (PL 83.802); Boglioni, "Scène de la mort," 280.

110. On rites of transition and the concept of liminality, see van Gennep, Rites of Passage; Huntington and Metcalf, Celebrations of Death, 11–13; and Turner, Forest of Symbols, 93–111.

111. Liber ordinum, 89: "Oremus ut huic famulo suo remissionem peccatorum, penitentie fructum et uite eterne remedium propitius tribuere dignetur. . . . Iungentes nostros cum fletibus fletus, fratres karissimi, misericordi Domino pariter supplicemus, ut hunc famulum suum, quem ad penitentie remedium satisfactionis excitat uotum, ipse qui perire neminem patitur, suscipere in hac humiliatione dignetur."

112. Luke 23:42. The central position of Psalm 50 is important. It is the fourth of the seven penitential psalms and figures prominently in most later death rituals from the ninth century on, as we shall see. The two manuscripts used by Férotin differ slightly, but they both suggest that the words of the thief were repeated after each verse of the psalm; Liber ordinum, 89–90.

113. This aspect of the ritual was taken over from the Holy Thursday ritual of reconciling public penitents, in which the antiphon was repeated after every verse of Psalm 50 and the assembled people shouted "Indulgentia!" (forgiveness) hundreds of times; see Gy, "Pénitence et la réconciliation," 122.

reward. By dramatically reminding God of the mercy shown by Christ to the thief—indeed, by assimilating the penitent to the figure of the thief in an eternal dramatic episode—the ritual action attempted to guarantee a repetition of that act of mercy and with it the forgiveness and salvation of the dying man.

If death seemed imminent, a ritual of incorporation, involving a reclothing in a clean garment and communion (6–7), completed the ceremony. (Otherwise, the final ritual actions and prayers were postponed, and the sick man remained in the liminal state.) After the Lord's Prayer was said, the attendant removed the sackcloth, reclothed the person in fresh garments, and sang the rest of Psalm 50.[114] The prayer of reconciliation, *Deus misericors*, begged God to reconstruct the penitent—to purify him within to match the purity of his *uestibus nitidis* and restore him to the body of the church.

> Merciful God, gentle God, you who restrain the multitude of your mercies through no law of time, and do not turn away those who knock at the door of your compassion, even at the very end of their life, look down favorably on this your servant N., begging in the full confession of the heart remission of all his sins. Renew in him, most pious Father, whatever has been violated through devilish deceit, and restore the member, perfected through this remission of sins, to the unity of the body of your church.[115]

The dying man received communion, presumably at the moment of death, after which a final prayer asked one last time for God's favor and aid.

Deathbed penance in Spain was a rite of preparation for death. Perhaps because it was so highly developed, there was no pressure to make rites for the sick appropriate for the care of the dying.

---

114. The reclothing in fresh garments at this point recalls the ritual of baptism, and links this last rite of passage to that first one; thus the title of the German edition of Bernard Poschmann's fundamental work: *Penitentia secunda: Die kirchliche Busse im ältesten Christentum bis Cyprian und Origenes* (Bonn, 1940). As penance became attached to the dying process, it naturally drew to itself elements derived from the *penitentia prima* of baptism.

115. Liber ordinum, 92: "Deus misericors, Deus clemens, qui multitudinem miserationum tuarum nulla temporum lege concludis, sed pulsantem misericordie tue ianuam, etiam sub ipso uite termino, non repellis: respice super hunc famulum tuum *Illum* propitius, remissionem sibi omnium peccatorum tota cordis confessione poscentem. Renoua in eum, piissime Pater, quicquid diabolica fraude uiolatum est, et unitati corporis Ecclesie tue membrum remissione perfecta restitue." On the Visigothic origins of this prayer, see Janini, "Oraciones visigóticas," 198.

Thus the Spanish ritual of anointing the sick remained a rite of healing, in line with the Roman traditions from which it sprung, and was in no way meant for use in deathbed ceremonies. In Ireland, precisely the opposite occurred.

Ireland

The Irish church in the early Middle Ages developed a variety of practices peculiar to itself. On an island without cities, it developed administrative structures organized around independent monasteries whose lifestyle tended toward the asceticism of the desert fathers rather than the more pragmatic style of St. Benedict of Nursia.[116] This asceticism found expression in the creation of "penitentials," intimate handbooks on care of souls, and in the practice of *peregrinatio,* voluntary pilgrimage in the service of God.[117] We have seen more than one example of the impact that Irish monasticism had on Merovingian Gaul in the seventh century, often directing ritual life into more penitential and otherworldly directions. This tendency is even more pronounced in the fragmentary remains of the native Irish liturgy of the period, which demonstrate the special character of Irish rituals for the dying.

From Anointing the Sick to Anointing the Dying

The Penitential of Finnian, oldest of the Irish penitential books (ca. 550), obliged the clergy to visit the sick.[118] The prologue to the Penitential of Cummean (d. 662), which sometimes circulated independently under the name of Caesarius of Arles, urged the visitation and anointing of the sick as one of twelve means to remit sin.[119] The biblical text cited in support of this practice was the

116. On the Irish church, see Kathleen Hughes, *The Church in Early Irish Society* (Ithaca, N.Y., 1966) and *Early Christian Ireland: An Introduction to the Sources* (Ithaca, N.Y., 1972).

117. *The Irish Penitentials,* ed. Ludwig Bieler, Scriptores latini Hiberniae 5 (Dublin, 1963); John T. McNeill and Helen M. Gamer, *Medieval Handbooks of Penance* (New York, 1938).

118. *Irish Penitentials,* ed. Bieler, 86, c. 33: "*infirmi sunt uisitandi.*" On this penitential book, see ibid., 3–4; Kenney, *Sources,* 240–45; McNeill and Gamer, *Medieval Handbooks,* 86–87.

119. *Irish Penitentials,* ed. Bieler, 6, 18–19, 108–10: "Octaba [remissio est] intercessio sanctorum, ut est illud: Si quis infirmatur . . ." The glossing of the James text as an "intercession of the saints" is interesting. Does it signal a peculiarly Irish use of litanies in rites of visitation and anointing at some time? The liturgical remains

passage from the letter of the apostle James (5:14–16)—the text on which Caesarius based his frequent exhortations to his flock to turn from folk-magical medicine to the ministrations of the church. Thus it is most probable that some Irish clerics in the sixth and seventh centuries practiced the visitation and anointing of the sick along the lines laid down by the bishop of Arles. In any case, when Irish rituals first appear in the written records in the second half of the eighth century, rites for the visitation of the sick are prominent among them.[120] Indeed, there are more surviving witnesses to rites for the sick than to any other ritual of the early Irish church.[121] One such rite is preserved as an addition to the mid-seventh-century Book of Mulling and in the eleventh-century Scottish Book of Deer.[122] Another appears in the Stowe Missal, written between 792 and 812, and as an addition to the Book of Dimma, which is contemporary with Stowe.[123]

---

of such rites from the eighth and ninth centuries contain no references to litanies, as we shall see, but that does not rule out their use in some instances, especially given the Irish tradition of apotropaic *loricae*. See Louis Gougaud, "Etude sur les *loricae* celtique et sur les prières qui s'en rapprochent," *Bulletin d'ancienne littérature et d'archéologie chrétiennes* 1 (1911): 265–81, 2 (1912): 33–41.

120. John Hennig, "Liturgy, Celtic," DMA 7.614, notes that among the fragmentary remains of the liturgy in Ireland, the "comparatively large number of texts relating to the sick and to women is remarkable."

121. Klaus Gamber was wrong, however, to follow Frederick Warren in claiming that the continental fragment on pp. 444–47 of St. Gall, Stiftsbibliothek, Cod. 1395, is part of a rite of visitation of the sick. Cf. Frederick E. Warren, *The Liturgy and Ritual of the Celtic Church* (1881), ed. Jane Stevenson (Woodbridge, Suffolk, and Wolfeboro, N.H., 1987), 182–83; CLLA 106; and Klaus Gamber, "Irische Liturgiebücher und ihre Verbreitung auf dem Kontinent," in *Die Iren und Europa*, ed. H. Lowe (Stuttgart, 1982), 539. The St. Gall fragment preserves portions of two of the *Suscipe* prayers *post obitum hominis* in the Vatican Gelasian (Gelasian, nos. 1610–11) whose Visigothic sources have been discussed above.

122. Warren, *Liturgy and Ritual*, 171–73 (Mulling), 164–65 (Deer). On these manuscripts, see Kenney, *Sources*, 632–33, 703–4. The text in Deer is fragmentary; it includes only part of the rite, from the prayer before the *Pater noster* until the end, but what is extant conforms closely to the rite in Mulling.

123. Stowe, 33–36. Warren edited the ritual as well, but with less fidelity to the manuscript, in *Liturgy and Ritual*, 220–25. On the Stowe Missal, see Kenney, *Sources*, 692–99. The ritual in the Book of Dimma is edited in Warren, *Liturgy and Ritual*, 167–71. On the Dimma manuscript, see Kenney, *Sources*, 632–33, 703–4. The dating of the handwriting of the sick ritual in the Book of Dimma has been a problem. Edmund O'Curry, *Lectures on the Ms. Materials of Ancient Irish History* (Dublin, 1871), 651, considered the inscription of the ritual to be contemporaneous with the writing of the book itself, which he dated to the mid–seventh century. Kenney, noting that the hand of the ritual was "of much later date" than the rest, dated the manuscript "saec. VII/VIII" and the ritual "saec. VIII/IX." R. I. Best, however, "On the Subscriptions of the 'Book of Dimma,'" *Hermathena*, no. 44 (1926), 84–100, placed the origin of the manuscript around the turn of the ninth

Irish Anointing Rituals

The visitation rite in both Mulling/Deer and Stowe/Dimma is a form of communion service for the sick, modeled after the corresponding portions of the mass, but with the addition of an unction.[124] There is a close correspondence between the texts in Mulling and Deer, and between those in Stowe and Dimma.[125] The rite in the first two is shorter, simpler, and closer to the spirit of the unction called for by Caesarius and the Penitential of Cummean. Yet both of them reveal the same blurring of the concepts of health and salvation which marked the Gallican prayers for the sick. Moreover, the rite in Stowe/Dimma makes explicit what that in Mulling/Deer does not: a ritual that had begun as a rite of physical healing gradually came to be used for the spiritual preparation of the dying.

The ritual preserved in the Book of Mulling and the Book of Deer opened with a bidding to the participants to pray for the spirit of the sick person "so that the lord may . . . grant her life, [and] bestow the protection of health, the reward of good works."[126] A second bidding beseeched God to send down "an angel of celestial medicine" to strengthen the ailing one.[127] After a prayer that is only partially preserved, the officiating priest recited a blessing

---

century and argued that the ritual was added as late as the tenth or eleventh century. Nevertheless, the close conformity of the Dimma rite to the one in Stowe proves that it originated in the eighth century. Cf. *Das irische Palimpsestsakramentar im CLM 14429 der Staatsbibliothek München*, ed. P. Dold and L. Eizenhöfer (Beuron, 1964), XVII, where they date the *Missa de visitatione infirmorum* in Dimma 750–850.

124. J. Pinsk, "Missa sicca," *Jahrbuch für Liturgiewissenschaft* 4 (1923): 90–118, showed that these rites are the source of the term *missa sicca*, which by the twelfth century referred to a commemorative office immediately following a service in which the formulas of the mass were said without the canon or communion service. The term *sicca* (dry) had been borrowed from communion services for the sick, such as those under discussion, to which only the host (consecrated earlier at a mass and dipped in wine) was brought. See also Michel Andrieu, *Immixtio et consecratio: La consécration par contact dans les documents liturgiques du moyen âge*, Bibliothèque de l'Institut de Droit Canonique 2 (Paris, 1924).

125. Although these rites have been cited from time to time, their historical relationships have not been investigated. See, e.g., Warren, *Liturgy and Ritual*, 167, where he calls them (misleadingly) *missae de infirmis*; Jungmann, *Mass*, 2.323, 332n, 371n, 389n; H. B. Porter, "The Rites for the Dying in the Early Middle Ages I," *JTS*, n.s. 10 (1959): 54; Chavasse, "Prière pour les malades," 580–81.

126. Warren, *Liturgy and Ritual*, 171: "Oremus, fratres carissimi, pro spiritu cari nostri .n. . . . ut dominus ei . . . uitam concedat, tutellam salutis remunerationem bonorum operum impertiat."

127. Ibid., 171–72: "Oremus . . . ut domini pietas per angelum medicine celestis uisitare et corrobare dignetur."

over water and the sick person and then anointed her with the following words: "I anoint you with sanctified oil in the name of the Father, and the Son, and the Holy Spirit, in order that you will be saved, in the name of the Holy Trinity."[128] When the sick person had sung the creed, she was to be told that she should forgive all who had offended her.[129] There followed the Lord's prayer and communion in both species. The formula accompanying the communion was as follows: "May the body with the blood of our Lord Jesus Christ be health [*sanitas*] for you unto eternal life."[130] The ritual ended with prayers and psalmody of thanks and exultation for God's gift of the Eucharist.

The prayers in Dimma and Stowe express a greater concern for the health of the soul than their counterparts in Mulling and Deer. The language tends to be generalized, so that, while forgiveness of sins is unquestionably sought, it is less clear that what is wished for is the return of bodily health. The first bidding in Stowe/ Dimma asks God to deign to cure the sick person, for "he who gave the soul may give also health."[131] One asks that God heal the body

---

128. Ibid., 172: "Unguo te deoleo [*sic*] sanctificationis in nomine dei patris, et filii, et spiritus sancti, ut saluus eris in nomine sanctae trinitatis." The *benedictio super aquam* that precedes the blessing of the person most probably stems from the use of a similar ritual for baptizing the sick. Cf. Warren's note to a similar blessing that precedes the rite in Stowe, ibid., 220n, and below on the communion formula.

129. Ibid., 172: "Tum dicitur ei ut dimittat omnia."

130. Ibid., 173: "Corpus cum sanguine domini nostri ihesu christi sanitas tibi in uitam aeternam." In the Book of Deer the words *et salutem* are added at the end; ibid., 164. Jungmann noted that when formulas for the distribution of communion first appear in Frankish sources in the eighth century, they have a similar wording: "May the body of our lord Jesus Christ be with you in life everlasting"; *Mass*, 2.389. What Jungmann did not notice is the normal context of the formula's appearance in the eighth-century witnesses—rites for the sick or dying. When the formula appears outside of the Irish visitation rites, as it does in the Frankish Gelasian sacramentaries, it is part of a special form of baptism *ad sucurrendum*—that is, for persons in danger of death. See Gelasian, no. 612: "Corpus domini nostri Iesu Christi sit tibi in uita aeterna"; Gellone, no. 2384: "Corpus domini nostri iesu christi in uitam aeternam." For examples in other eighth-century Gelasians, see Gellone, Introductory volume, xxxii, 107. In Stowe (p. 32) it appears in the general baptismal rite as "Corpus et sanguinis d. n. i. c. sit tibi in uitam aeternam." It is also possible that the wording of the distribution formula for the sick in the baptismal and anointing rites derives from the fact that the communion was given as bread dipped in wine. The formula accompanying the commingling of the bread and wine in the ceremony of the communion of the priest ran "Fiat commixtio et consecratio corporis et sanguinis D. n. J. C., accipientibus nobis in uitam aeternam." Cf. Jungmann, *Mass*, 2.315 and 389. That, however, while possibly accounting for its origin, does not account for its use. When the sources cite the communion formula for normal distribution at mass, starting in the ninth century, they present the form as it appears in earlier rituals for the sick; Jungmann, *Mass*, 2.390.

131. Warren, *Liturgy and Ritual*, 167: "Oremus fratres, dominum deum nostrum

and give health to the soul.[132] Another asks specifically for the
forgiveness of sins, but without linking it to the health of the
body.[133] The others use ambiguous images. One introduces a curious turn of phrase to ask that "the creature may feel the hand of
the creator, either being healed or being received [or gathered
up]."[134] Another imagines God as an artificer who has the power to
remake his creation.[135] A third begs God to visit his creature "with
the medicine of celestial grace."[136]

These are the same images as those that appear in the eighth-
century Frankish prayers for the sick and the exorcisms and benedictions of oil used in anointing rites. Indeed, they cannot be separated
from them. We find numerous echoes and shared texts in all four
witnesses to the Irish visitation rites and the eighth-century Frankish mass books, especially the *Missale Gothicum*.[137] While the
Visigothic sources took the ritual care of the sick toward the bodily
side, the Irish and the Frankish seem to have moved toward increasing spiritualization. That spiritualization is given an explicit otherworldly tone in the readings that are recorded for the rites in Stowe
and Dimma.[138] Unlike those that accompany the early Roman mass

---

pro fratre nostro . . . ut eum domini pietas caelestibus dignetur curare medicinis;
qui dedit animam det etsalutem [*sic*]"; cf. Stowe, 33.

132. Warren, *Liturgy and Ritual*, 168: "Deum in cuius manu tam alitus uiuentis
quam uita morientis, fratres dilectissimi, deprecemur, ut corporis huius infirmitatem sanet et animae salutem prestet"; cf. Stowe, 34.

133. Warren, *Liturgy and Ritual*, 168: "Deus qui non uis mortem peccatoris, sed
ut conuertatur et uiuat, huic ad te ex corde conuerso peccata dimite, et perennis
uitae tribue gratiam"; cf. Stowe, 34.

134. Warren, *Liturgy and Ritual*, 167: "Deum uiuum . . . oremus, quo creatura
manum sentiat creatoris aut inreparando aut inrecipiendo"; cf. Stowe, 33.

135. Warren, *Liturgy and Ritual*, 167–68: "Domine . . . qui es artifex, pie exerce
in hoc plasmate tuo"; cf. Stowe, 33.

136. Warren, *Liturgy and Ritual*, 168: "Deus qui . . . uisita eum . . . caelestis
gratiae ad medicamentum." For the difference between the text in Dimma and
Stowe, see Stowe, 34n. This prayer also appears in the Vatican Gelasian (Gelasian,
no. 1535) as the first prayer in a visitation rite, whence it passed to Benedict of
Aniane's Supplement (1388).

137. The bidding *Oremus, fratres carissimi, pro spiritu* in Mulling = Gothicum,
no. 240, *Oratio pro infirmis*; the prayer after communion in Mulling, *Custodi intra
nos* = a prayer *Consummacio missae* in Gothicum (509); the prayer after the unction in Dimma and Stowe = the prayer *Ante oracionem dominica* in the immediately preceding mass in the Gothicum (495); a prayer that is common to all the
Irish sources and ends the rite in all but Stowe = the *Consumaccio missae* in that
same mass in Gothicum (498); the blessing that precedes the unction in Mulling
and comes at the end of the rite in Stowe and Dimma = the *Benedictio populi* in a
mass for the week after Easter in the Gallicanum vetus (228).

138. No readings for the rite appear in Mulling/Deer.

for the sick, the readings by-pass Christ's healing of the sick as well as James's exhortation to prayer and anointing in favor of explicitly eschatological texts. In Dimma, the first reading is from Paul's first letter to the Corinthians (15:19–22), where Paul plays on the meaning of death and life, noting that as all died in Adam, so all will live in Christ. The life referred to is of course the life of the resurrected body, not the earthly one. In the same place the Stowe Missal has Matthew's (24:29–31) record of Jesus' prophecy on the end of time. Finally, both texts present for the second reading Jesus' words to the Sadducees concerning the state of the bodies of the resurrected (Matt. 22:29–33).[139] There is simply no way to assimilate these readings to a healing ritual. Their purpose was to focus attention on the spiritual rather than the physical welfare of the sick person. In such a context the phrasing of the communion formula is entirely appropriate. The reference to health (*sanitas*) of the earlier formula in Mulling/Deer has been dropped so that it reads: "May the body and the blood of the lord Jesus Christ son of the living God preserve your soul in life everlasting."[140] In the Stowe Missal, a prayer after communion reiterates the eschatological meaning of the readings. "Having received the food of the divine saving body, we give thanks to our saviour Jesus, because through the sacrament of his body and blood he has liberated us from death and he has seen fit to grant to the human race the remedy of both the body and the soul."[141] The death referred to is not the death of the body to this world but the ultimate death of the soul; and the remedy is the saving grace by which humankind is granted a new life in the resurrection.[142] The visitation and anointing in Stowe/Dimma are aimed not at the return of physical health but at the preparation for death and eternal life; together they comprise a rite for the dying, not for the sick.

139. Warren, *Liturgy and Ritual*, 168–69 (Dimma); Stowe, 34–35.

140. Warren, *Liturgy and Ritual*, 170: "Corpus et sanguis domini nostri ihesu christi filii dei uiui conseruat animam tuam in uitam perpetuam"; cf. Stowe, 35.

141. Stowe, 35–36: "Accepto salutari diuini corporis cibo salutari nostro iesu christo gratias agimus quod sui corporis et sanguinis sacramento nos a morte liberauit et tam corporis quam animae humano generi remedium donare dignatus est."

142. Cf. the definition of communion in the *Collectio hibernensis*, which assimilates communion in general to viaticum and resurrection; *Irische Kanonensammlung*, ed. Wasserschleben, 17 (bk. 2, c. 16): "Communionis nomen hoc est, viaticum, id est viae custodiam; custodit enim animam usque dum steterit ante tribunal Christi, cui refert sua. . . ." Variants in other manuscripts listed by Wassserschleben preface the foregoing with "Communio dicitur, quia omnium fidelium in exitu vitae communis est victus, ergo quod comviaticum nominant, i. e. vitae custodiam. . . ."

Reformers and Rituals

How did this ritual change come about? A curious passage in Adomnan's *Life of St. Columba*, written at the end of the seventh century, shows the saint reluctant to be at the bedside of a dying man at the moment of death. "At another time, when the holy man was living in the island of Io, one of his monks . . . was attacked by a bodily affliction, and brought to the point of death. When the venerable man visited him in the hour of his decease, after standing a little while beside his couch, and blessing him, he quickly left the house, being unwilling to see him die."[143] The exact nature of Columba's blessing is left unstated, as is the reason for his reluctance to see the monk die, but a similar reluctance is both mentioned and explained in documents that stem from the eighth-century movement in Ireland associated with the reformers known as Célí Dé.[144] The name eventually came to be applied to a wide variety of ascetic reformers, but in the eighth century it is associated first with the community of Darinis under Abbot Ferdacrich (d. 747) and then with the monks of Tallaght, which was founded by Ferdacrich's disciple Maelruain in 774.[145] The Célí Dé sought to revive the practice of asceticism in religious institutions that they felt had grown lax, emphasizing piety, learning, and poverty.[146] Although the ravages of the Vikings eventually undermined the institutional basis of the reform, it was an important force from the second quarter of the eighth to the beginning of the tenth century. The ideals and practices of the Célí Dé are preserved in the form of prose and verse rules and collections of notes and exempla from the acts of respected spiritual ancestors and contemporary masters of the reform dating from the early ninth century.[147]

143. *Adomnan's Life of Columba*, ed. A. O. and M. O. Anderson (London, 1961), 476–77.
144. On the reform, see Kenney, *Sources*, 468–72; W. Reeves, "On the Célí-dé, Commonly Called Culdees," *Transactions of the Royal Irish Academy* 24 (1873): 119–263; Hughes, *Church in Early Irish Society*, 173–93; P. O'Dwyer, *Célí Dé: Spiritual Reform in Ireland, 750–900*, 2d ed. (Dublin, 1981); and D. A. Binchey, "Penitential Texts in Old Irish," in *Irish Penitentials*, ed. Bieler, 47–51.
145. On Ferdacrich and Maelruain, see Reeves, "On the Célí-dé," 125–28, and O'Dwyer, *Célí Dé*, 4, 30, 55–56.
146. Reeves, "On the Célí-dé," 125; O'Dwyer, *Célí Dé*, 15–16; Binchey, "Penitential Texts," 48.
147. Reeves, "On the Célí-dé," 200–215, printed the text and a translation of a short metrical and a longer prose "Rule of the Célí Dé." E. J. Gwynn and W. J. Purton, "The Monastery of Tallaght," *Proceedings of the Royal Irish Academy* 29,

Various passages in the documents concerning the Célí Dé and the way of life at Tallaght suggest that the pastoral care of the sick and dying was of central importance in their spirituality. A collection of reminiscences of Maelruain (d. 792), one of the acknowledged leaders of the Célí Dé, records that his disciple Maeldithruib (d. 840) "makes much of going the thousand paces, or more, to visit the tenantry on Sunday; and the thousand paces have been left as an ordinance for watching a sick man, and for administering the communion for him."[148] In a life of St. Moling, the founder of the monastery of Tech-Moling, who died in 697, the saint reproaches a figure in purple raiment who appears to him claiming to be Christ, saying that "when Christ comes to converse with the Céli-nDé," he does so in the form of the wretched, as a sick man or a leper. W. Reeves took this episode to mean that Moling's associates "were chiefly to be found among the miserable, to wit, the sick and lepers." The Irish annals record that when a Viking army plundered Armagh in the year 921, they spared "the houses of prayer with their people of God, that is the Céli-dé, and the sick."[149]

The emphasis on the care of the sick among the Célí Dé can explain why in Ireland the rite for visiting and anointing the sick became a rite for the dying. They needed such a ritual, because they did not allow priests to come into contact with the dead. This is apparent in another story:

> Now, to eat a meal with a dead man (though saintly) in the house is forbidden; but instead there are to be prayers and psalm singing on such occasions. Yet one in orders who brings the sacrament to a sick man is obliged to go out of the house at once thereafter, that the sick man die not in his presence; for if he be present in the house at the death, it would not be allowable for him to perform the sacrifice until a bishop should consecrate him. It happened once to Diarmait and to Blathmac mac Flaind that it was in their hands that Curui expired. When he died, they were about to perform the sacrifice thereafter, without being consecrated, till Colchu hindered them from doing so.

---

sec. C (1911–12): 115–79, published a document they characterized as a "collection of memorabilia, probably jotted down from time to time" (121) by someone intimate with the reformers. In *The Rule of Tallaght*, in *Hermathena*, no. 44, 2d suppl. vol. (Dublin, 1927): 1–109, Gwynn published a version of a related document and a new and superior edition and translation of the rule.

148. Gwynn and Purton, "Monastery of Tallaght," 156–57, c. 71.

149. Reeves, "On the Céli-dé," 195–96, 120, 128–29; and 197–98, from the Annals of Ulster and the work of the Four Masters.

The authority is Leviticus; and Diarmait also, the abbot of Iona, was with him on that occasion.[150]

The reference to the Old Testament book of Leviticus is the key to understanding the Célí Dé attitude, for it recorded the injunction of the Lord to Moses that the sons of Aaron—that is, the priests— should not defile themselves by contact with the dead.[151]

The evidence is indirect, but the following process suggests itself as reasonable. In contrast to earlier monastic practice in Ireland, the eighth-century reformers urged men with an ascetic calling to become priests.[152] Since priests had to shun the dead in order to avoid ritual pollution, they were led to give special attention to the sick and the dying. This practice resulted in the rewriting of an old ritual for the visitation of the sick to make it appropriate as a rite of preparation for death—the last time a dying individual would be attended by a priest. The manuscripts indicate that this was indeed the case, for both the Book of Dimma and the Stowe Missal are connected with centers of the Célí Dé reform. The Stowe Missal is generally acknowledged to be a product of the scriptorium of the monastery of Tallaght, written within two decades of the death of Maelruain.[153] The Book of Dimma, moreover, is a product of the monastery of Roscrea, "another Célí Dé stronghold," as one scholar has called it.[154] J. F. Kenney concluded that the text of the visita-

150. Gwynn and Purton, "Monastery of Tallaght," 153, c. 65. Gwynn and Purton tentatively identify Colchu with the reformer Colchu ua Duinechda (d. 789) (173– 74).

151. Lev. 21:1–12; cf. Ezek. 44:25. Menahem Haran, "Priests and Priesthood," *Encyclopaedia Judaica* (Jerusalem, 1971) 13.1081. On the place of the Old Testament, especially the Mosaic law, in the spirituality of the Irish church, see Paul Fournier and Gabriel Le Bras, *Histoire des collections canoniques en occident*, 2 vols. (Paris, 1931), 1.62–64; Paul Fournier, "Le Liber ex Lege Moysi et les tendances bibliques du droit canonique irlandais," *Revue celtique* 30 (1909): 221–34; R. Kottje, *Studien zum Einfluss des alten Testamentes auf Recht und Liturgie der frühen Mittelalters* (Bonn, 1970); Michael J. Enright, *Iona, Tara, and Soissons: The Origin of the Royal Anointing Ritual*, Arbeiten zur Frühmittelalterforschung 17 (Berlin/New York, 1985), 41–48; and the "Canones Adomnani" in *Irish Penitentials*, ed. Bieler, 176–81, which, while not unquestionably the work of Adomnan, link his name with decisions derived from Mosaic law (9). Février, "Mort chrétienne," 893, cites a twelfth-century sacramentary that alludes to this same prohibition.

152. Kenney, *Sources*, 472–73, says that the Célí Dé were all priests; Hughes, *Church in Early Irish Society*, 180, notes that "some, however, were laymen."

153. Kenney, *Sources*, 469, 699; Hennig, "Liturgy, Celtic," 614; Binchey, "Penitential Texts," 47; but cf. J. Ryan, "The Mass in the Early Irish Church," *Studies* 50 (Dublin, 1961): 376, who argues that Stowe originated at Lorrha, where the manuscript was in the eleventh century.

154. Jane Stevenson, Introduction to Warren, *Liturgy and Ritual*, p. lxxiin; Ste-

tion ritual in the Book of Dimma "constitutes, doubtless, the office of the visitation of the sick as used in the monastery of Roscrea in the second half of the eighth or the first half of the ninth century."[155] Whether that ritual was used with the merely sick or, as is more likely, with the dying, its purpose was to prepare the recipient for death and eternal life.

Deathbed Penance

Perhaps because priests were forbidden contact with the dead, the early Irish sources contaiu almost nothing on other rituals surrounding death. A chapter in the Penitential of Finnian addresses the question whether or not communion as viaticum was to be denied to persons who had been on the point of death, had recovered, and had not fulfilled the terms of a penance prescribed at that time. "If the sinner should not fulfill his or her debt to God, the consequences will be on his or her own head, and [yet] we will not deny him or her what we owe. We must not cease to snatch prey from the mouth of the lion or the dragon, that is the devil, who does not cease to snatch away the prey of our souls, even if we have to strive and struggle at the last moment of a person's life."[156] It is unlikely that the penance referred to here had the character of the Visigothic rite, for no tradition of public penance was ever established in Ireland. The deathbed confession referred to by Finnian was more likely modeled on the private confession that was the norm in Ireland. Thus the vow made would entail only the fulfillment of the terms of the penance, and not the complete break with lay life which followed upon the Spanish ritual. That communion as viaticum was always given is supported also by other texts connected with the Célí Dé. One of the documents from the reform period discusses the various positions on giving communion *in articulo mortis*, while another invokes the authority of Colchu to rule on the issue. "This is what Colchu approves, to give the

---

venson goes on to say, "There may be mere accidents of survival involved, but it is perhaps possible that the reforming activities of the Célí Dé included a particular interest in liturgy."

155. Kenney, *Sources*, 703–4.

156. *Irish Penitentials*, 86, c. 34: "Si . . . peccatrix uel peccator . . . non impleat uotum quod uouerit Deo, in caput suum erit et nos quod debemus non negabimus ei. Non cessandum est eripere predam ex ore leonis uel draconis, id est de ore diabuli, qui predam nostre anime deripere non desinit, licet in extremo line [*sic; fine?*] uite hominis adfectandum et nitendum est."

sacrament to those that are lying sick at the hour of death, provided they have made a renunciation of every vanity. Leave it, however, to God to judge the mind of such, whether it be true conversion; and if it be so, [be sure that] the sacrament can bring salvation to them in that moment. It is not proper, however, to repeat the sacrament thereafter in extremis."[157] As we have seen, the reception of viaticum in eighth-century Ireland, at least among the Célí Dé, would have occurred at the conclusion of the ritual of anointing, which itself entailed the forgiveness of sins, if not an explicit confession and reconciliation.

Death and Ritual before the Carolingian Reform

The new rituals in preparation for death which developed in Ireland and Spain between the mid-sixth and the mid-eighth centuries had no immediate effects on ritual practice in Francia. Nevertheless, the correspondence between the attitudes expressed in Gallican prayers and in Irish sources of the seventh and eighth centuries points to the cultural interchange between Irish and Frankish monasticism in the period. The exact movements of that interchange are hard to ascertain, but their effects are clear. Irish and Gallican clerics alike tended to take a spiritual approach to rites for the sick, emphasizing ritual purification and eternal salvation more than the return of physical health. Since we find no evidence that the Irish rite of anointing the dying penetrated Francia before the late eighth century, the correspondence seems to derive from a common attitude toward penance and ritual purification in general and from changing attitudes toward anointing in particular. By the middle of the eighth century, anointing with oil was becoming an increasingly familiar ritual of spiritual transformation in the Frankish lands. The early eighth-century *Missale Francorum* records an ordination ceremony for priests which includes the earliest example of consecration with oil, and ordination anointings became a standard part of the Frankish liturgy during the eighth and ninth centuries.[158] The anointing of Pippin in 751 and of his whole family in 754 was a powerful symbol of the

157. Gwynn and Purton, "Monastery of Tallaght," 148, c. 56. For the discussion to which this text is clearly a response, see *Rule of Tallaght*, ed. Gwynn, 11, cc. 13–14.

158. Missale Francorum, nos. 33–34, p. 10; Gerald Ellard, *Ordination Anointings in the Western Church before 1000 A.D.* (Cambridge, Mass., 1933).

transformative powers of consecrated oil.[159] The Irish background to both of these uses of consecrated oil has been pointed out by the historians who have studied them, although Visigothic precedents cannot be ruled out completely.[160] One must also consider the resonances of the symbolic lexicon of baptism in any anointing ceremony; in baptism anointing with oil not only strengthened but separated, liminalized, set apart the recipients from the non-Christian world and enlisted them in the higher circle of the Christian community. In this respect, Spanish influence may be central, for the Spanish church placed special emphasis on the notion that the chrism used in the baptismal rite of confirmation was what made one a Christian—that is, an anointed one.[161]

Fully developed rites of deathbed penance seem to have been confined to the Spanish church. Some form of deathbed penance may have been in use in Rome in the sixth and seventh centuries, as appears evident from the language of the second and third of the five mass formulas *super defunctos* in the so-called Verona sacramentary (ca. 600). These masses were said for persons who had desired but had not received penance before death, or, having received it, had been unable to fulfill the terms of the penance before they died.[162] With the proliferation of Irish Columbanian monastic foundations in Gaul in the seventh century, it is likely that Frankish practices tended toward Irish rather than Spanish models, eschewing a formal rite of deathbed penance for a more informal confession and reconciliation as part of the preparation for death.

159. Enright, *Iona, Tara, and Soissons*, 137–59. While Enright argues that royal anointing replaced long hair as a symbol of life-giving abundance, he insists that its effects were taken on a purely physical level: "In a society which regarded consecrated oil as the sovereign medicine and restorative, the increasing carnalization of this Mediterranean spiritual concept was a very nearly ineluctable process" (154). The evidence from rituals for the sick suggests that this is an oversimplification; in Mediterranean Spain and Italy the effects of anointing the sick were understood as considerably more carnal than spiritual.

160. The question of cultural interchange among Ireland, Spain, and Francia in the seventh century is hotly debated. See Edward James, "Ireland and Western Gaul in the Merovingian Period," in *Ireland in Early Medieval Europe* (Cambridge, 1982), 362–86; and J. N. Hillgarth, "Ireland and Spain in the Seventh Century," *Peritia* 3 (1984): 1–16. The problem of priority of influence on which this debate has centered is less important here than the abundant evidence it provides of mutual interchange among the three areas.

161. Isidore, *De ecclesiasticis officiis*, 2.27 (PL 83.823–24); Ildefonsus of Toledo, *De cognitione baptismi*, c. 123 (PL 96.162); Liber ordinum, 34.

162. Verona, nos. 1141–50. Cf. 1141: "ut paenitentiae fructum, quem uoluntas eius optauit, praeuentus mortalitate non perdat," and 1145: "ut deuotio paenitentiae, quam gessit eius affectus, perpetuae salutis consequatur effectum." See also Sicard, *Liturgie*, 239–48, and above, n. 60.

That is not to say, however, that the Gallican rituals were not penitential. In lieu of a compressed penitential rite of passage on the Spanish model, the church in both Ireland and Merovingian Francia emphasized the purification of the soul throughout the ritual sequence and devised new forms of prayer for the dead which would follow the soul through the long process of purification and incorporation into the other world with prayers, alms, and commemorative masses.

But what about Roman rites for the dying? The old Roman *ordo defunctorum* prescribed only the reading of the Passion of Christ and the reception of viaticum before death. Its rich and expressive psalmody began after death and continued throughout the funeral services. Two stories in the *Dialogues* of Gregory the Great indicate the development of a tradition of singing psalms for the dying as well. The first concerns a pious layman named Servulus, who, realizing that death was near, asked the people around him to stand and recite psalms with him "in expectation of death." In the second story, the holy nun Romula dies to the accompaniment of two choirs of heavenly beings chanting psalms in the street outside her door.[163] In the seventh and eighth centuries, the chanting of psalms for the dying became common far from Gregory's Rome. The death ritual in the Spanish *Libri ordinum* prescribes a selection of thirty-six psalms to be sung during the agony, ending with Psalm 50, *Miserere mei, Domine*.[164] A note in one of the Célí Dé documents directs the singing of the Song of Solomon "when a man was at the point of death, or immediately after his soul departed," inasmuch as the canticle "signified the union of the Church with every Christian soul."[165] Texts from monastic centers, especially from Anglo-Saxon England in the early eighth century, present the deaths of abbots in the context of continuous psalmody. Wilfrid, bishop and abbot of Hexham, died surrounded by monks chanting the psalter.[166] Benedict Biscop's monastic

163. *Dialogues*, 4.15.4, ed. de Vogüé, 3.50: "Cumque se iam morti proximum agnouit, peregrinos uiros atque in hospitalitate susceptos admonuit, ut surgerent et cum eo psalmos pro expectatione exitus decantarent"; 4.16.7, 3.66: "uiaticum petiit et accepit . . . et ecce subito in platea ante eiusdem cellulae ostium duo chori psallentium constiterunt . . . cumque ante fores cellulae exhiberentur caelestes exsequiae, sancta illa anima carne soluta est."

164. Liber ordinum, 108–9. Cf. Fernández Alonso, *Cura pastoral*, 582–87; Hillgarth, "Popular Religion," 30.

165. *Rule of Tallaght*, ed. Gwynn, 19, c. 29. See also John Ryan, *Irish Monasticism: Origins and Early Development*, 2d ed. (Dublin, 1972), 401–3.

166. *The Life of Bishop Wilfrid by Eddius Stephanus*, trans. and ed. by Bertram

brethren similarly attended him on his deathbed with psalmody and readings from the Gospels.[167]

Thus, although the history of rituals around dying and the dead between the sixth and the eighth centuries is obscured by the uneven quality and quantity of source material and the web of crosscurrents that flowed among Italy, Spain, Francia, and Ireland, certain developments stand out. The work of Caesarius of Arles in propagating the anointing of the sick and the care of the dying and the dead is well documented. The Spanish and Irish developed clerical rituals of anointing the sick on the basis of his preaching efforts but along different lines, the Spanish emphasizing ritual healing, the Irish purification and preparation for death. The Spanish church developed a rite of deathbed penance. Roman ritual traditions certainly moved across the Alps throughout the period, and to Anglo-Saxon England, where the successors of the monk Augustine self-consciously maintained close ties with the Roman church. Though prayers around the deathbed and grave continued to draw their imagery from late antique models, Gallican sources display a tendency on the one hand to elaborate the ritual process into several distinct steps and, on the other, to include penitential themes not previously present, a phenomenon that affected burial practices as well. As Christian ritual activity was brought into conformity with the intensive communal relations of northern society, new forms of commemoration appeared to ease the incorporation of souls into the community of the dead. With the coming to power of the Carolingians, a field would be created where these developments could meet. In the hands of Carolingian churchmen, the innovations and crosscurrents of the preceding centuries would become the foundation of a unified response to death and dying for the Latin Middle Ages.

Colgrave (Cambridge, Eng., 1925), 140, c. 65: "illi vero in choro die noctuque indesinenter psalmos canentes et cum fletu miscentes."

167. *Venerabilis Bedae opera historica,* ed. Carolus Plummer (Oxford, 1896), 1.378: "Conueniunt fratres ad aecclesiam, insomnes orationibus et psalmis transigunt umbras noctis, et paternae decessionis pondus continua diuinae laudis modulatione solantur. . . . Euangelium tota nocte pro doloris leuamine . . . a presbytero legitur."

CHAPTER THREE

The Beginnings of Ritual Consolidation
in the Frankish Lands, ca. 740–800

Ritual and Reform in the Eighth-Century Frankish Church

The rise to power of the Carolingians, intimately connected with the penetration of Anglo-Saxon missionaries into the lands beyond the Rhine and the reigns of popes willing and able to direct such activities, created the conditions under which the more or less independent traditions of the past—Roman, Visigothic, Irish, Anglo-Saxon, Gallican—could interact and influence one another.[1] Such interaction did of course antedate the middle of the eighth century. Roman ritual traditions were exported to Anglo-Saxon England, Visigothic books crossed the Pyrenees, and there is no question that the Irish foundations that proliferated on the continent from the time of Columbanus brought about a lively interchange of ideas and forms of piety between Franks and Irish. But the creation of a powerful Christian center around the court of the Carolingian kings marked the beginning of something new. Consciously committed to the creation of a Christian society, a "new Israel," the leaders of the Frankish church and commonwealth drew on all the traditions and talents of their neighbors and

---

1. See Wilhelm Levison, *England and the Continent in the Eighth Century* (Oxford, 1946), 70–131; John Michael Wallace-Hadrill, *The Frankish Church* (Oxford, 1983), 143–80; Geary, *Before France and Germany*, 179–220; Rosamond McKitterick, *The Frankish Kingdoms under the Carolingians, 751–987* (London/New York, 1983), 16–38.

subject territories. Guided by the urge to reform church and society, Frankish schools and scriptoria became centers of attraction for all the ritual developments of the preceding centuries.

In the past, historians have held that under the rallying cry of *more romano*—the custom of the Roman church—the Carolingians and their clerical advisers set out to forge a Christian society unified by conformity to the Roman liturgy and common allegiance to king and pope.[2] Theodor Klauser drew a sharp line between the period before 750, when liturgical change was a matter of individual initiative at the local level, and after, when the Frankish kings played a dominant role.[3] Cyrille Vogel credited Pippin with the introduction into Francia not only of the Roman style of chant but of the whole of the Roman liturgy.[4] But the results of the reform efforts did not always depend either on the activities of the kings or on the desire for "Romanization," and more recent discussions have tended to play down both of these aspects. Rosamond McKitterick, for example, has argued that in the second half of the eighth century the role of the kings was less important than the continued work of individual clerics. For Carloman and Pippin, and even for Charlemagne, the main task was not so much to Romanize as to Christianize. The goal of the kings was to extirpate pagan rites and promote the production of correct texts. The actual work was carried out in a variety of places under local conditions. Given the enormous task of transforming the people of the far-flung Frankish lands into a Christian society, changes in sacramentaries and other liturgical books were made, as McKitterick put it, "with the needs of the task to be performed by the clergy for the people primarily in mind."[5] Thus, while the attempts at Romanization by the Carolingian rulers succeeded to a degree—the Roman

2. See, e.g., Edmund Bishop, "The Liturgical Reform of Charlemagne," *Downside Review* 38 (1919): 1–16; Theodor Klauser, "Die liturgischen Austauschbeziehungen zwischen der römischen und der fränkish-deutschen Kirche vom achten bis zum elften Jahrhundert," *Historisches Jahrbuch* 53 (1933): 169–89; and the following works by Cyrille Vogel: *La réforme cultuelle sous Pepin le Bref et sous Charlemagne* (Graz, 1965); "La réforme liturgique sous Charlemagne," in *Karl der Grosse: Lebenswerk und Nachleben*, vol. 2, *Das geistige Leben*, ed. Bernhard Bischoff (Düsseldorf, 1965), 217–32; and *Medieval Liturgy*, 147–50.

3. Klauser, "Liturgischen Austauschbeziehungen."

4. Vogel, *Réforme cultuelle*, 178–213, esp. 178–80.

5. Rosamond McKitterick, *The Frankish Church and the Carolingian Reforms, 789–895* (London, 1977), 118–19, 123–24. And see p. 129: "The production of liturgical texts continued to be a largely individual affair conducted by the different monasteries and dioceses, in which the clergy were left with a great deal of freedom to determine by actual use the proportion in which Frankish and Roman elements were to be mingled."

liturgy of the Mass replaced the old Gallican rite and books with Roman cores became the common carriers of rituals and prayers— they did not always eradicate local traditions or replace older texts.

Texts and traditions concerning rituals for the dead and dying were among those that tended to survive. Roman liturgical books, often restricted to materials for papal use, did not cover the full ritual life of the church. Such books transmitted Roman prayers and rites for the sick, with their emphasis on the restoration of physical health, but these rites came into conflict with the Irish and Gallican tendency to treat sickness in the context of spiritual health or as a preparation for death. The old Roman *ordo defunctorum* may have been in use in Rome or elsewhere, but no direct evidence for such use survives from the period. In any case, its optimistic celebration of Christian salvation in the face of death did not reflect the more penitential, less self-assured faith of early medieval Christians. Thus, although the Roman liturgy played a role in the development of ritual responses to death and dying in the Carolingian Church, it did so as a source less of ritual models than of a dynamic tension that accentuated anomalies and led to experimentation, synthesis, and the preservation of local traditions.

Conciliar and Royal Decrees

Although the Carolingian reform did not lead to official attempts to promote comprehensive rituals for the dying and the dead, canons from the first reform councils and royal decrees recorded in early capitularies reflect the centrality of such ritual behavior in defining Christian Frankish society. An Austrasian council held by Pippin's brother Carloman in the year 742, which stands at the very beginning of Carolingian conciliar history, took up the problem of pagan practices surrounding sickness and death. In language reminiscent of Caesarius of Arles, the council admonished bishops to see that the people not perform mortuary sacrifices or resort to divination, the casting of lots, or the wearing of phylacteries.[6] A council presided over by Pippin in 755 at the royal palace of Verberie, while affirming episcopal control over baptism, nevertheless gave priests permission to perform the rite when necessary "so that

6. MGH, Capitularia 1.25, c. 5: "Decrevimus, ut . . . episcopus in sua parrochia sollicitudinem adhibeat . . . ut populus Dei paganias non faciat, sed . . . abiciat et respuat; sive sacrificia mortuorum sive sortilegos vel divinos sive filacteria et auguria sive incantationes sive hostias immolatitias."

no one at all may die without baptism."[7] A similar ruling, issued a few years later, permitted even degraded priests to administer baptism to the dying in an emergency.[8] Charlemagne issued a capitulary between 775 and 790 concerning the administration of recently conquered Saxon territories which made pagan cremation funerals a capital crime and insisted that Christian Saxons be buried in church cemeteries and not in pagan burial grounds.[9] Such measures made the manner of one's death and burial a fundamental sign of membership in the new society.

At a Bavarian council held during the 740s, the assembled fathers addressed the nature of reciprocal responsibilities in a Christian community in broad terms. The laity must obey the priests and bishops and strive to live in accordance with the decrees reached in holy councils. In return, the clergy would provide the "medicine of penance" (paenitentiae medicamenta) and act as intercessors for the people as a whole. In urging the people to regular confession, the fathers cited the words of St. James: "Concerning which the apostle instructs us, dearest ones, in these words, 'Confess your sins one to another and pray for each other so that you will be saved.' So let them not delay turning to the lord their God, so that no one will die without viaticum and confession; for no man knows the hour of his death and it is very dangerous to make that long journey, where we migrate to either eternal life or eternal death, without receiving viaticum."[10]

This passage suggests that, as in the time of Caesarius, people generally waited until they were gravely ill before requesting the rites of penance, and thus that deathbed penance was a common

7. MGH, Capitularia 1.34, c. 7: "Ut publicum baptisterium in ulla parrochia esse non debeat, nisi ibi ubi episcopus constituerit cuius parrochia est; nisi tantum si necessitas evenerit pro infirmitate aut pro necessitate, illi presbyteri, quos episcopus in ipsa parrochia constituerit, in qualecumque loco evenerit, licentiam habeant baptizandi, ut omnino sine baptismo non moriantur."

8. MGH, Capitularia 1.41, council at Verberie, 758–68(?), c. 15: "Presbiter degradatus, certa necessitate cogente, pro periculo mortis, si alius non adest, potest infirmum baptizare."

9. MGH, Capitularia 1.69, c. 7: "Si quis corpus defuncti hominis secundum ritum paganorum flamma consumi fecerit et ossa eius ad cinerem redierit, capitae punietur"; c. 22: "Iubemus ut corpora christianorum Saxanorum ad cimiteria ecclesiae deferantur et non ad tumulus paganorum."

10. MGH, Concilia 2.52, c. 2: "Unde nos, dilectissimi, monet apostolus dicens: Confitemini alterutrum peccata vestra et orate pro invicem ut salvemini. Et ne tardent converti se ad dominum Deum ipsorum, quia nescit homo diem exitus sui, ut nullus absque viatiquo et absque confessione vitam istam excedat, quia maximum periculum est, ut longum illud iter, ubi ad aeternam migramus sive ad mortem sive ad vitam absque viatico faciamus."

form of ritual behavior in Frankish Bavaria, as it had been in Visigothic Spain. It further suggests the council's desire to ensure a good death for all Christians by encouraging them to do penance beforehand, so as not to be caught unprepared. Thus penance was understood as a rite of preparation for death whenever it was received, for it restored the health of the soul (salus animae).[11] The evocation of the journey of the soul after death (a striking feature of Gallican funeral prayers), during which its destination might still be altered, recalls the changes in the understanding of commemorative rituals and the possibilities of intercession current in the Frankish lands since the seventh century.[12] The citation of the words of St. James is particularly interesting, for the verse cited (James 5:16) immediately follows the exhortation on anointing the sick.[13] Its appearance here does not imply the currency of a ritual of anointing the dying in mid-eighth-century Bavaria, yet it points to the kinds of associations that would eventually lead to such a use. The limits of the passage between this life and the next were expanding in both directions out from the moment of death. This expansion both required and offered the opportunity for more ritual activity. Rites of penance and purification were highly adaptable to meet such requirements, especially if one interpreted James's references to healing as spiritual rather than bodily in intent.

The Frankish Sacramentaries

The period of reform that began with the Austrasian and Neustrian councils of the 740s was to be as rich in the production of liturgical manuscripts as in conciliar activity. And whereas the decrees of the councils often expressed only hopes and expectations, the rituals inscribed in sacramentaries were nearly always expressions of or models for actual practice, at least within the clerical or monastic communities that produced them. The first phase of this productive activity encompassed the last half of the eighth century and resulted in the creation of a tradition of Frankish-Gelasian ritual books represented by two main types. Al-

11. Ibid., c. 3.

12. Another canon urges offerings for oneself and one's relatives, both living and dead; ibid., c. 4: "Ut oblationes suas adferre usum adsumant atque pro se ipsis et pro parentibus, seu vivis seu defunctis, offerre non pigeat."

13. On the unity of the verses that make up James 5:13–16 in the standard numbering, see Edouard Cothenet, "La guérison comme signe du royaume et l'onction des malades (Jc 5, 13–16)," in La maladie et la mort, 101–25; trans. Matthew J. O'Connell in Temple of the Holy Spirit (New York, 1983), 33–51.

though these so-called Gelasian sacramentaries were built around Roman sources, their creation and dissemination originated in the Frankish lands and cannot be separated from the activity that marked the early stages of the restructuring of church and society under the Carolingians. Furthermore, they are most Roman in their transmission of the liturgy of the mass and least so in precisely the area of main interest here—the rituals around death and dying.

The first type, usually referred to as the "old" Gelasian, is represented by only one extant manuscript, now in the Vatican; but fragments of others show it not to have been unique.[14] The second type, the "young" or eighth-century Gelasian, is represented by at least five complete manuscripts from the two decades before the year 800 (or just after) and fragments of varying lengths.[15] The two types are distinguished by their structures. Both are primarily mass books, arranged according to the calendar; but the first type, represented by the Vatican Gelasian, runs through the year twice, giving one book to the sequence of Sundays and great feasts of the church throughout the year and another to individual saints' days. The eighth-century Gelasians combine these two cycles in one book. Both types provide directions and prayers for rituals connected with the liturgical year (especially for the baptismal rites around Easter) as well as miscellaneous prayers, masses, blessings, and rituals, including those for the sick, dying, and dead. In the Vatican Gelasian the miscellaneous material appears as the third of its three books. In the eighth-century Gelasians it is appended to the cycle of annual masses and feasts, sometimes without a break in the manuscript and sometimes as a second book.[16] The importance of distinguishing the two types lies in the fact that the eighth-century Gelasian books are younger than the Vatican Gela-

14. On the Vatican Gelasian, MS Reg. lat. 316, see Vogel, *Medieval Liturgy*, 64–70. Bernard Moreton gives a good summary of the evidence for the type in *The Eighth-Century Gelasian Sacramentary: A Study in Tradition* (Oxford, 1976), 198–205; cf. CLLA 610–15. The best edition is that of Mohlberg, Eizenhöfer, and Siffrin (i.e., Gelasian).

15. On the eighth-century Gelasians, see Vogel, *Medieval Liturgy*, 70–78; CLLA 801–95; Deshusses, "Sacramentaires," 39–40; and Moreton, *Eighth-Century Gelasian*, esp. 175–98. Moreton's list, while admittedly incomplete, comprises all the important eighth-century manuscripts; the three not edited when he was writing have now appeared in the Corpus christianorum, series latina (i.e., Gellone, Autun, and the sacramentary of Angoulême [ed. Patrick Saint-Roch, CCL 159C], which does not contain material pertinent to this study).

16. Indicated by the title: *Incipit liber secundus de extrema parte.* See M. B. Moreton, "The Liber Secundus of the Eighth Century Gelasian Sacramentaries: A Reassessment," *Studia Patristica* 13 (Berlin, 1975): 382–86.

sian and in part dependent on it. Comparison of the common features of the eighth-century Gelasian rites for the dying and the dead with those in the Vatican Gelasian will serve, therefore, as an indication of the development of ritual in Francia between the middle and the end of the eighth century.

New Forms of Commemoration

The Frankish sacramentaries of the period 740–800 did not add greatly to the commemorative masses that had developed in the Latin church up to that time. As we have seen, most of the masses for the dead in the Vatican Gelasian are Roman creations that drew on the masses of the Verona "sacramentary" and presumably arrived in Francia as part of the Roman material on which the Frankish Gelasian books are based. These masses—for dead clerics, the recently baptized, and the laity, and for the third, seventh, and thirtieth days after burial—were carried over with little change to the eighth-century Gelasian books. Growth is most visible among the related group of "votive masses." Although not all votive masses were sung in the name of the dead, their ultimate purpose was to fulfill the penitential obligations incurred by sin, usually for dead members of the family that requested the mass. Arnold Angenendt sees the general development of votive masses as proceeding apace with the new penitential practices introduced into the life of the Frankish church by Irish and Anglo-Saxon missionaries. Thus it should come as no surprise that they were placed among the sequence of rites for the sick, dying, and dead in the eighth-century Gelasian sacramentaries of Rheinau and St. Gall, both of which show strong Irish and Anglo-Saxon connections. But Angenendt takes the proliferation of these votive masses primarily as a sign of the "materialization" of early medieval spirituality, part of a process by which more primitive forms of religiosity gained ascendancy over the theology of the New Testament and the fathers.[17] From a theological point of view, he may be right, but more than theology was at stake in these ritual practices, and an understanding of their theological implications should be matched by what they tell us of the social and interpersonal structures of Frankish society. Prayer for the dead had no less a social purpose than deathbed

17. Angenendt, "Missa Specialis," 181–91, 212–21; idem, "Theologie und Liturgie," 90–91, 99, 198–99; see also Vogel, "Deux conséquences de l'eschatologie grégorienne."

rituals, and both types of ritual behavior tended to create communal ties among the living which issued forth in permanent structures that bound together scattered groups of men and women in a common enterprise. The conception of the mass as a gift to God which he would reciprocate arose not from a fall into a materialistic understanding of sin and penitence but from the natural tendency of northern Christians—Irish, Anglo-Saxons, Franks—to model their religious behavior on the structures of their social life, in which gift giving played a central role. The evolving rituals for the dying and the dead mirrored the construction of a religious identity that overrode ethnic, legal, and linguistic differences to bind people one to another in the hope of a common salvation.[18] Such feelings led to the inclusion in the eighth-century Gelasian sacramentary of Gellone of a mass for souls whose condition after death was uncertain. This mass was offered for persons whom the congregation suspected of grave crimes, in the hope that if they did not merit glory, their torments might at least be made more tolerable.[19] Such activities may have disturbed a few theologians, but they flowed from faith in God's mercy, charity toward the very present dead, and the strength of communal bonds in the new society of Carolingian Christendom.

The change in attitude toward the care of the dead apparent in the proliferation of votive masses led, in mid-eighth-century Francia, to the creation of a new type of social institution whose growth would parallel that of the death rituals over the following century—confraternities of prayer for the dead.[20] These confraternities emerged as voluntary associations among groups of clergy

18. Cf. Gerd Tellenbach, "Die historische Dimension der liturgischen Commemoratio im Mittelalter," in *Memoria*, ed. Schmid and Wollasch, 200–214, esp. 210–12; and Oexle, "Gegenwart der Toten," 20–77, esp. 26–35.

19. Gellone, nos. 2923–31, *Missa pro cuius anima dibitarum* (sic, recte *dubitatur*); note the language of the first prayer, no. 2923: "et forsitan grauitate criminum non meretur gloria . . . uel tolerabiliora fiant ipsa turmenta." The language comes from Augustine, *Enchiridion*, 110, perhaps mediated through the *Collectio Hibernensis*. See *Irische Kanonensammlung*, ed. Wasserschleben, 42, bk. 15, c. 2.

20. The bibliography on this topic is growing steadily. Fundamental works are Adalbert Ebner, *Die klösterlichen Gebetsverbrüderungen bis zum Ausgange des karolingischen Zeitalters* (Regensburg, 1890); A. Molinier, *Les obituaires français au moyen âge* (Paris, 1890); and Bishop, "Some Ancient Benedictine Confraternity Books," in *Liturgica Historica*, 349–61. New work from the members of the Münster project *Societas et Fraternitas*, begun by Gerd Tellenbach, appears regularly in the journal *Frühmittelalterliche Studien* and the series Münstersche Mittelalter-Schriften; see, e.g., Karl Schmid and Joachim Wollasch, "Die Gemeinschaft der Lebenden und Verstorbenen in Zeugnissen des Mittelalters," FS 1 (1967): 365–401, and their edited volume *Memoria*.

for the purpose of contracting liturgical services in the event of the death of any of their members. The practice of requesting prayers from monastic houses had developed among the Irish and Anglo-Saxons, especially among those missionaries whose work had taken them far from their native lands and religious communities. The Anglo-Saxon missionary Lullus, for example, sent the archbishop of York the names of men he wished to be remembered in the prayers of those at home in England, and Boniface asked to be included in the "sweet fraternity and spiritual fellowship" of the community of Monte Cassino.[21] Analysis of the late eighth-century Salzburg confraternity book, moreover, suggests that Irish monks had been keeping lists of their dead for liturgical commemoration since the turn of the eighth century.[22]

The rapid development of the Frankish church in the years of Pippin's ascendancy and reign led to the institutionalization of the informal arrangements for commemoration which had developed among the Irish and Anglo-Saxons. There is evidence from 750 on that monastic communities regularly circulated lists of their members, living and dead, for commemoration by other houses.[23] The earliest known reference to a formal agreement to do so appears in a letter from Lullus to some priests of Thuringia requesting that they fulfill the terms of *constitutionem nostram* and sing the requisite number of psalms and masses for the repose of the soul of Bishop Romanus of Meaux, who died in 755.[24] Then, sometime between 760 and 762, a group of forty-four Frankish bishops, abbot-bishops, and abbots gathered at the royal villa at Attigny and made formal arrangements for commemorative services after each other's death. Under the terms of the agreement, when one of the signators had died, the others were to see to it that their priests sang one hundred masses and the same number of psalters for his soul. Each bishop was to sing personally thirty masses; those ab-

21. Levison, *England and the Continent*, 102. See also J. Wollasch, "Die mittelalterliche Lebensform der Verbrüderung," in *Memoria*, ed. Schmid and Wollasch, 215–16; and Angenendt, "Missa Specialis," 203–4.

22. Dagmar O Riain-Raedel, "Spuren irischer Gebetsverbrüderungen zur Zeit Virgils," in *Virgil von Salzburg: Missionar und Gelehrter*, ed. H. Dopsch and R. Juffinger (Salzburg, 1985), 141–46.

23. Karl Schmidt and Otto Gerhard Oexle, "Voraussetzungen und Wirkung des Gebetsbundes von Attigny," *Francia* 2 (1974): 71–122.

24. *Die Briefe des heiligen Bonifatius und Lullus*, ed. Michael Tängl, 2d ed., MGH, Epistolae selectae 1 (Berlin, 1955), letter 113, p. 245: "Misimus vobis nomen domni Romani episcopi, pro quo unusquisque vestrum XXX missas cantet et illos psalmos et ieiunium iuxta constitutionem nostram"; cited by Angenendt, "Theologie und Liturgie," 175.

bots who were not themselves bishops were to find bishops to sing the thirty masses for them.[25] The singing of thirty masses derives from the story in the *Dialogues* of Pope Gregory the Great in which Gregory used such means to gain the release of the soul of a dead monk from torment.[26] While the confraternity of Attigny involved only the highest ranks of the Frankish clergy and gave a central role to the bishops, a confraternity established in 772 at Dingolfingen in Bavaria eliminated the distinction between bishops and abbots and included ordinary monks and priests among the recipients of commemoration.[27] Arrangements of this type were then adapted for use within congregations, as at the Alsatian monastery of Wissembourg in 776/77, and between them, as in the confraternity created between Reichenau and St. Gall in 800.[28]

Karl Schmid has pointed out the features that distinguish the developments at Attigny and Dingolfingen from the practices of the Anglo-Saxons: their hierarchical and organizational tendencies, their synodal character, and the important part they played in defining the structure of the Carolingian *Reichskirche*.[29] The creation of reciprocal ties among the high clergy of the Frankish territories marked both the lines of the hierarchy and its unity of purpose in the development and governance of the Frankish kingdoms. But it would be a mistake to lose sight of the basic religious dimension of these activities and their function within the large structure of death rituals—that is, as rites of incorporation. The confraternities were set up not to define structures of power and authority—although they certainly mirrored such things—but to guarantee aid to souls in the transition from this world to the next. They took advantage of the evolving structures of communication,

25. MGH, Concilia 2.72: "Unusquisque . . . quando quislibet de hoc saeculo migraverit, centum psalteria et presbiteri eius speciales misas centum cantent. Ipse autem episcopus per se XXX misas impleat. . . . Abbates vero, qui non sunt episcopi, rogent episcopos, ut vice illorum ipsas XXX misas expleant."
26. *Dialogues*, 4.57.8–16, ed. de Vogüé, 3.188–95; Vogel, "Deux conséquences de l'eschatologie grégorienne."
27. MGH, Concilia 2.96–97: "In Christi nomine . . . decrevimus . . . ut eorum quis de hac luce migraretur, unusquisque superstitum episcoporum vel abbatum pro defuncto in domo sua, id est episcopale vel coenubio, C missas speciales et eodem numero psalteria cantare faciat, ipse vero de propria persona sua XXX speciales conpleat missas. . . . Presbiteris autem sive monachis, cum de hoc saeculo migraverint, episcopus seu abbas uno presbitero vel uno monacho XXX missas speciales, totidem psalteria faciant celebrare." This agreement may have led to the creation of the Salzburg confraternity book; see Ó Riain-Raedel, "Spuren irischer Gebetsverbrüderungen," 141.
28. Angenendt, "Missa Specialis," 205–6; idem, "Theologie und Liturgie," 175.
29. Schmid and Oexle, "Voraussetzungen und Wirkung," 85–86, 94–95.

conciliar action, and religious institutions to refine and intensify the ritual process and make it a more powerful symbol of Christian passage. That this heightening of symbolic power was recognized is evident from the rapid dissemination of membership in confraternities from the exclusive core of high clergy at Attigny to all the members of the monasteries and dioceses whose bishops and abbots met at Dingolfingen ten years later. And that is not all. If the creation of confraternities among the higher clergy and institutions of the realm represents a movement from the top down, there was a corresponding movement from the bottom up. Within the monasteries and cathedral churches of the later eighth century numerous men and women worked at the composition, copying, and transmission of ritual books for everyday use. Analysis of the prayers and rubrics concerning the sick, the dying, and the dead in the extant sacramentaries of the period reveals a sustained and growing interest not only in new ways of ritually incorporating the dead into the next world but also of helping them in their separation from this one.

Sickness, Death, and Burial in the Vatican Gelasian

The question of date and provenance of the Vatican Gelasian has received various answers, but most scholars agree that it was created by the nuns of the abbey of Chelles in the years just before Pippin took the throne as king of the Franks.[30] The community had been established by the Merovingian queen Balthildis around the year 658 as a royal villa nineteen kilometers east of Paris. In the eighth century it forged close ties with the Carolingians. Charles Martel's wife took the veil there, and the most high-born of Carolingian women would continue to fill the office of abbess right into the tenth century.[31] While the Vatican Gelasian probably does not represent an official product of the early reform, it is the earliest example of a Frankish ritual book created around a Roman core.[32] Given the importance of the abbey and its links with the

---

30. Vogel, *Medieval Liturgy*, 65; Deshusses, "Sacramentaires," 28; Moreton, *Eighth-Century Gelasian*, 198–99; Sicard, *Liturgie*, 336; Ulla Ziegler, "Das Sakramentar Gelasianum, Bibl. Vat. reg. lat. 316, und die Schule von Chelles," *Archiv für Geschichte des Buchwesens* 16 (1976): 1–124, esp. 95. It is not known whether or not the book was used at Chelles itself.

31. R. van Doren, "Chelles," DHGE 12.604–5.

32. Chavasse, in *Sacramentaire gélasien*, attempted to reconstruct the earlier Roman book that lay behind the Vatican Gelasian, but his views have not gone

court, it is hardly likely that this is a coincidence. The Roman and Gallican prayers and rituals preserved in the Gelasian sacramentary thus provide an idea of the range of ritual material available and in use in the central Frankish lands around 750. Although it is unclear whether the nuns of Chelles altered or simply copied their exemplar (or even if they had one),[33] analysis of the book they produced sheds light on the confluence of Roman and indigenous prayers and rituals in mid-century and forms the basis for comparison with all later developments.

The various prayers and rubrics for the visitation of the sick, the reconciliation of penitents *ad mortem*, and the prayers for death and burial are spread throughout the Vatican Gelasian. The reconciliation of penitents on their deathbeds is treated in the first book as a digression in the material on the general reconciliation of penitents on Holy Thursday. The third book groups the prayers and masses for the sick with other prayers said "in the home." The death and burial service and the commemorative masses that follow them form a separate section near the end of book 3.

The material on the ritual care of the sick in the Vatican Gelasian reveals the state of affairs brought about by the confluence of Gallican and Roman traditions in Francia in the first half of the eighth century. The basic stock of prayers and ritual actions is Roman, but it is mixed with material expressing the peculiarly Gallican understanding of the efficacy of anointing and the ritual care of the sick. We have already seen how the Roman formula for blessing the oil for the sick was altered in the hands of Gallican clerics to emphasize its spiritual effects. The same tendency is apparent in the set of four prayers in the Vatican Gelasian to be said "over a sick person in the home."[34] Only the third and fourth of these prayers are clearly Roman in provenance, a fact attested by

---

unchallenged. Cf. José Janini's review in *Analecta Sacra Tarraconensia* 31 (1958): 12–14; C. Coebergh, "Le sacramentaire gélasien ancien," ALW 7 (1961): 45–88; and J. D. Thompson, "The Contribution of Vatican Reginensis 316 to the History of Western Service Books," *Studia Patristica* 13 (Berlin, 1975): 425–29.

33. Moreton suggests that there were no sacramentaries at all in Francia before the independent redactions of the Gelasian books of the second half of the eighth century, but only more or less complete collections of mass sets and ritual-pontifical material circulating independently. In his view, the difference between the "old" and "young" Gelasians is that the latter drew from two such collections of Roman material and the former from only one. Moreton, *Eighth-Century Gelasian*, 168–69; idem, "Roman Sacramentaries and Ancient Prayer-Traditions," *Studia Patristica* 15 (Berlin, 1984): 577–80.

34. Gelasian, nos. 1535–38.

their presence in the mass for the sick in the Bobbio Missal. The other two have their roots in the native Gallican liturgy.[35] The first uses language drawn from the Gallican tradition of prayer for the sick: "God . . . look down upon your servant laboring in the ill health of the body; visit him in your health and grant him the medicine of celestial grace."[36] The second repeats the words of the Frankish benediction of the oil—*non solum corpore sed etiam amina*—thus emphasizing the spiritual as well as the physical efficacy of the ritual care of the sick: "God . . . preserve for your servant the gifts of your virtues and grant that he may feel your healing not only in the body but also in the soul."[37] The appearance of these Gallican prayers within the structure of a visitation rite may indicate the emergence of a Frankish rite of anointing the sick, but if so the ritual action was directed at least as much at the "health" of the soul as at the cure of bodily infirmity.[38]

The Vatican Gelasian has few indications of rituals for the dying. As in the case of rites for the sick, it mixes old Roman texts with more recent material developed outside of Rome. Roman prayers for sick catechumens and a shortened form of the baptismal rite for the sick or dying appear as additions to the instructions for the feast of Pentecost.[39] The four prayers appended to the instructions for the reconciliation of public penitents on Holy Thursday, and headed "the reconciliation of penitents at death," form a special group.[40] The first originated in Spain before the conversion of the

35. Chavasse, *Sacramentaire gélasien*, 460–61, regards all four prayers as Roman, but the language of the first two and the fact of their independent transmission to other Frankish Gelasian books (Rheinau, nos. 1274–75; St. Gall, nos. 223–24) argue otherwise. It is not without interest that portions of these two prayers eventually came to rest in masses for the terminally ill in the Roman missal; i.e., masses beseeching "the grace of dying well." See P. Siffrin, *Konkordanztabellen zu den römischen Sakramentarien*, vol. 2, RED, series minor 5 (Rome, 1959), 197.

36. Gelasian, no. 1535: "Deus . . . famulum tuum ex aduersam ualitudinem corporis laborante . . . respice et uisita in salutari tuo et caelestis gratiae praesta medicina [sic]."

37. Ibid., no. 1536: "Deus . . . conserua famulo tuo tuarum dona uirtutum et concede, ut medellam tuam non solum in corpore sed etiam in anima sentiat."

38. Martimort, "Prières pour les malades," 143, argues that the prayers *super infirmum in domo* in the Vatican Gelasian became associated with the Roman sacramentary in the last half of the seventh century, and mark the beginning of the organization of ritual visitation in the Latin Church. See also Chavasse, *Etude*, 170–75, 190–200.

39. Gelasian, nos. 592–617. Most of these prayers are not found outside of the Gregorian-Gelasian tradition; see Siffrin, *Konkordanztabellen*, 2.75–78, and Chavasse, *Sacramentaire gélasien*, 172–76, where he argues against his own earlier view that they were not Roman.

40. Gelasian, nos. 364–67. Chavasse's claim that all four of the prayers in the Vatican Gelasian are "incontestably Roman" (*Sacramentaire gélasien*, 150–53)

Visigoths as a prayer for the reconciliation of Catholics who had been rebaptized as Arians; the second and third are North Italian prayers for reconciling public penitents.[41] The last originated as a rewritten form of the first for use in the deathbed penance ritual from seventh-century Spain.[42] None of these prayers, however, is explicitly connected with the normal ritual for death and burial in the Vatican Gelasian, and thus the question of what, if any, ritual preparation for death was current among the compilers of the sacramentary remains open. In any case, the simultaneous recognition and rejection of Spanish traditions of deathbed penance suggests that they had made little headway among the Frankish clergy in the early eighth century. Perhaps the severity of their effects if the sick should recover, combined with the growing acceptance of repeatable private confession under the influence of Irish and Anglo-Saxons, precluded its acceptance. On the other hand, the presence of the Spanish and North Italian prayers of reconciliation attests to an awareness of their beauty and utility. Their transmission through the Vatican Gelasian would eventually guarantee for them a place within a fully developed ritual sequence around death and dying which recognized the value of confession and reconciliation within a deathbed ceremony but did not attach to them the consequences entailed by the old Spanish rite.[43]

As we saw in Chapter 2, groups and collections of prayers for death and burial—the ritual of Caesarius of Arles, the prayer service in the Bobbio Missal, and various prayers of Spanish or mixed provenance—circulated in the Frankish lands in the seventh and

---

must be corrected. First, he based his opinion on the Roman origin of the *Statuta ecclesiae antiqua,* which have since been shown to be a late fifth-century Gallican creation; see C. Munier, *Les "Statuta ecclesiae antiqua"* (Paris, 1960). Second, José Janini has provided alternative origins; see his "Oraciones visigóticas," 191–204.

41. Janini, "Oraciones visigóticas," 194–99, 202–3.

42. Ibid., 198, and chap. 2 above, n. 115. The Latin of the Vatican Gelasian is far less clear than that of the original; cf. Gelasian, no. 367.

43. The Vatican Gelasian does, however, contain one other indication of the practice of deathbed penance in the mid–eighth century—a special mass to be said for a person who had wished to receive penance before death but had lost the power of speech; Gelasian, nos. 1658–61. The source for this mass is eminently Roman, since it was taken from the private collection of mass sets known as the Verona sacramentary; cf. Verona, no. 1141 (= Gelasian 1658), 1142–43 (= 1659), and 1146 (= 1661). The prayer *Infra actionem* (Gelasian 1660) in this mass, whose source is not in the Verona book, has the unusual feature of using the feminine to refer to the person bringing the offering and the masculine in reference to the dead person: "Hanc igitur oblacionem, quam tibi offeret famula tua illa pro anima famuli tui illius. . . ." Does this reflect the circumstance of a wife offering a mass for her dead husband, or a nun for a brother or father?

early eighth centuries. Most of these prayers were gathered together at some time to form a single burial service, which was in
circulation between 740 and 750, when the compilers of the Vatican Gelasian reproduced it.[44] The result was a rite for death and
burial in five moments: an initial response to death, including the
washing and laying out of the body; a ceremony before the procession to the cemetery; one before burial; one after burial; and a
final commendation. The structure of the whole suggests that the
original *libellus* integrated into the Vatican Gelasian was created
at Chelles, or another community of women, for its base is clearly
the burial service for nuns which became appended to Caesarius of
Arles's rule for his sister's community. It opens, as does the
Caesarian service, with the prayer *Pio recordationis affectu*, and
both the first of the prayers after burial and the first of the two
commendations of the soul were taken from the Caesarian service.
The remaining prayers were woven into this framework from other
sources.[45]

In sum, although the Vatican Gelasian's Roman core did not
present numerous opportunities for the insertion of non-Roman
prayers and rituals, some nevertheless appear. The book preserved
certain Gallican prayers for the sick and subtle alterations in the
Roman blessing of the oil for the sick in order to express a more
spiritualized understanding of the effects of anointing than was
traditional in the Roman church. It included Visigothic prayers
that could be used in a form of deathbed penance. And it presented
the first of a series of fully developed Frankish postmortem rituals,
drawing on a wide variety of sources. Overall, however, the material shows no consistent pattern. Roman, Gallican, and Visigothic
elements jostle one another in uneasy juxtaposition. The compilers of the Vatican Gelasian collected and transmitted material,
but did not transform it into a coherent whole.

Sickness, Death, and Burial in
the Eighth-Century Gelasians

The origins of the eighth-century Gelasian type are obscure. Most
scholars agree that its archetype appeared sometime after the cre-

---

44. Gelasian, nos. 1607–27. That there must have been a preexisting rite is evident from Sicard's collation of the Vatican Gelasian rite with that in the lost sacramentary of St-Remy of Reims and the Gallican and Gelasian rituals as a group; see
Sicard, *Liturgie,* 335–39.
45. E.g., Gelasian, no. 1616 = Gothicum, no. 248, *Oracio pro spiritibus pausan-*

ation of the Vatican Gelasian. According to Cyrille Vogel, the creation of the original eighth-century Gelasian sacramentary represented the most important product of the official attempt to Romanize the liturgy of Francia under Pippin. As he put it, sometime in the decade 750–760, under the direction of the king, a Frankish cleric blended a sacramentary of the type of the Vatican Gelasian (for the structure of the mass and its wealth of non-eucharistic Gallican materials) with a Gregorian sacramentary (for the general disposition of the liturgical year), thus establishing the basic character of the type. Vogel regarded the creation of the new sacramentary as an attempt to eliminate the local Gallican liturgy and end an assumed rivalry between Gelasian and Gregorian books in circulation at the time, while still providing room for indigenous Gallican rituals such as the death ritual.[46] Vogel's assumption of royal sponsorship has not found wide acceptance, but his description of the distinguishing features of the type is accurate.[47] As for the archetype itself, there is consensus on the time of its creation—in the third quarter of the eighth century—but not on the place, some investigators arguing for the monastery of Flavigny and others for a Benedictine community in the Rhaetian Alps.[48]

Four extant eighth-century Gelasian books contain ritual material on death, dying, and the dead. They were all created at the end of the eighth or in the first years of the ninth century. A book now in Paris and known by the name of the monastery of Gellone, where it arrived sometime after 804, was written at Meaux or Cambrai, and shows familiarity with the Gregorian sacramentary that had arrived in Frankland from Rome before 791.[49] A manu-

---

cium. Individual *libelli* could have carried the prayers that appear in the Bobbio Missal and/or those in Sicard's third source; cf. Sicard, *Liturgie,* 304–32.

46. According to Vogel, *Réforme cultuelle,* 186–95, the compiler could have been either Bishop Remedius of Rouen, the brother of Pippin, who spent time in Rome studying the liturgy around 760, or Chrodegang of Metz. Cf. the updated remarks by the translators of Vogel's *Medieval Liturgy,* 73–76. In 1961 Jean Deshusses introduced the hypothesis that Charlemagne may have encouraged the copying of eighth-century Gelasian books as an initial response to the inadequacy of the papal sacramentary sent by Pope Hadrian, but he has not reiterated it in his recent work; cf. "Le sacramentaire de Gellone dans son contexte historique," EL 75 (1961): 193–210, with "Sacramentaries," and his Introduction to Gellone. Moreton has argued that the popularity of the type depended solely on its usefulness and comprehensiveness; *Eighth-Century Gelasian,* 173–74.

47. There is still a question, however, as to whether its Roman sources were fully developed sacramentaries or independent collections of liturgical material; see n. 33 above.

48. On Flavigny, see Deshusses, Introduction to Gellone, p. xxiii; on the Rhaetian Alps, Moreton, *Eighth-Century Gelasian,* 173.

49. Paris, Bibliothèque Nationale, MS lat. 12048; Gellone. For codicological in-

script now in Berlin was written at Autun.[50] The Rheinau sacramentary, now in Zürich, and the St. Gall sacramentary, in that monastery's library, were written in the lands around Lake Constance.[51]

Up to now, the search for the archetype of the eighth-century Gelasians has focused entirely on the main body of the sacramentary: that is, the *liber primus*, containing the mass formulas for the Sundays and feasts of the liturgical year.[52] As we shall see, the unity in presentation of the rites for the sick, the dying, and the dead in the manuscripts that include such material suggests that a structural unity also underlies the *liber secundus*. Within that structural unity, however, a striking degree of diversity is created by the alteration, omission, and addition of material.[53] Since the materials vary significantly from manuscript to manuscript, I will look to the late eighth-century Gelasian sacramentaries as representative of local traditions in or around the communities that produced them.

These four books differ in important ways from their forerunner, the Vatican Gelasian. The most obvious change is organizational. Unlike the Vatican Gelasian, which treats the liturgy of the sick in the general context of clerical visits and blessings "in the home" and makes no connection between rites of penance and those for death and burial, the eighth-century Gelasian books place rites and prayers for the sick, the dying, and the dead in a continuous sequence. Although the mixture of Roman and Gallican prayers is retained, the materials are arranged to lead logically from the cere-

---

formation and bibliography, see Deshusses's Introduction to the companion volume to Dumas's edition. See also CLLA 855.

50. Berlin, Öffentliche Wissenschaftliche Bibliothek, MS lat. 105 (Phillips 1667); Autun (CLLA 853).

51. Zürich, Zentralbibliothek, codex Rheinau 30 (Rheinau; CLLA 802); and St. Gall, Stiftsbibliothek, MS lat. 350 (CLLA 831). The Rheinau book was produced at St. Gall or Reichenau, or at an unknown scriptorium under their influence; see Rheinau, pp. 48–63. The St. Gall book was produced at Chur and used at St. Gall; see also A. Bruckner, *Scriptoria medii aevi Helvetica: Denkmäler Schweizerischer Schreibkunst des Mittelalters*, vol. 1, *Schreibschulen der Diözese Chur* (Genf, 1935), 36, 89–91.

52. Antoine Chavasse, "Le sacramentaire gélasien du viii⁰ siècle: Ses deux principales formes," EL 73 (1959): 249–98, and *Le sacramentaire dans le groupe dit "Gélasiens du viii⁰ siècle,"* 2 vols., Instrumenta Patristica 14 (The Hague, 1984); Deshusses, Introduction to Gellone, xxiii–xxvi.

53. Cf. Moreton, "Liber Secundus" and *Eighth-Century Gelasian*, 171, where he characterizes "the ritual-pontifical material" as "local additions to the sacramentaries proper, coming out of a widespread and variable libellus tradition."

monies for the sick to those for the dying and then to those for the dead. Moreover, some manuscripts reveal significant additions to this basic ritual structure. These changes are indicated in Table 1.

Rites for the Sick

Why did the compilers of the eighth-century Gelasian sacramentaries bring the rites and prayers for the sick together with those for the dying and the dead? Perhaps they were simply exercising a Benedictine penchant for order, as Bernard Moreton has suggested.[54] On the other hand, the spiritualization of the liturgy of the sick in the Frankish lands in the seventh and early eighth centuries—the tendency of such prayers and rituals to give as much emphasis to the purification of the soul and preparation for eternal life as to the return of physical health—would naturally suggest such a change. Given the development of an anointing ritual for the dying among the reformed Irish clergy during the same period, moreover, one would expect to find the process of joining rites for the sick with those for the dying most highly developed in areas of Irish influence. This is in fact the case.

In the Gellone and Autun books, the prayers for the home and for the mass for the sick were taken directly from the older Gelasian tradition (represented by the Vatican Gelasian) without alteration, and express the same predominantly Roman attitudes with slight Gallican overtones.[55] As we saw earlier, those Gallican overtones are carried in the two prayers *super infirmum in domo* in the Vatican Gelasian which did not derive from its Roman sources. In the two books written in the Swiss lands around 800, the sacramentaries of Rheinau and St. Gall, however, only the Gallican prayers are presented.[56] Although they include some of the Roman

54. Moreton, "Liber Secundus," 383, 386.
55. Gellone, nos. 2878–87, and Autun, nos. 1896–1905, correspond to Gelasian, nos. 1535–43, with the exception that Gellone and Autun add a preface (2885/1903) to the mass prayers based on a prayer *post infirmitatem* in the Verona sacramentary: "Qui famulos tuos ideo corporaliter uerberas ut mente proficiant, potenter ostendens quod sit pietatis tuae praeclara saluatio, dum praestas ut operetur nobis etiam ipsa infirmitas salutem"; cf. Verona, no. 1060, and nos. 308, 314, 334, 465.
56. Rheinau, nos. 1274–75; St. Gall, nos. 223–24. In both books these prayers appear under the separate rubric *super infirmo in domo*. Anton Hänggi and Alfons Schönherr have discovered various indications that the exemplar for much of the material in Rheinau came from the monastery of Nivelles, founded in the seventh century under the supervision of Irish monks and one of the "bevorzugten Durchgangspunkten von wandernden Iroschotten"; Rheinau, pp. 48–57, quotation on 51. This is the case, for instance, with the fourth of its nine votive masses, if not for the whole series; ibid., 56.

Table 1. Organization of rites for the sick, dying, and dead in Frankish Gelasian sacramentaries

Rite	Vatican Gelasian (book and section nos.)	Later sacramentaries (item nos.)			
		Gellone	Autun	St. Gall	Rheinau
Prayers in the home	3.69	2877–81	1895–99	222–24	1273–75
Blessing of bread/water	—	—	—	225–26	—
Mass for the sick	3.70	2882–86	1900–1904	227–31	1276–79
Prayers for return of health	3.71	2887	1905	232	1280
Anointing	—	—	—	233	—
Votive masses	—	—	1906–9	234–49	1281–1324
Prayers for the dying	—	—	—	—	1325–26
Deathbed reconciliation	1.39	2888–91	1910–13	250–51	1327–29
Rite for the agony	—	2892–98	1914	—	1330
Death and burial	3.91	2899–2922	1914–38	252–60	1331–41
Commemorative masses	3.92–105	2923–3010	1939–2020	—	1342–1405

SOURCES: *Liber sacramentorum Romanae aeclesiae ordinis anni circuli*, ed. Leo C. Mohlberg, L. Eizenhöfer, and P. Siffrin, 3d ed. (Rome, 1981); *Liber sacramentorum Gellonensis*, ed. Antoine Dumas (Turnhout, 1981); *Liber sacramentorum Augustudonensis*, ed. Odilo Heiming (Turnhout, 1984); *Ein St. Galler Sakramentar-Fragment*, ed. Georg Manz (Münster, 1939); *Sacramentarium Rhenaugiense*, ed. Anton Hänggi and Alfons Schönherr (Fribourg, 1970).

material, both books distinguish between Roman prayers of healing and Gallican (or Irish-Gallican) prayers and acts of purification in preparation for death.

The ritual visitation of the sick in the St. Gall sacramentary presents the only example of a formula for anointing in a Frankish sacramentary before the mid–ninth century, and is thus the closest continental analogue to the anointing rituals in contemporary Irish sources. Expanding on the common basis within the tradition of the eighth-century Gelasians, it includes blessings of bread and water (unique to the St. Gall manuscript), which suggest a ritual purification of the sick person's food, and directions for the anointing.[57] Although the unction formula follows the prayer "for the return of health," it expresses more than the expectation of physical healing.

> I anoint you with sanctified oil so that in the manner of a warrior prepared through anointing for battle you will be able to prevail over the aery hordes. Do your work, creature of oil, in the name of the Father and the Son and the Holy Spirit, so that no unclean spirit will remain either in the limbs, marrow, or joints of this man, but let work in him the power of Christ the son of the most high God, who lives and reigns forever with the Father and the Holy Spirit.[58]

This formula, with its reference to anointing before battle, has its roots in the baptismal liturgy—the long second sentence appears in the Stowe and Bobbio missals as part of the baptismal rite—but its peculiar reference to the demons of the air also suggests the migration of the soul after death.[59] Thus both of its clauses suggest that the anointing symbolized a spiritual transformation rather than a physical one. Nonetheless, the meaning of the ritual is still ambiguous. Tensions remain between the images and language of the Roman mass and prayer "for the return of health" on the one

57. St. Gall, nos. 222, *Oracio in domo infirmorum* (= Gellone, 2877); 223–24, *Oratio super infirmos in domo* (= Gellone, 2878–79); 225, *Benedictio panis ad egrotum*; 226, *Benedictio aquae ad egrotum*; 227–31, *Oratio ad missam pro infirmis* (= Gellone, 2882–86); 232, *Oratio pro redita sanitate* (= Gellone, 2887); 233, *Ad infirmum unguendum*.

58. Ibid., no. 233: "Ungo te de oleo sanctificato, ut more militis uncti praeparatus ad luctam possis ereas superare catervas. Operare, creatura olei, in nomine Patris et Filii et Spiritus sancti, ut non lateat spiritus immundus nec in membris nec in medullis nec in ulla conpage membrorum huius hominis, sed operetur in eum virtus Christi, Filii Dei altissimi, qui cum eterno Patre et Spiritu sancto vivit et regnat."

59. Cf. Enright, *Iona, Tara, and Soissons*, 148–49 (anointing before battle); Stowe, p. 31, and Bobbio, no. 243; Ntedika, *Evocation de l'au-delà*, 46–83 (demons).

hand and the Gallican prayers and the anointing formula, with their emphasis on spiritual well-being, on the other. This ambiguity may have been intentional, so that the ritual could be used for both the merely sick and the dying; or it may have its basis in the efforts of liturgists to preserve their sources while experimenting with new ritual gestures and contexts.

Another innovation in the St. Gall book is shared with Rheinau—the inclusion of a series of votive masses between the rites for the sick and the deathbed reconciliation (Table 1). There are three such masses in St. Gall and nine in Rheinau. Many of the prayers in these masses are found only in these books and other Frankish sources.[60] Their tone is overwhelmingly penitential and supplicatory, and many have to do with sickness and death. Their inclusion within the ritual sequence is a further indication of the expansion of ritual activity in the second half of the eighth century, especially in terms of intercessory prayer for the dead and dying.

The Rheinau ritual presents one final innovation. In Chapter 2 I discussed two prayers from the *Missale Gothicum* as exemplifying the Gallican ritual attitude toward the sick, which focused on spiritual as much as on physical healing.[61] In the Rheinau book, these two prayers appear following the votive masses and immediately preceding the deathbed reconciliation. This placement shows a recognition of the differences between the Roman and old Gallican prayers for the sick and goes beyond the simple conjoining of the rites for the sick, the dying, and the dead in the other eighth-century Gelasians. The scribes of the Rheinau manuscript kept the prayers from the Gelasian tradition associated with the visitation of the sick and the return of physical health together, and separated them from the rites of the dying and the dead by appropriate votive masses. They then included the two prayers from the old Gallican

60. Rheinau, secs. CCLV–CCLXIII: "Missa pro salute uiuorum" (= St. Gall, nos. 244–46); "Missa uotiua pro remedium animae"; "Missa pro tribulantibus de quauislibet extra flagella corporis"; "Missa uotiua pro eos qui sibi in corpore uiui missam cantare rogant"; "Item alia missa uotiua"; "Missa uotiua cum lectiones"; "Item alia missa pro deuoto"; "Missa uotiua"; "Missa in natale sanctorum uel pro memoria uiuorum siue agenda mortuorum fidelium in Christo." The prayers of the second mass are found only in other eighth-century Gelasians. Almost all of the third, fourth, and fifth masses are found only in the Rheinau book. Most of the sixth is in Padua, Biblioteca Capitolare MS D 47, a mid-ninth-century Gregorian sacramentary derived from a Roman original, but with much later material; the seventh is from Gellone (1847–53). The first two prayers in the eighth mass are from Bobbio (438–39); the last prayer of the ninth is shared with most of the eighth-century Gelasians, but the first two are unique to the Rheinau sacramentary. See the *Konkordanztabelle* at the end of Rheinau.

61. Gothicum, nos. 240–41 = Rheinau, nos. 1325–26.

liturgy which most clearly expressed the Gallican emphasis on "celestial medicine" and spiritual healing. In so doing, they recorded a version of the second prayer which is more explicitly directed toward spiritual health than that in the *Missale Gothicum:* "Lord for whom it is easy to raise the dead, restore to the sick their previous health, lest those who beg the cure of your mercy lack the remedies of eternal medicine."[62] As a result, the Gallican prayers stand out from the previous prayers for the sick as specifically related to the rites that follow—those for death. Although they are styled prayers *pro infirmo,* their ritual placement and language reveal them as prayers for the dying.

In sum, the rearrangement of the ritual material concerning the sick in these four late eighth-century Frankish Gelasian books points to the continued tension between two models of ritual healing within the Frankish church—one centered on the return of physical health, the other on the health of the soul and preparation for eternal life. This tension was variously dealt with in the centers that produced the sacramentaries. The compilers of the rituals in the Gellone and Autun books maintained the dynamic tension brought about by the mixture of Roman and Gallican prayers for the sick in the Gelasian tradition as a whole. At the home of the St. Gall and Rheinau books, perhaps because of the strength of Irish and Irish-Gallican traditions there, the liturgists struggled with that dynamic tension while trying to remain more or less faithful to their sources. The tension is heightened in the St. Gall book by the introduction of an anointing ritual that presents the oil as an aid to the soul in an upcoming battle with the demons of the air and draws on the imagery of spiritual transformation in baptismal anointings. The sacramentary of Rheinau achieved a resolution of a sort by separating the two streams, Roman and Gallican, letting them flow into the channels most suited to each—the Roman toward the sick and the Gallican toward the dying. Nevertheless, the Rheinau achievement was tentative and localized. A final resolution would require a full articulation of rites of preparation for

62. Rheinau, no. 1326, with Gothicum variants italicized in brackets: "Domine [cui] uiuificare mortuos facile est, restitue egrotantibus pristine sanitatem [*pristinae sanitati*], [ne] aeternae [*ne terreni*] medicaminis remedia desiderent, quicumque medillam tuae misericordiae [*caelestis misericordiae tuae*] depraecantur, saluatur mundi [*dipraecantur*]." The editors of Rheinau give the reading [*ut*] *aeternae,* but given the text in Gothicum, the proper restoration is more likely to be [*ne*] *aeternae,* though neither word appears in the manuscript (cf. Zürich, Zentralbibliothek, codex Rheinau 30, fols. 150v–151r). Either way, however, the alteration of meaning remains.

death and the incorporation of ritual anointing as one of their essential features.

Death and Burial

Damien Sicard has carried out a thorough analysis of the burial services in all the Frankish Gelasian sacramentaries and grouped them into families.[63] When his work on the textual history of the individual prayers and groups of prayers is viewed from the wider perspective taken here, the historical process that produced the variations in the manuscripts emerges more clearly. As we have seen, the eighth-century Gelasian books agree on the overall arrangement and presentation of the various rites for the sick, dying, and dead. Within that organizational scheme, however, there is a great deal of diversity in the contents of the individual rites. These variations could have been produced in one of two ways: either the original form of each of these burial services circulated as a small booklet (*libellus*), and continued to do so well into the ninth century, or the services were excerpted from full sacramentaries and circulated as *libelli*.[64] Either circumstance would explain why some sacramentaries created in the ninth century, otherwise up to date in structure and content, contain burial services that are the same as those in sacramentaries of an earlier period and of a less developed type. The eighth-century Gelasian sacramentary of St-Remy, for example, although written around 800, contained the same burial service that was written into the Vatican Gelasian over a half century earlier.[65] The burial service added to an important mid-ninth-century Gregorian sacramentary now in Padua repro-

63. Sicard, *Liturgie*, 334–51; and see the tables headed "La structure des rituels gallicans et gélasiens de la mort," at the end of his book.

64. Short *libelli* excerpted from full sacramentaries for pastoral work are extant from this period; e.g., the *Liber sacramentorum excarsus* of Brussels MS 10127–44 and the *Liber sacramentorum romane ecclesiae ordine excarpsus* of Paris, B.N. lat. 2296, in *Testimonia orationis christianae antiquioris*, ed. P. Salmon, C. Coebergh, and P. de Puniet, CCCM 47 (Turnhout, 1977), 79–177. Although neither of these *libelli* contains a death ritual, the first, the vade-mecum of a parish priest of northeastern France (ibid., 81), has a rite of baptism for the sick, and the second, created at St-Amand ca. 800 for an abbatial church or one dependent on the abbey (ibid., 117), contains the prayers for the visitation of the sick common to most of the Gelasian sacramentaries.

65. This sacramentary is no longer extant, but its burial service is printed in the notes to Ménard's edition of the Gregorian sacramentary in PL 78.467–68. Because it very nearly reproduces the burial rite in the Vatican Gelasian, Sicard regards both as members of the same family, A; *Liturgie*, 335–39.

duces the burial service in the Autun sacramentary, but does not take account of any of the other changes made in the intervening period.[66] On the other hand, there are clear indications of development over time, for when individual scribes created new ritual books, they often altered what they found in their models whether *libelli* or complete sacramentaries. Thus it is that the tradition represented by the ritual in the Vatican Gelasian was slightly revised in some of the eighth-century Gelasians and extensively so in others. Certain innovations had a lasting appeal, and were then further copied into later books, most often those from the same or related scriptoria, and disseminated for use in surrounding communities.

Three such important innovations in death and burial rites are evident in the late eighth-century Gelasian books. The first is the general rearrangement of ritual material to bring the old North Italian and Visigothic prayers for the deathbed reconciliation of penitents, which first appeared together in the Vatican Gelasian, into a new location immediately before the rites for death, burial, and commemoration (Table 1). This rearrangement took place in two stages. The Gellone sacramentary represents the first stage, in which the deathbed reconciliation prayers were reproduced in both their original position—as additions to the general reconciliation of penitents on Holy Thursday—and the new, before the rite for death and burial.[67] In the second stage—represented by the Autun sacramentary, for example—the deathbed reconciliation prayers were edited out of the Holy Thursday rites and appear only in their new position.[68] This was surely in acknowledgment of an increasing recourse to penance before death among the Frankish clergy of the time. The second innovation is also organizational. It is represented in the sacramentary of Autun and in the Prague sacramen-

---

66. Sicard, *Liturgie*, 340–42, 348, groups the rites in the Padua manuscript (Biblioteca Capitolare D 47; CLLA 880) and Autun in family *B*, along with the Prague sacramentary (MS O.83; *Das Prager Sakramentar*, vol. 2, *Prolegomena und Textausgabe*, ed. Alban Dold and Leo Eizenhöfer, Texte und Arbeiten 38–42 [Beuron, 1949]). Note also that in Sicard Autun = Ph (i.e., Phillips 1667).

67. Cf. Gellone, nos. 588–610 and 2888–91, with Gelasian, nos. 352–74.

68. Cf. Autun, nos. 465–81, with the rites in Gellone and the Vatican Gelasian cited in n. 67; only in the Autun sacramentary does the Holy Thursday reconciliation ritual appear in its full integrity. Of the other eighth-century Gelasians, St. Gall, Stiftsbibliothek MS 348, and the Sacramentary of Angoulême (neither of which, because of their lack of a *liber secundus*, figure otherwise in this analysis), both follow Autun; see the *Konkordanztabelle* at the back of Dumas's edition of Autun.

tary, a Bavarian product that is known to have been at Regensburg in the year 794.[69] Although the burial service in these books is only slightly developed from the rite in the Vatican Gelasian, rubrics have been added to distinguish more clearly the separate moments of the ritual process, and prayers have been rearranged accordingly.[70] The third innovation deserves detailed consideration, for it signals a fundamental change in ritual structure and tone. In one way or another, these books all record the development of a ritual accompaniment to death itself which focused the power of communal prayer on the deathbed as an aid to the dying person in his or her final agony.[71] The ritual process around the deathbed mirrored the increasingly dense network of reciprocal ties between the living and the dead which marked the Frankish society of the eighth century, and placed each individual and the whole community within a sacred history stretching from the Old Testament covenant to the final judgment.

Gellone: A New Ritual Moment—the *Commendatio animae*

Up to the time the Gellone sacramentary was compiled, and even in some of the other eighth-century Gelasians, the rites for death and burial were introduced by a rubric denoting the fact that death had occurred.[72] Similarly, the ending of the burial ritual was marked by a commendation of the soul. A commendation still appears at the end of the service in the Gellone book, but the rites bear the general heading "Prayers over the dead and commendation of the soul" (*Orationis* [sic] *super defunctum vel commendatio animae*) and the prayers that immediately follow are clearly meant to be spoken before death and during the final agony.[73] That this

69. Autun, nos. 1914–38; and *Prager Sakramentar*, secs. 286–91. The Prague book has a service for death and burial but nothing on the sick or the reconciliation *ad mortem.*

70. Both add a rubric for the ritual washing of the corpse and reorganize prayers from the Vatican Gelasian ritual for a church vigil and before departure for the burial site; cf. Gelasian, nos. 1608–19, with Autun, nos. 1917–24, and *Prager Sakramentar*, secs. 287–89.

71. The significance of this innovation has been noted by Louis Gougaud, "Etude sur les *ordines commendationis animae*," EL 49 (1935): 3–27, and Rowell, *Liturgy of Christian Burial*, 62–63. Cf. Sicard, *Liturgie*, 348–49; this innovation is the distinguishing feature of his family C.

72. Appendix to Caesarius's rule for nuns: *Incipiunt orationes super defunctae corpus*; Bobbio: *Orationes ad defunctum*; Vatican Gelasian: *Orationes post obitum hominis*; Prague: *Orationes super defunctos*; Autun sacramentary: *Orationes super defuncto*; St-Remy: *Incipit officium pro defunctis.*

73. Gellone, nos. 2892–98; they are followed by the rubric *orationes post obitum super defunctum.*

was a radical innovation is indicated by the fact that the scribe did not have a customary rubric for this new ritual moment and had to employ an older expression in a new context. The term *commendatio animae* in the heading seems to have been meant to cover the whole ritual from agony to burial and final commendation, but its appearance in Gellone ultimately led to its employment as a heading for rites for the agony in ritual books throughout the Middle Ages.[74] The explanation for its use here may be that one of the prayers for the agony in Gellone is precisely that prayer, *Deus apud quem,* which in the Prague sacramentary is introduced with the rubric *Oratio super defunctos vel commendatio animae* and takes its position at the end of the burial service, not around the death itself.[75] The similarity between the two rubrics is telling. The Prague book must have picked up the prayer from a source in which it was separately transmitted as the sole prayer for the dead—just as the Vatican Gelasian may have done. Gellone drew on a similar source, inserted the one prayer into an already evolving rite for the agony, and used the rubric to refer to this new ritual moment. The prayers for the laying out and the funeral follow in Gellone after a section *post obitum super defunctum,* now reduced to a single prayer.

Let us look closely at this new moment in the death ritual signaled by the Gellone sacramentary. It begins with a prayer that eventually became part of the *Rituale Romanum* at this point in the ritual process—the *Proficiscere anima.*[76] This prayer exhorts the soul to "Go forth from this world, in the name of the Father Almighty who created you, and in the name of Jesus Christ, the son of the living God who suffered death for you, in the name of the Holy Spirit who has been poured out upon you, in the name of the angels and archangels," and so on from the court of the heavenly king down to the "monks, anchorites, virgins, and faithful widows" on earth. A litany in the form of a prose prayer, the *Proficiscere* connects the people gathered around the deathbed with the entire community of the blessed: the immortal denizens of heaven, "all those of the human race who have been received by God," and those on earth most worthy of paradise, the ascetics and

74. Gougaud, "Etude sur les *ordines.*"
75. *Prager Sakramentar,* sec. 291, no. 2.
76. Gellone, no. 2892. Cf. Sicard, *Liturgie,* 361–64; Gougaud, "Etude sur les *ordines,*" 12. And see the frontispiece to this volume, which reproduces the illuminated initial *p* from the word *Proficiscere* in the Gellone manuscript, which is in the form of a dead man lying next to a shield.

the cloistered. The final words, "Today a place for him has been made in peace, and a house for him in the celestial Jerusalem. Receive, Lord, your servant into goodness," echo Christ's words on the cross to the good thief (Luke 23:42) and recall the rite of deathbed penance from the old Spanish *Libri ordinum.*[77]

Another prose litany follows, whose invocations have the form "Free, Lord, the soul of your servant."[78] Over and over again, eleven times in all, the attendants invoke God to free the soul of the dying person. What is most remarkable about the prayer is the repetition of the person's name, also eleven times. The dying person is the center of attention, body and soul. The chant begins with a call to free the soul from "all the dangers of the nether regions." It then turns to a list of comparisons with biblical persons: "Free, Lord, the soul of your servant N., . . . just as you freed Noah from the deluge . . . Enoch and Elijah from the common death of this world . . . Moses from the hand of Pharaoh, king of the Egyptians . . . Job from his sufferings . . . Daniel from the lion's den . . . the three boys from the fiery furnace and the hands of the evil king . . . Jonah from the stomach of the whale . . . Susanna from false testimony . . . David from the hands of King Saul, Goliath, and all his chains . . . Peter and Paul from prison and torments. Thus may you see fit to free the soul of this person and grant it a place with you in heavenly delights."[79] Each of the com-

77. Gellone, no. 2892: "Proficiscere anima de hoc mundo, in nomine dei patris omnipotentis qui te creauit, et in nomine iesu christi fili dei uiui qui pro te passus est, in nomine spiritus sancti qui in te effusus est, in nomine angelorum et archangelorum, in nomine thron[or]um et dominationum, in nomine principatum et potestatum et omnium uirtutum cęlestium, in nomine cęrubyn et seraphyn, in nomine omnis humanu generis quod a deo susceptus est, in nomine patriarcharum et prophetarum, in nomine apostulorum et martyrum, in nomine confessorum et episcuporum, in nomine sacerdotum et lęuitarum, et ominis ęcclęsię catholicę gradum, in nomine monachorum et anichoritarum, in nomine uirginum et fidelium uiduarum. Hodię factus est in pace locus ęius, et habitatio ęius in hyerusalem cęleste. Suscipe domine seruum tuum in bonum."

78. Gellone, no. 2893. Cf. Ntedika, *Evocation de l'au-delà,* 72–83; Sicard, *Liturgie,* 364–72, and "Préparation à la mort et prière pour les agonisants," in *Maladie et la mort,* 327–37; and Gougaud, "Etude sur les *ordines,*" 13–14.

79. Gellone, no. 2893: "Libera domine animam serui tui *illi* ex omnibus periculis infernorum et de laqueis poenarum et omnibus tribolationibus multis. Libera domine animam serui tui *ill.* sicut liberasti Noę per diluuium . . . hęnoch et Hęliam de conmuni morte mundi . . . moysen de manu pharaonis regis ęgyptiorum . . . iob de passionibus suis . . . danihęlem de lacum leonis . . . tres puęrus de camino ignis ardentis et de manibus regis iniqui . . . ionam de uentre c[o]eti . . . susannam de falso testimento . . . dauid de manu saul regis et golię et de omnibus uincolis ęius . . . petrum et paulum de carceribus [et] turmentis. Sic liberare digneris animam hominis istius et tecum habitare concede in bonis cęlestibus." The irregular Latin of the scribe was corrected for only the first part of this prayer.

parisons is to a person, to a moment in human history in which God intervened to save one of his faithful. The rhythmic repetitions of these prayers helped to concentrate the minds of the participants on the ritual action. Their shared recitation created community, not only among the attendants at the death but between them and those who had gone before them in sacred history. They mark the point at which dying has become for Christians a participatory act, requiring (and benefiting from) the presence of others, not just to supply the "necessary viaticum" but to help the dying person through the power of communal prayer. Though such prayers may have been in use in rites for the dying for some time before they were written into the Gellone and other eighth-century Gelasian books, their inclusion there points to the growing importance of participatory rituals in the Frankish church and marks the beginning of a long tradition.[80]

Autun: The *Commendatio* and Roman *ordo defunctorum*

A similar elaboration of the antemortem phase of the death ritual is apparent in the Autun sacramentary. Although the Autun book does not record the prayers found in Gellone, it has, squeezed in between the deathbed reconciliation and the burial service, a peculiar form of the old Roman *ordo defunctorum*.[81] Given the romanizing ideals of the reformers around Pippin and Charlemagne, it is not surprising that the Frankish ritual books of the period would show interest in this tradition. But that interest was limited; evidence of it survives only in the Autun and Rheinau sacramentaries, and both books present important differences from other witnesses.[82] Careful attention to the precise manner of the reception and use of the Roman *ordo*, moreover, reveals a great deal about the process of Romanization, the persistence of local traditions, and the nature of attitudes toward death and dying in the Frankish church at the inception of the Carolingian reform.

The Roman service in the Autun sacramentary has the unusual heading, "On the migration of the soul" (*de migratione animę*). Sicard believes that its peculiarities are of Roman provenance and

---

80. Ntedika, *Evocation de l'au-delà*, 79–80, has noted the forerunners of the *Libera* prayer in Gallican and Visigothic traditions of the seventh century, but his examples come either from the mass or from the funeral services, not from antemortem rites.

81. Autun, no. 1914.

82. Ibid. and Rheinau, nos. 1331–41. These portions of Rheinau and Autun were first edited by Hieronymus Frank in "Älteste erhaltene *ordo defunctorum*," 362–65. Sicard has reedited them in *Liturgie*, 6–11 (Autun), 20–22 (Rheinau).

that the differences between it and the other witnesses of the Roman *ordo* are the result of its creation and use by a clerical or monastic community.[83] It is a monastic or clerical rite, but there is no reason to believe that its peculiar form is anything other than a Frankish creation, or much older than the time of its inscription in the Autun sacramentary. On the contrary, its analogues with the *commendatio animae* in Gellone suggest that it is a manifestation of late eighth-century Frankish interest in communal aid for the dying, for all its unique features cluster around the antemortem ritual activities. The Autun rite added three more rubrics to the two Roman ones directing the reception of viaticum and the reading of the passion until death (Ritual 4). These rubrics provide for the chanting of a litany preceded by a psalm and antiphon, and the recitation of a prayer of commemoration.[84]

The chant pieces indicated after the reading of the passion appear in other witnesses to the Roman *ordo* as part of the funeral procession to the church, but are entirely appropriate to an antemortem ritual.[85] The attendants sing, in the name of the dying, "You ordered me to be born, Lord; you promised that I would rise again," followed by the song of hope that is Psalm 41. The litany that is indicated, beginning *Christi audi nos,* is nowhere attested in Roman sources, but appears in the baptismal liturgy of this same sacramentary and as a preparation for the mass in the Stowe Missal.[86] It fulfills the same function here as the *Proficiscere* and *Libera* chants in Gellone. The attendants forge a symbolic bond between themselves and the angels, patriarchs, and saints in heaven, into whose company the dying person will soon pass. A prayer of commendation is to be said before death rather than after, just as in Gellone. Finally, the Autun rite reverses the relationship of the two antemortem acts in the Roman *ordo*—the reception of viaticum

83. Sicard, *Liturgie,* 27, 49. Sicard did not consider whether it might not be a Frankish adaptation of the old Roman *ordo* or if it was the usage of the church where Autun was written; cf. ibid., 7, and CLLA 853. The recent editor of the manuscript (Odilo Heiming) argues that the Autun book was created for the bishop of Autun and is not monastic in origin; Autun, pp. xii–xvii.

84. Autun, no. 1914: "Primitus enim ut adpropinquaret hora exitus incipiunt legi evangelium Iohannis de passione domini. Deinde incipiunt canere psalmum *Quemadmodum* cum antephona *Tu iussisti nascere mi domine*. Postea letania. *Christe audi nos.* ipsa expleta, dicit sacerdus orationem anime commemorationis. Inde uero antequam egrediatur a corpore, communicet eum sacerdus corpus et sanguinem illum praeuidentes ut sine uiaticum non exeat. Hoc est corpus domini." Cf. Sicard's edition, *Liturgie,* 8.

85. On the chant piece *Tu iussisti—Quemadmodum,* see Sicard, *Liturgie,* 132–33, 141.

86. Autun, no. 537; Stowe, p. 3; Bishop, "The Litany of the Saints in the Stowe Missal," in *Liturgica Historica,* 137–64.

Ritual 4. Preparation for death in the Roman *ordo defunctorum* and the Autun sacramentary

Roman *ordo defunctorum*	Autun sacramentary
	On the migration of the soul
As soon as they should see him approaching death he is to be given communion, even if he has eaten that day, because the communion will be his defender and advocate at the resurrection of the just. It will resuscitate him.	As the hour of his death draws near they begin to read the passion of the Lord from the Gospel of John.
After the reception of communion, the Gospel accounts of the passion of the Lord are to be read to the sick person by priests or deacons until the soul departs from the body.	Then they begin to chant the psalm *Quemadmodum* [41] with the antiphon *Tu iussisti nascere mi domine.*
	Afterward, the litany *Christe audi nos.*
	When that is finished, the priest recites the prayer of commemoration of the soul.
	Just before the soul leaves the body, the priest should give him the body and blood, seeing that he should not die without viaticum, that is, the body of the Lord.

SOURCE: Damien Sicard, *La liturgie de la mort dans l'église latine des origines à la réforme carolingienne* (Münster, 1978), 34–52.

and the reading of the Passion. The rubricist apparently felt it necessary to justify this change in sequence by paraphrasing the language of papal and conciliar decrees (*sine viaticum non exeat*) that insisted on the right of everyone to the viaticum.[87] He may also have acted on the mistaken impression that it was a Roman custom to have the host in the mouth at the moment of death. Such a notion is belied by the usual form of the Roman *ordo*, but it can be seen at work again in a tenth-century addition to the fifth-century life of St. Melania, wherein it is affirmed that it was a

87. Cf. Nicaea, c. 13 (above, chap. I, n. 71), and the decretals of Gregory the Great, *Gergorii I papae registrum epistolarum*, 2 vols., ed. Paul Ewald and Ludwig Hartmann, 2d ed., MGH, Epistolae 1–2 (Berlin, 1957), 2.5, 58, 410.

Roman custom that the eucharist should be in the mouth at the moment of death.[88]

Although the Autun sacramentary does not have Gellone's rite for the dying, its peculiar treatment of the Roman *ordo* reveals a similar intent. The placement of the *ordo* between the *reconciliatio ad mortem* and the *orationes super defuncto*, the unusual heading given it (*de migratione animae*), and the variations from all other witnesses indicate the same tendency as in Gellone toward the elaboration of a rite for the dying. The process of ritual development, however, is still incomplete in Autun. Its version of the Roman *ordo* is sandwiched between the deathbed reconciliation and the burial service so that the Roman psalmody for the postmortem phase of the ritual is not integrated into the Gelasian prayer service. Thus one is left wondering how the ritual process actually proceeded.[89] Its various pieces are not quite integrated into a coherent whole.

Rheinau: Ritual Integration

Integration was achieved in the sacramentary of Rheinau. We have already seen the elegant solution reached by the compilers of the Rheinau book to the problem created by the confluence of the Roman and Gallican prayers for the sick. Their achievement no less elegantly clarifies and orders the various tendencies apparent in the way its cognates presented the rites around the deathbed. Rheinau follows the Gellone manuscript closely in its disposition of the death ritual and its creators clearly drew on the Roman tradition found in the Autun book, but they went beyond both of them to indicate precisely the nature of the rite for the agony and to absorb the words and acts of the Roman *ordo* into the structure of older Frankish death rites.[90] They skillfully wove the Roman rubrics with their indications for psalms and antiphons into the fabric of the Gelasian prayers (Ritual 5).

88. *Vita S. Melaniae*, c. 68: "Consuetudo est . . . Romanis ut cum animae egrediuntur, communio Domini in ore sit"; cited by Rush, *Death and Burial*, 92n. Rush, along with Browe, "Sterbekommunion," 15–16, and Rush, "Eucharist: The Sacrament of the Dying," 32–33, used this text to argue that the practice was of great antiquity. They did not realize, however, that it is a tenth-century addition to the original Life; see *Vie de Sainte Melanie*, ed. Denys Gorce, Sources chrétiennes 90 (Paris, 1962), 101, 265.

89. Cf. Moreton, review of Sicard, *Liturgie*, JTS 31 (1980): 235.

90. Rheinau, nos. 1330–41. Sicard included the Rheinau sacramentary in his analysis of the Roman *ordo* (*Liturgie*, 20–22) and its burial service in his discussion of Gelasian rites (343–44), but did not explore the implications of its fusion of the Roman *ordo* and the Gelasian prayers.

Ritual 5. Rites for the sick, dying, and dead
in the Rheinau sacramentary

Rite	Item nos.
Prayers for the sick	
Old Gallican prayers of spiritual healing	1325–26
Deathbed reconciliation	
Old Gelasian/Visigothic prayers	1327–29
Ordo ad commendationem animae	
Proficiscere/Libera chant prayers	1330
[Moment of death]	
Orationes super defunctis uel commendatio anime	
Deus apud quem	1331
Gelasian prayer	1332
Laying out of the corpse	
Gelasian prayers	1333–35
Roman rubric and psalmody	1336a
Gelasian prayer	1336b
Procession to church	
Roman rubric and psalmody, Gelasian verse set,	1337a
Psalm 50: *Miserere mei*	
In church	
Gelasian prayers	1337b–38
Roman rubric directing mass and continuous	1339a
psalmody	
Gelasian prayer	1339b
Procession to grave	
Roman rubric and psalmody	1340a
Burial	
Roman rubric, Psalm 50: *Miserere mei*	1340b
Rubric and Gelasian prayer	1340c–d
Roman rubric and psalmody	1341a
Commendatio anime	
Tibi domine commendamus	1341b

<small>SOURCE: *Sacramentarium Rhenaugiense,* ed. Anton Hänggi and Alfons Schönherr (Fribourg, 1970), 271–76.</small>

In creating a mixed rite from the Gelasian prayers and the Roman psalmody, the compilers of the Rheinau sacramentary made three significant changes. First, they included only the rubrics and psalmody from the Roman *ordo* for the postmortem rites, beginning with the laying out of the body.[91] Why? It is possible, of

---

91. Sicard, *Liturgie,* 21, noted that the Rheinau sacramentary did not include the rubrics for the death itself, but drew no conclusions from the fact.

course, that they had access only to a partial copy of the *ordo;* but given the highly developed structure of the rites as a whole, it seems more likely that they intentionally omitted the beginning of the Roman *ordo,* preferring to emphasize the new rite for the agony. Second, the invocational prayers for the agony were separated from what comes after by their own rubric: *Ordo ad commendationem anime* [*sic*], here used in the specific meaning of a rite for the dying. The postmortem ritual was then given the general heading of the rites in Gellone: *Orationes super defunctis uel commendatio anime.* Finally, they altered the tone of the Roman psalmody by the addition of Psalm 50 as part of the funeral procession and the prayers at the grave.[92] This psalm, which was to become one the most common in all subsequent rituals, appears for the first time in the Rheinau sacramentary. It is the most penitential of all the psalms.[93] As we have seen, it was central to the rite of deathbed penance in the Visigothic church. It provided the first line to the prayer of reconciliation included there and in all the Gelasian sacramentaries: "Merciful God, gentle god, who in accordance with the multitude of your mercies wipes out the sins of the repentant."[94] It also appears as an introduction to part of an Irish litany of confession.[95] Its inclusion in the Romanized funeral rite in the Rheinau sacramentary maintained the Frankish emphasis on sin and forgiveness while drawing on the triumphant optimism of the Roman psalmody.

If the compilers of the sacramentary of Rheinau meant to Romanize the Gallican death ritual through the use of the old Roman *ordo,* the sum total of their work was to add its psalmody to the postmortem ceremonies. Yet even there they made these rites more supplicatory, more penitential than the Roman *ordo* had intended. Moreover, they organized the ritual so that the *Proficiscere* and *Libera* chants, introduced in the Gellone book, would replace the reading of the passion and the viaticum of the Roman *ordo* as aid to the dying soul. Since communion as viaticum would have been given at the conclusion of the deathbed reconciliation, the

92. Rheinau, nos. 1337a, 1340b. Cf. Sicard, *Liturgie,* 137–38.
93. Sicard, *Liturgie,* 139, calls it "le psaume de la pénitence par excellence."
94. Gelasian, no. 364: "Deus misericors, deus clemens, qui secundum multitudinem miserationum tuarum peccata paenitencium deles"; cf. Liber ordinum, 92; Gellone, no. 2888; Rheinau, no. 1327, and Ps. 50:3: "Miserere mei Deus secundum magnam misericordiam tuam et secundum multitudinem miserationum tuarum dele iniquitatem meam."
95. Charles Plummer, *Irish Litanies,* HBS 62 (London, 1925), 6; from a manuscript of the ninth to tenth centuries.

ritual accompaniment to death itself became a communal chant. The recital of litanies around the beds of the dying was becoming an essential part of the death ritual for Frankish clerics and monks in the late eighth century,[96] and the new prayers for the dying in these sacramentaries were taken from such litanies. The ultimate source of that practice was the Irish monks who dominated the church of Gaul in the seventh century, for whom litanies were a lively form of private devotion.[97]

In sum, the ritual structures of the Gellone, Autun, and Rheinau sacramentaries all point to a widespread desire to expand the ritual preparation of the dying and the role of the community in the death of one of its members. This innovation led to a substantial reworking of the Roman *ordo* by Frankish liturgists who were aware of it. Two of the eighth-century Gelasians took account of the old Roman death *ordo,* but neither replaced Gallican rites with it. The compilers of the Autun sacramentary included the *ordo* in something like its Roman form, but not without substantial changes to take account of the new rite for the agony. In the one case in which the Roman *ordo* was merged with the Gallican rites—the Rheinau sacramentary—the rubrics for the death agony were omitted in favor of prayers built in the style of litanies for the aid of the departing soul (which first appeared in the Gellone sacramentary), and the psalmody of the processions was augmented by Psalm 50 to reflect the more penitential faith of the northern lands. To the extent that the Roman *ordo* was incorporated in the changing ritual structure, the Roman psalmody tended to alleviate the penitential aspect of the Gallican rites. Nonetheless, to the extent that it was used at all, the Roman *ordo* was incorporated into an evolving ritual structure that either ignored or greatly expanded its simple preparations for death and aid to the dying, and stressed the need for penance and absolution over the confident expectation of salvation.

Of all the eighth-century Gelasian books, the sacramentary of

96. See Gougaud, "Etude sur les *ordines,*" 11, 27; most scholars now date the *Vita Austrebertae,* in which a litany is sung at the deathbed of the saint, not to the early eighth century but to the early ninth. See Eligius Dekkers, *Clavis Patrum Latinorum,* 2d ed. (Steenbrugge, 1961), no. 2089a; and Angenendt, "Theologie und Liturgie," 169.

97. Gougaud, "Etude sur les *loricae* celtiques"; H. Leclercq, "Litanies (Celtiques)," DACL 9.2511–16; Wilhelm Levison, "Die Iren und die fränkische Kirche," *Historische Zeitschrift* 109 (1912): 1–22, repr. in *Mönchtum und Gesellschaft in Frühmittelalter,* ed. Friedrich Prinz (Darmstadt, 1976), 91–111. See also Hughes, "Some Aspects of Irish Influence," 48–61.

Rheinau is the most highly developed. It organized the rites in a coherent sequence from sickness through death, burial, and commemoration. It separated the Roman prayers for the sick from the Gallican, and placed the latter directly before the reconciliation *ad mortem*. It unambiguously presented the new rite for the agony under its own heading. And it successfully combined the Roman *ordo* with the evolving structure of Frankish death and burial rites. It does not signal the end of the process of ritual development, however, for it took no account of ritual anointing as a preparation for death, which had made some impact on Frankish practice by this time. Moreover, the ritual innovations and solutions in Rheinau and the other eighth-century Gelasian sacramentaries were to be thrown into disarray within a few years by the introduction of new rites and by a new ritual carrier, the Gregorian sacramentary of Pope Hadrian, which would set in motion another series of adjustments and experiments.

Death and Ritual at the End of the Eighth Century

The fundamental innovations of the late eighth-century Frankish church were the reorganization of rites for the sick, the dying, and the dead in the ritual books, the realization of a rite for the agony (the *ordo ad commendationem animae*), and the institutionalization of commemorative rites in the confraternities of prayer. Common to all these elements is an emphasis on ritual continuity and communal participation. The community stepped forth to aid the dying at the deathbed. It invoked the presence of that other community to which the soul would pass, compelling the souls already departed to attend to the fate of the dying person; accompanying the soul on its journey to the other world; keeping up a constant stream of supplication and sacrifice until the soul safely reached its heavenly home. After being carefully washed, clothed, and buried, the body was incorporated into the community of bodies awaiting resurrection in the unmarked graves of Carolingian churches and churchyards.[98] The soul's incorporation into the other world was no less carefully attended to, so much so that institutions were created to see to its successful passage—institutions, incidentally, that would long outlive the political

98. On Carolingian cemeteries, see Bullough, "Burial, Community, and Belief," 175–201, and Young, "Exemple aristocratique et mode funéraire," 401.

structures of the Carolingian empire. The performance of these rituals bound together the people who took part in them just as it bound together the communities of the living and the dead in a seamless whole.

At the center of all these developments stood the clergy. There is no evidence from the eighth century that these rituals reached beyond the walls of cathedral or monastery and into the lives of the laity. But the goals of the Carolingian reform were always expressed in language that included not only clerics but all Christian men and women, and the ninth century would see a concerted effort to involve the laity in the new *artes moriendi*. The ninth century would also see confusion, however, as new rituals for the sick and the dead were promulgated in the second phase of the reform, under the direction of Benedict of Aniane. Benedict's contributions to the history of the death ritual would seriously complicate things and put off the final synthesis until a later time, when the products of the high reform period could be woven into the process of ritual development already well under way at the end of the eighth century.

CHAPTER FOUR

New Rites for Old: Benedict of Aniane and Ritual Reform, 800–850

Ritual and Reform in the Early Ninth Century

When Charlemagne took up the work left uncompleted by his father, he set his goals higher. The conciliar decrees and capitularies that survive from his reign, especially those issued between the *Admonitio generalis* of 789 and the reform councils of 813—held simultaneously in five major cities in the year before the emperor's death—amount to a complete program for the education of the clergy and laity in the basic precepts of Christian living.[1] The decisions of the councils and the court were transmitted locally by the bishops, who issued instructions to their subordinates in the form of capitularies, and, ideally, by the parish clergy, the final link between the reformers and the general populace.[2] These sources reveal that one of the major thrusts of the reform program in the early ninth century was the encouragement of the anointing of the sick.

Anointing the Sick

Numerous decrees on anointing the sick appear in legislative sources after the year 800. In the first of three capitularies issued to

1. Vogel, *Réforme cultuelle*, 214–22; idem, "Réforme liturgique"; McKitterick, *Frankish Church*, 2–44.
2. McKitterick, *Frankish Church*, 45–114.

his diocesan priests (801–802), Bishop Gerbald of Liège alluded to the text of St. James while prescribing unction and prayers for the sick. "In accordance with the decrees of the holy fathers, if anyone is sick, she is to be anointed carefully by the priests with sanctified oil to the accompaniment of prayers."[3] In his third capitulary (802–809) Gerbald was more precise, quoting James 5:15 in support of his decree: "When priests visit someone who is sick, they should take consecrated oil and anoint him in the name of the lord and pray for him and, as it is written, 'the prayer of faith will save the sick man and the lord will raise him up; and if he has sinned, his sins will be forgiven.'"[4] An anonymous *Capitula ecclesiastica*, dated to the same period, also quotes from James (5:14), decreeing that each priest should obtain the oil of the sick from his bishop on Holy Thursday so that "when someone is ill, he might bring in the priests of the church, and they might pray over him, anointing him with oil in the name of the Lord."[5]

Even more than the similar pronouncements of the mid–eighth century, these decrees display an unequivocal regard for the apostolic tradition of St. James (mediated by Caesarius of Arles) as the foundation for ritual practice. The most complete and direct statement of the doctrine was set forth at the council of Chalon-sur-Saône in 813. "In accordance with the example of blessed James the apostle, with which also the decrees of the fathers concur, priests ought to anoint the sick with oil that has been blessed by bishops . . . (James 5:14–15). . . . And so this form of medicine, which heals the sufferings of body and soul, ought not to be taken lightly."[6] A corresponding decree from the council of Tours held in the same year echoes the sermons of Caesarius. It admonished the faithful not to avail themselves of the traditional magical forms of

3. MGH, Capitula episcoporum, 21, c. 21: "Ut secundum diffinitionem sanctorum patrum, si quis infirmatur, a sacerdotibus oleo sanctificato cum orationibus diligenter unguatur."

4. Ibid., 42, c. 19: "Ut presbyteri, quando ad infirmum accedunt, cum oleo consecrato veniant et oleo sancto unguent eum in nomine domini et orent pro ipso et *oratio fidei*, sicut scriptum est, *salvet infirmum et allevet eum dominus et, si in peccatis fuerit, dimittentur ei*."

5. MGH, Capitularia 1.179, c. 17: "Ut presbyter in coena Domini duas ampullas secum deferat, unam ad chrismam, alteram ad oleum ad cathecuminos inunguendum vel infirmos iuxta sententiam apostolicam; ut, quando quis infirmatur, inducat presbyteros ecclesiae, et orent super eum, unguentes eum oleo in nomine Domini."

6. MGH, Concilia 2.283, c. 48: "Secundum beati Iacobi apostoli documentum, cui etiam decreta patrum consonant, infirmi oleo, quod ab episcopis benedicitur, a presbyteris ungui debent. . . . Non est itaque parvipendenda huiuscemodi medicina, quae animae corporisque medetur languoribus."

healing, such as incantations and bundles of herbs or bones, for such things were "unable to provide a remedy" and were in fact "snares and traps of the ancient enemy."[7]

What was the intention behind these decrees? Clearly, they were part of a more general call for pastoral work among the clergy. Just as clearly, they rested on a tradition in Gaul going back to Caesarius of Arles. Indeed, they seem to restore that tradition in its pure form. In doing so they imply that ritual anointing of the sick was to be a means of physical healing and spiritual cleansing for the living. Although nothing would have prevented the dying from receiving ritual anointing, its institution within the context of the Carolingian reform seems to have been meant primarily as a ritual aid to recovery, not as a preparation for death and the transition to the other world.

Rites in Preparation for Death

On the whole, the reform councils and capitularies of the early ninth century had little to say about rites specifically meant for the dying. They urge the clergy to see that no one should die without baptism and communion, and sometimes mention reconciliation as well.[8] Bishop Gerbald, for example, warned his priests to be ready day and night to minister to the needs of the dying, either with baptism or with penance and communion.[9] There are, however, some interesting hints regarding the *commendatio animae.* An anonymous program of study for priests dating from 802 to 813 includes knowledge of the commendation of the soul among the

7. Ibid., 292, c. 42: "Admoneant sacerdotes fideles populos, ut noverint magicas artes incantationesque quibuslibet infirmitatibus hominum nihil posse remedii conferre, . . . non ligaturas ossuum vel herbarum cuiquam mortalium adhibitas prodesse, sed haec esse laqueos et insidias antiqui hostis, quibus ille perfidus genus humanum decipere nititur."

8. E.g., the Capitula ecclesiastica (810–813?), MGH Capitularia 1.179, c. 16: "Ut presbyter semper eucharistiam habeat paratam, ut, quando quis infirmaverit aut parvulus infirmus fuerit, statim eum communicet, ne sine communione moriatur"; and the diocesan statute (<813) edited by de Clercq from Vesoul, MS 73 (*La législation religieuse franque,* 1 [Louvain/Paris, 1936], 374), c. 34: "Morientibus iam sine cunctamine communio et reconciliacio praebeatur." The language of the first canon illustrates the necessity of looking for contextual clues to determine when the sources mean to discuss the merely sick or the dying, since the word *infirmus* could clearly refer to both.

9. MGH, Capitula episcoporum, 39, c. 8: "Ut unusquisque presbyter omni hora sive die sive nocte ad officium suum explendum paratus sit, ut, si fortuitu aliquis infirmus ad baptizandum venerit, pleniter possit implere officium suum. . ."; cf. ibid., 21, c. 20; 40, c. 11; 41, c. 15; 42, c. 20; 68, c. 21.

basic requirements of clerical preparation—the creed, the Lord's Prayer, the sacramentary with the canon of the mass and the votive masses for the commutation of penances, and the manner of writing charters and letters.[10] The appearance of the term without any explanation implies that its meaning was obvious. In the last years of Charlemagne's reign Bishop Waltcaud of Liège composed a capitulary to his diocesan clergy which expands on the laconic style of the previous text. Though Waltcaud also did not define the commendation, it is significant that he included it among clerical activities of a distinctly pastoral nature: "Priests should know how to admonish the people with exhortatory words, how to preach homilies appropriate to Sundays and the feasts of the saints, the penitential, computus, chant and commendation of the soul, and the reconciliation."[11] Do these texts refer to the final commendation of the soul at the end of the burial service, which is a common feature of all the Gelasian sacramentaries, or to the developing ritual moment around the agony, which, as we have seen, was taking shape in some contemporary ritual books?[12] Or was the *commendatio* meant more generally to refer to the whole of the death ritual? We have no way of knowing. Nevertheless, these capitularies attest to the use of the term to denote rites around death and burial in the early ninth century, as well as the importance of those rites within the reform program of clerical training and pastoral work.

Death and Burial: The Supplement to the Gregorian Sacramentary

As is well known, one of the central acts in Charlemagne's reform program was his request for a sacramentary from the apostolic see in Rome. Pope Hadrian I responded between 784 and 791 by sending a copy of a Gregorian sacramentary now referred to as

10. MGH, Capitularia 1.235: "Haec sunt quae iussa sunt discere omnes ecclesiasticos. Fidem catholicam sancti Athenasii et cetera quaecumque de fide; Symbolum etiam apostolicum; Orationem dominicam. . . . Librum sacramentorum pleniter tam canonem missasque speciales ad commutandum pleniter; Exorcismum super caticuminum sive super demoniacos; commendationem animae; . . . Scribere cartas et epistulas."

11. MGH, Capitula episcoporum, 47, c. 11: "Verba exortatoria ad plebem, quomodo unusquisque admonet vel intellegit, omelias de dominicis diebus et sollemnitatibus sanctorum ad praedicandum, paenitentiale, compoto, cantu vel commendatione animae et reconciliatione."

12. De Clercq, *Législation*, 1.226, assumes that it refers to the rite for the agony, but gives no reason for his opinion.

the *Hadrianum*.[13] But if Charlemagne had hoped to get a book that he might use as a model for the ritual life of the Frankish kingdom, and that would replace the Gelasian books, he must have been disappointed, for the *Hadrianum* was quite specifically arranged for the use of the pope himself as he made the rounds of the various stational churches in Rome, and thus was totally inadequate to the needs of the Frankish clergy.[14] Jean Deshusses once suggested that the initial response to the inadequacy of the *Hadrianum* was to encourage copying of the eighth-century Gelasian books, and he may be right,[15] but the prestige of the papal book, linked as it was with the name of Pope Gregory the Great, was not to be denied. Given the difficulties involved in copying and transmitting both types of book together, the only plausible solution was to combine them. This task called for supplementary additions that could be copied along with the Gregorian text in one manuscript; most such supplements derived from the eighth-century Gelasian tradition. Almost every extant ninth-century manuscript of the *Hadrianum* has been supplemented in this manner.[16] One of these supplements, however, was to prove of greater importance and influence than any of the others. Known by the first word of its preface, *Hucusque*, this supplement had long been believed to be the work of Alcuin of York.[17] That assumption has been dealt a decisive blow, however, by the researches of Deshusses, who has proved that the real author was the monk Benedict of Aniane.[18]

Benedict of Aniane was born around 750 to the family of the count of Maguelonne in the Narbonnais and given the Visigothic name Vitiza. He spent his youth at the court of Pippin the Short and became a monk at St-Seine, near Dijon, around the year 774. After returning to the southern lands of his ancestry around 779–780, he established a monastery at Aniane, near Narbonne. At first

13. Vogel, *Medieval Liturgy*, 80–85; the new edition of Jean Deshusses (Hadrianum), based on a manuscript copy made for Bishop Hildoard of Cambrai in 811–812 (Cambrai, Bibliothèque Municipale, MS 164), supersedes all previous editions.

14. McKitterick, *Frankish Church*, 130–32.

15. His hypothesis would explain the clustering of most of the extant manuscripts around the year 800; Deshusses, "Sacramentaire de Gellone," 200–204.

16. Deshusses, "Sacramentaires," 40–41.

17. Vogel, *Medieval Liturgy*, 85–86; Gerald Ellard, *Master Alcuin: Liturgist* (Chicago, 1956).

18. Deshusses, "Le 'Supplément' au sacramentaire grégorien: Alcuin ou Saint Benoît d'Aniane?" ALW 9 (1965): 48–71. Initial hesitation over this ascription has been replaced by general scholarly agreement; see, e.g., ALW 26 (1984): 52–53; and the remarks of Vogel's translators in *Medieval Liturgy*, 86.

a disciple of Eastern monastic traditions, he gradually became convinced of the worthiness of St. Benedict's rule. From around 787, he began to work for monastic reform on the model of the Benedictine rule. He became a close counselor to Louis, Charlemagne's son and at that time king of Aquitaine. Louis made Benedict head of all the monasteries of his kingdom. In the late eighth century, Benedict worked on a collection of prefaces to be used with the eighth-century Gelasian sacramentaries, and between 810 and 815 he created his Supplement to the *Hadrianum*, using an eighth-century Gelasian together with older Gregorian and Visigothic texts. After 814, when Louis became emperor, he built Benedict the monastery of Inden, near the royal chapel in Aachen, and extended Benedict's authority to cover all the monasteries of the empire. Benedict worked for monastic reform continually thereafter and, with Louis, established definitive guidelines for monks, nuns, and canons at two great councils at Aachen in 816 and 817. He died in 821.[19]

The identification of Benedict of Aniane as author of the Supplement to the *Hadrianum* has two important ramifications for this study. First, it suggests that Charlemagne himself was not totally committed to centralization and unification around the ideal of the Roman liturgy, remaining content with the papal book as a symbol and the Gelasian books as the reality. Consequently, it would seem that it was a specific party, centered on Benedict, that pushed unity and standardization around the Gregorian text, and that that party did not gain the upper hand until Louis the Pious had come north from Aquitaine to take over the imperial throne in 814.[20] Second, and most important, the identification of Benedict as the author of the Supplement provides a basis of interpretation for the rituals and prayers it contains, especially those after death, which are quite idiosyncratic and represent a departure from previous traditions. His idiosyncratic work in the supplement, in turn, makes it possible to identify Benedict as the author of a ritual for anointing the sick in accordance with the goals of the Carolingian reform. We will look in detail at Benedict's contributions to ritual life shortly. For the moment, let us turn to rites of

19. Philibert Schmitz, "Benoît d'Aniane," DHGE 8.177–88; Josef Narberhaus, *Benedikt von Aniane: Werk und Persönlichkeit*, Beiträge zur Geschichte des alten Mönchtums und des Benediktinerordens 16 (Münster, 1930); Deshusses, "Supplément," 60–65. Deshusses has redated Benedict's work on the Supplement from 800–810 (58) to 810–15 (Gregorian, 1.68).

20. McKitterick, *Frankish Church*, 132–33.

commemoration, which developed rapidly in the Frankish realms during Benedict's lifetime and increasingly gave shape to Frankish Christian society in both this world and the next.

Commemoration and Prayer for the Dead

Whereas the introduction of the Gregorian sacramentary as the official carrier of ritual instruction and prayer added to the diversity of responses to sickness, dying, and death in the first half of the ninth century—precisely because the *Hadrianum* needed to be supplemented if it was to be useful—the commemorative practices of the Frankish church and its religious communities continued to develop on the foundations laid in the previous generation. Familiarity with the votive and commemorative masses for the living and the dead in the sacramentaries became an expected requirement of clerical training.[21] In addition to the proliferation of such *missae speciales*, new rituals arose which sprang from and took advantage of the more highly organized nature of cloistered living in the reformed Frankish church. The increasing importance of prayer directed toward the good of souls after death can be seen in the gradual development of a special office for the dead as part of the daily round of monastic prayer.[22] The continued growth and expansion of the confraternity movement called forth whole new genres of written record—confraternity books, annals of the dead, and *libri memoriales*—all of which had ritual character.[23] Together these phenomena continued to dissolve the borders between this world and the next and to redefine Frankish Christian society.

The office for the dead developed out of the commemorative practices of monastic communities. Before the end of the eighth century, the monks of Monte Cassino had begun to commemorate their dead brothers daily, the priests offering a mass and the monks singing Psalm 50 at each of the offices.[24] The ritual order of Angilbert, abbot of St-Riquier in Picardy and intimate friend and

21. MGH, Capitularia 1.110, c. 3; MGH, Capitula episcoporum, 47–48, c. 13.
22. Roger E. Reynolds, "Dead, office of the," DMA 4.117–18; Camille Callawaert, "De officio defunctorum," in *Sacris Erudiri: Fragmenta liturgica collecta a monachis Sancti Petri de Aldenburgo in Steenbrugis* (Steenbrugge, 1940; repr. 1962), 169–77; Bishop, *Liturgica Historica*, 212–20.
23. N. Huyghabaert, *Les documents nécrologiques*, Typologie des sources du moyen âge occidental (Turnhout, 1972); Oexle, "Gegenwart der Toten," 31–48.
24. *Theodomari abbatis Casinensis epistula ad Theodoricum gloriosum*, ed. D. J. Winandy and K. Hallinger, in *Initia consuetudinis Benedictinae*, CCM 1.136: "ab eisdem sacerdotibus pro omnibus quiescentibus fratribus quotidie fit commemoratio, quodque pro eis per singula officia psalmus quinquagesimus ab omni congregatione cantatur."

counselor to Charlemagne, written around the year 800, tells us that his community included special commemorations of the dead during the night offices.[25] When the monks of Fulda wrote to Charlemagne in 812, begging him to support their adherence to their house customs, they put commemorative rituals at the top of their list. It was the practice at Fulda, they said, to commemorate the dead members of the house twice daily, after matins and vespers, with a short office comprising the antiphon *Requiem aeternam*, part of Psalm 64, a verse, and a prayer.[26]

The most elaborate office for the dead from the early ninth century is described in a letter sent to Abbot Haito of Reichenau between 817 and 821 by two of his monks, who reported on the practices of an unidentified monastery: "They celebrate vespers with antiphons for the dead after the usual vespers are finished. And after compline they sing most fully and sweetly a vigil with antiphons and responses. And after nocturns, in the intervening period, they sing matins for the dead."[27] It is possible that the monastery referred to in their report was Benedict of Aniane's own house of Inden.[28] Whatever the case may be, Benedict did not attempt to establish similar practices in all the cloistered communities of the empire, at least not at the great reform councils at Aachen over which he presided in 816 and 817. The Aachen decrees restrict themselves to the implication that the office for the dead should be regularly sung, and to the demand that, in general, the seven penitential psalms be sung for the dead.[29] Nonetheless, the place of the office for the dead in monastic services was as-

25. Bishop, *Liturgica Historica*, 314–32; *Institutio sancti Angilberti abbatis de diuersitate officiorum*, ed. K. Hallinger, M. Wegener, and H. Frank, in *Initia consuetudinis Benedictinae*, CCM 1.302; "ob memoriam cunctorum fidelium defunctorum per singulos dies ac noctes Uespertinos, Nocturnos, atque Matutinos deuotissime eo ordine, ut in sequentibus declaratur, celebrare studerent."

26. *Supplex libellus monachorum Fuldensium Carolo imperatori porrectus*, ed. J. Semmler, in ibid., 321: "quotidie bis habuimus, id est post matutinam celebrationem et vespertinam, quae est antiphona videlicet *Requiem aeternam* et prima pars psalmi *Te decet hymnus deus*, versus et collecta."

27. *Capitula in Auuam directa*, ed. H. Frank, in ibid., 336, c. xi: "Vespera solito finita Uesperam cum antiphonis celebrant pro defunctis. Et post Completorium Uigiliam cum antiphonis uel responsoriis plenissime atque suauissime canunt. Et post Nocturnas interuallo Matutinos pro mortuis faciunt."

28. Bishop, *Liturgica Historica*, 217, thought so, but the most recent editor makes no such claim; cf. *Initia consuetudinis Benedictinae*, CCM 1.332.

29. *Synodi primae Aquisgranensis decreta authentica*, ed. J. Semmler, in *Initia consuetudinis Benedictinae*, CCM 1.460, c. xi: "Ut si necessitas poposcerit . . . quando officio mortuorum celebratur . . . bibant"; *Synodi secundae Aquisgranensis decreta authentica*, ed. J. Semmler, in ibid., 475, c. xii: "psalmi speciales pro elemosinariis et defunctis cantentur." On the Aachen decrees, see also McKitterick, *Frankish Kingdoms*, 112–24.

sured. Amalarius of Metz, writing in the 830s, described the variety of forms in which it was practiced. He puzzled over a sacramentary in which he had read that the office for the dead was to be sung on the third, seventh, and thirtieth days after a death, concluding that it must mean that on those days a more elaborate office should be sung, since it would be spiritually lazy not to make supplications for the dead daily during the first thirty days.[30] One collection of the decrees of the reform councils, written around 850, added three new chapters in order to give authority to the practice, first introduced by Benedict of Aniane at Inden, of beginning each day with the recitation of three groups of five psalms, one each for the living, the dead, and the recently deceased.[31] By the middle of the tenth century, the daily singing of the office of the dead was a universal feature of Benedictine monasticism.[32]

The growth in offices for the dead in the monasteries is closely related to the development of the confraternity system, which continued to expand during the first half of the ninth century. Taking their cue from the agreements reached at Attigny and Dingolfingen, monastic communities began to draw up contracts of commemoration such as the convention between Reichenau and St. Gall, signed in 800.[33] Under its terms, the monks and priests of the two communities agreed not only to commemorate their common dead as usual on the third, seventh, and thirtieth days following, but also to perform vigils for all at the beginning of each month, with special attention to the recently deceased. They also agreed to set aside one day in the year, November 14, for a general commemoration.[34] A Bavarian council meeting in 805 added a new element to local traditions by prescribing not only masses and psalmody for the dead but also the giving of alms.[35] Thus was

---

30. Amalarius of Metz, *De officiis*, bk. 4, chap. 42.1, in *Amalarii episcopi opera liturgica omnia*, ed. J. M. Hanssens, Studi e Testi 139 (Vatican City, 1948), 2.535.

31. *Legislationis monasticae Aquisgranensis collectio Sancti Martialis Lemovicensis*, ed. J. Semmler, in *Initia consuetudinis Benedictinae*, CCM 1.561, cc. LXXVI–LXXVIII; cf. Bishop, *Liturgica Historica*, 214.

32. Bishop, *Liturgica Historica*, 219.

33. *Libri confraternitatum Sancti Galli, Augiensis, Fabariensis*, ed. Paul Piper, MGH (Berlin, 1884), 140, "Confraternitatum syngraphae" 10.

34. Ibid.: "Ceterum vigilias pro defunctis in capite singulorum mensium ex more iugiter celebremus, in quibus vigilias omnium simul defunctorum fratrum, qui in nostro consortio coadunati sunt, commemoratio fiat, eoque die commemoretur et nomen nuper defuncti. . . . Preter haec quoque semel in anno sub die XVIII Kal. Decemb. commemoratio omnium simul fiat pro annuali singulorum videlicet defunctorum memoria."

35. MGH, Concilia 2.233: "Episcopi autem et abbates pro alio defuncto det unusquisque solidos XX aestimatione argenti in elimosinam eius, presbiteri autem pro

initiated a revival of the antique Christian connection between commemoration of the dead and care of the poor. As before, feeding the poor in the earthly community symbolized, and was felt to aid, the incorporation of souls into the heavenly community. Charitable giving in commemoration of the dead would continue to grow along with the confraternity movement, reaching its culmination at Cluny in the late eleventh and early twelfth centuries, when the poor who benefited from it numbered in the tens of thousands annually.[36]

The activities of Benedict of Aniane did not include the official promotion of relationships of confraternity, but the unification of Frankish monasticism around the Benedictine rule at Aachen in 816 indirectly led to the production of the oldest of the medieval memorial books, the *Liber memorialis* of Remiremont. It was after accepting the rule of St. Benedict in 817 that the nuns of the convent of Remiremont, on the Moselle River, began to record the names of their predecessors, their relations and benefactors, and those of other communities linked with them in memorial lists that were continually expanded by more than fifty scribes over a period of almost four hundred years.[37] The Remiremont book recorded the names of the people, both living and dead, for whom a special daily mass of commemoration was to be offered.[38] Its presence on the altar was a symbol of the dissolution of the borders between the living and the dead. Those whose names appeared therein enjoyed a special relationship with one another; they were joined, in life and death, in the common enterprise of supplication, which was the only means of ensuring their eventual incorporation into the blessed community of the saints around the throne of almighty God. The communal prayers of living men and women expressed ties reaching beyond death to the other world; the forging of new communities among the living symbolically represented the continuity between the communities of the living and the dead.

---

episcopis suis det unusquisque solidum unum, pro presbitero autem conparrochiale tremissem unum."

36. Joachim Wollasch, "Gemeinschaftbewusstsein und soziale Leistungen im Mittelalter," FS 9 (1975): 268–86, esp. 280–82.

37. *Liber Memorialis von Remiremont*, ed. Eduard Hlawitschka, Karl Schmid, and Gerd Tellenbach, MGH, Libri Memoriales 1 (Dublin/Zürich, 1970), xvi–xxii; Giles Constable, "The *Liber Memorialis* of Remiremont," *Speculum* 47 (1972): 261–77.

38. *Liber Memorialis*, 1: "Decreuimus pro omnibus his utriusque sexus missam cotidie caelebrari . . . tam pro uiuis quam et pro defunctis."

Benedict of Aniane made little contribution to this wider cultural movement. We have seen his reticence on the subject of the office of the dead at the reform councils. His treatment of commemorative masses in the Supplement to the *Hadrianum* reveals a similar lack of interest in the needs of the dead. Where the Vatican Gelasian had seventeen masses and the eighth-century Gelasians from eleven to sixteen, Benedict included only nine.[39] Similarly, when he set his hand to the composition of a service for death and burial to include in his Supplement, he took no notice of the Gelasian tradition of communal prayer to aid the dying, introducing new prayers and new themes into the rites for the dead and for burial. Because he was out of step with certain major cultural preoccupations of his age, Benedict's ritual contributions sometimes worked against prevailing trends. Nonetheless, Benedict spoke to other equally important concerns of his age, and his position in the Frankish church guaranteed that whatever he created would play a major role in later developments.

Death and Burial in Benedict of Aniane's Supplement

In the overall structure of the rites in the Supplement to the *Hadrianum*, Benedict followed the lead of the eighth-century Gelasians. Prayers for the sick, deathbed reconciliation, rubrics and prayers for death and burial, and the series of commemorative masses follow one another in logical sequence. The prayers for the sick were carried over from the Gelasian tradition with the addition of two from the *Hadrianum* itself. The prayers and ritual indications for deathbed reconciliation and for death and burial are more varied and bear the marks of his particular attention. Benedict included only two of the four prayers for the *reconciliatio ad mortem* that had been part of the Gelasian tradition.[40] The reason is obscure. Benedict may have sought to oppose the loose penitential practices of the day and support the reinstatement of the ancient discipline of public penance. Some of the decrees of the later councils of Charlemagne's reign, especially canon 25 of the council of Chalon-sur-Saône (813), urged a return to the ancient system of penitential discipline for certain public crimes.[41] That would ex-

39. Supplement, secs. CIIII–CXII.
40. Supplement, nos. 1396–97 = Gellone, nos. 2888–89 = Gelasian, nos. 364–65.
41. MGH, Concilia 2.278: "Si qui publice peccat, publica multetur paenitentia et secundum ordinem canonum pro merito suo et excommunicetur et reconcilietur."

plain his choice of two of the three prayers derived from reconciliation rites for public penitents and his avoidance of the last prayer, which derived from the Visigothic rite of deathbed penance. The prayers that he chose would suffice to reconcile public penitents still undergoing penitential discipline at the time of their death. In all, it appears that Benedict did not expect deathbed penance to be a normal part of a ritual preparation for death.[42]

The idiosyncratic nature of the prayer service over a dead body and for funerals in the Supplement to the *Hadrianum* was underscored long ago by Edmund Bishop, who noted that, in contrast to the great majority of the Supplement's material, taken almost completely from the eighth-century Gelasian tradition, the prayers for death and burial derived from the Visigothic (Mozarabic) liturgy: "Out of the eight prayers for one just deceased four are taken from Mozarabic sources. . . . Of the nine prayers of the remainder of his burial service six are found in Mozarabic books. . . . In a word, Alcuin made a clean sweep of nearly the whole of the twenty or twenty-one prayers found in these services in Gaul throughout the eighth century, and substituted for them new Mozarabic material."[43] We can now substitute the name of Benedict of Aniane for that of Alcuin here, thus solving the puzzle of why the Anglo-Saxon monk would be so drawn to old Spanish prayers, especially given his energetic opposition to the Spanish liturgy set off by the adoptionist controversy.[44] But questions remain over the extent to which Benedict participated in, altered, or redirected the structure and meanings of the rites. What did his turn to the Visigothic ritual tradition entail for the development of rituals of death and burial?

Benedict's rite for death and burial merits sustained consideration, for it represents a conscious break from the ritual action and prayers of such eighth-century Gelasians as the sacramentaries of Gellone, Rheinau, Autun, and St. Gall. Given that Benedict's main sources were the Gregorian sacramentary of Hadrian, which contained no developed death ritual, and, presumably, an eighth-century Gelasian, his rejection of most of the Gelasian prayers and

---

42. Rites of deathbed penance may have been dying out in Spain in the first half of the ninth century because of an upsurge in Novatianist tendencies among Spanish clergy. A treatise in response to these tendencies—*De caput poenitentiae agendae*, written in Gerona about 850—argued for a return to the tradition of deathbed penance. See Lozano Sebastián, "Legislación canónica sobre la penitencia," and G. Martínez Díez, "Un tratado visigótico sobre la penitencia," *Hispania Sacra* 19 (1966): 88–98.

43. Bishop, *Liturgica Historica*, 168.

44. Wilhelm Heil, "Der Adoptionismus, Alkuin und Spanien," in *Karl der Grosse*, 2.95–155.

his omission of any reference to ritual aid to the dying betrays a surprising lack of interest in current developments.[45] Instead of referring to the ritual process as the *commendatio animae*, Benedict chose the more prosaic heading *Orationes in agenda mortuorum* and provided only the barest of rubrics, dividing the ritual into four moments: when the soul has left the body, after the washing of the corpse, at the grave before burial, and after burial (Ritual 6). He apparently took the heading from the *Hadrianum*, where it appears before a series of three prayers after the papal mass for a dead bishop.[46] He included these three prayers in his own ritual, but no other Roman material.[47] Although Benedict ended his ritual with a prayer of commendation, the term never appears in his descriptive rubrics. He seems to have made little use of any contemporary versions of the Gelasian death ritual, such as appear in the Gellone, Autun, and Rheinau sacramentaries, but apparently turned instead to an older structure around which he could weave his own additions and changes.[48]

The first prayer spoken after death in Benedict's ritual is the *Pio recordationis affectu*, the bidding that had originated in his native southern lands and had been the response to death in every Frankish ritual book up to the Rheinau sacramentary. But Benedict changed the text of the prayer. By introducing terms with legal connotations (*reatus, delinquere*), Benedict brought a new element of personal guilt and responsibility into the penitential quality of the prayers for the dead.[49] This suggestion of guilt contrasts sharp-

45. Deshusses once suggested that Benedict had used a sacramentary of the Gellone type ("Sacramentaire de Gellone," 208), but in his edition of the Gregorian he says that it was one of the Autun type (Gregorian, 1.68). If Benedict's source had a death ritual like that in either of these books, however, he clearly ignored it.

46. Hadrianum, heading to sec. 225: *Item alia oratione ad agendam mortuorum.* This designation is also common to witnesses to the old Roman *ordo* from the late ninth century on. Given the limited use of the *ordo* up to and including the time of Benedict, however, it is most likely that the later witnesses of the *ordo* got the designation from the *Hadrianum* through Benedict rather than vice versa.

47. Supplement, nos. 1403–5 (= Hadrianum, nos. 1015–17). Benedict seems to have had no Roman sources to draw on other than these three prayers. The old Roman *ordo*, available to liturgists in the north for use in the sacramentaries of Rheinau and Autun, may have been unknown in the south at the beginning of the ninth century.

48. It is possible that Benedict used an old ritual in use in the south at the time which had its roots in the cultural interchange between Visigothic Spain, northern Italy, and southeastern Gaul. The correspondence between the list of nine prayers appended to the death ritual in a mid-ninth-century North Italian manuscript and the prayers of Benedict's ritual not found in Roman or Gelasian books implies the existence of such a rite; see below, n. 113.

49. The variants in the apparatus to Sicard's edition of the prayer (*Liturgie*, 263)

Ritual 6. Rites for the sick, dying, and dead in Benedict of Aniane's Supplement

Rubrics and Prayers	Item no.	Source
Prayers for visitation of the sick		
Deus qui famulo tuo	1386	Gregorian
Respice domine	1387	Gregorian
Deus qui facturae tuae	1388	Gelasian
Deus qui humano generi	1389	Gelasian
Virtutum caelestium deus	1390	Gelasian
Domine . . . qui fragilitatem	1391	Gelasian
Mass for the sick		
Omnipotens . . . deus salus	1392	Gelasian
Deus cuius nutibus	1393	Gelasian
Deus infirmitatis	1394	Gelasian
Prayer for return of health		
Domine . . . qui benedictionis	1395	Gelasian
Reconciliation of a penitent at death		
Deus misericors deus clemens	1396	Gelasian
Maiestatem tuam domine	1397	Gelasian
Prayers *in agenda mortuorum*		
When the soul has left the body		
Pio recordationis affectu	1398	Gelasian
Deus cui omnia uiuunt	1399	Gelasian
Suscipe domine animam	1400	Visigothic
Non intres in iudicio	1401	Visigothic
Fac quaesumus domine	1402	Visigothic
Inclina domine aurem tuam	1403	Gregorian
Absolue domine animam	1404	Gregorian
Annue nobis domine	1405	Gregorian
Verse set	1406	Gelasian/new
In memoria aeterna erit iustis		Ps. 111:17
Ne tradas bestiis animas confitentium tibi		Ps. 73:19
Preciosa in conspectu domini mors sanctorum eius		Ps. 115:15
Non intres in iudicio cum seruo tuo		Ps. 142:2
Requiem aeternam dona ei domine		Visigothic
After washing of the body		
Deus uitae dator	1407	Visigothic
Deus qui humanarum	1408	Visigothic
At the grave before burial		
Obsecramus misericordiam	1409	Visigothic
Deus apud quem	1410	Visigothic
After burial		
Oremus fratres carissimi	1411	Gelasian
Deus qui iustis supplicationibus	1412	Gelasian
Debitum humani corporis	1413	Gelasian
Temeritas quidem est	1414	Visigothic
Tibi domine commendamus	1415	Gelasian
Commemorative masses	1416–50	Gelasian

SOURCE: *Le sacramentaire grégorien,* ed. Jean Deshusses, vol. 1 (Fribourg, 1971), 453–72.

ly with the traditional language, in which sin is represented as the result of earthly fragility and the snares of the devil.[50] The new tone in Benedict's opening prayer suggests a more juridical approach to sinfulness as well as a heightened sense of personal responsibility. Sin is the result not of corporeal fragility in the face of the devil's wiles but of conscious choice and responsible action. Thus one has a greater need to rely on the absolute mercy of God, all the more awesome given the obstinate and freely chosen sinfulness of his children.

There is another change in this prayer. The final formula in the earlier sources reads "through our lord Jesus Christ your son," so that the prayer addressed God the father through Christ the son. Although such formulas were ubiquitous in the Latin liturgies, they might give pause to someone writing around the turn of the ninth century in the southern Frankish lands who wished to avoid any hint of the Spanish heresy of adoptionism. A christology that distinguished between the divine and human nature of Jesus, so that, insofar as he was human, he was an adopted rather than a natural son of God, adoptionism had developed in the eighth century among the Christians of Muslim Spain and been condemned by two popes and several councils in Rome and the Frankish realm in the 780s and 790s.[51] Benedict, who wrote against adoptionism and twice accompanied royal Frankish missions to Spain to investigate the matter, reveals his sensitivity to the issue in the new ending that he gave to this prayer: "That he deign to answer who lives and reigns with the Father and the Holy Spirit God for ever and ever."[52] The new formula avoids any direct reference to Christ as the son of the father, while presenting Christ as high god together with the other persons of the trinity. As we shall see, this characteristic of Benedict's liturgical style is important not only for its orthodox trinitarian theology but also as a personal signature of his reworking of traditional prayers and rites.

---

establish Benedict's change in the text from the earlier wording: "quicquid hoc saeculo proprius error adtulit" to "quicquid in hoc saeculo proprio (vel alieno) reatu delequit."

50. See above, chap. 2, n. 60.

51. Various explanations of the origins of adoptionism have been advanced, among them the idea that the old Spanish liturgy itself suggested the separation of Jesus' divine and human natures; see D. W. Johnson, "Adoptionism," DMA 1.57–58; Heil, "Adoptionismus," 102–8.

52. Narberhaus, *Benedikt von Aniane*, 5, 34; Supplement, no. 1398: "Quod ipse praestare dignetur qui cum patre et spiritu sancto uiuit et regnat deus per omnia saecula saeculorum." Cf. Sicard, *Liturgie*, 263, for variant readings in older texts.

The characteristic changes that Benedict made in the first prayer of his ritual reappear in those that follow, many of which reiterate Benedict's attitude toward sin and carry the new formula at the end. Sicard noted the hand of the author of the Supplement in the changes made in the next prayer, *Deus cui omnia uiuunt*, pointing out how the phrasing has been altered to accentuate human responsibility for sin.[53] In two other texts, the bidding *Oremus fratres* and the prayer *Debitum humani corporis*, both spoken after burial, Benedict repeated his final formula, stressing the role of Christ as both mediator and equal to the father and the holy spirit.[54]

In a number of instances Benedict pared down some of the rich eschatological imagery of the older rituals. He ignored the *Suscipe* prayers spoken after death and during the laying out in the Gelasian tradition (which were themselves Visigothic in origin) in favor of another form of the same basic prayer which gives a simpler vision of the fate of the soul: "Receive Lord the soul of your servant N. which you have deigned to call from the prison of this world, and free it from the princes of darkness and the places of punishments, that, absolved from the chain of all sins, it may enjoy to the full the blessedness of quiet and eternal light, and deserve to be resuscitated among the saints and his elect in the glory of the resurrection."[55] Gone are references to the *prima resurrectio* and the celestial Jerusalem. The imagery does not describe the heavenly world in great detail, as do the *Suscipe* prayers of the Gelasian tradition, but limits itself to the old notions of peace and light. More emphasis is given to this world, which is defined as a prison, and to the intervening places, where the princes of darkness dwell and the evil are punished. It is sparing of detail, and the focus is juridical.

The next two prayers, also taken from Visigothic sources, continue and amplify the legalistic turn taken by Benedict in his ritual. The first prayer addresses the Lord God in his role as high judge,

53. Sicard, *Liturgie*, 90–95.

54. Supplement, no. 1411 (see Sicard, *Liturgie*, 320–21, for variant readings) and no. 1413 (Sicard, 269–71). Deshusses's apparatus to no. 1413 (Gregorian, 1.462) reveals that certain scribes did not know quite what to make of these changes. Some omitted the doxology; some changed it.

55. Supplement, no. 1400: "Suscipe domine animam serui tui *illius* quam de ergastulo huius saeculi uocare dignatus es, et libera eam de principibus tenebrarum et de locis poenarum, ut absoluta omnium uinculo peccatorum, quietis ac lucis aeternae beatitudine perfruatur, et inter sanctos et electos suos in resurrectionis gloriam, resuscitari mereatur." This prayer occurs in the office of the dead in the Visigothic Breviary (PL 86.986). The earlier forms are discussed in chap. 2.

begging him not to enter a judgment against the dead person, since before God "no one will be justified." The speaker does not wish to offend by asking for mercy when no basis for it exists. He hopes only that the supplication of faithful Christians will induce God to turn aside his just vengeance from one who, "while living, was marked with the sign of the Trinity"—that is, at baptism.[56] The second prayer again begs mercy from God as high judge, so that the dead person "may not receive a return in punishment for his deeds, . . . so that, just as here true faith joined him with the crowds of the faithful, so there your mercy will allow him to associate with the angelic choirs."[57]

The group of three prayers for a dead bishop which Benedict transferred from the end of the *Hadrianum* to this place in his death ritual are not so old as the psalmody of the Roman *ordo defunctorum*.[58] Sicard has dated them to the first half of the eighth century, when the peculiar form of the Gregorian sacramentary that became the *Hadrianum* took shape.[59] Their directness and simplicity mark them as Roman, but they make no direct reference to the Roman *ordo defunctorum*, which seems never to have found a place in Gregorian sacramentaries before they left Rome. The first is a simple plea in the form of many late antique prayers. "Incline your ear, Lord, to our prayers through which as suppliants we beg your mercy, so that you will establish the soul of your servant N., whom you have ordered to depart from this world, in

56. Supplement, no. 1401: "Non intres in iudicio cum seruo tuo domine *ill.*, quoniam nullus apud te iustificabitur homo, nisi per te omnium peccatorum tribuatur remissio, non ergo eum tua quaesumus iudicialis sententia praemat, quem tibi uera supplicatio fidei christianae commendat, sed gratia tua illi succurrente mereatur euadere iudicium ultionis, qui dum uiueret insignitus est signaculo trinitatis." It also appears in the oldest (<711) Visigothic liturgical manuscript, Verona, LXXXIX, ed. José Vives, *Oracional visigótico*, Monumenta Hispaniae sacra, serie litúrgica 1 (Barcelona, 1946), no. 1211. Sicard (*Liturgie*, 200–202) argues that it is Roman, not Visigothic. Its rhymed couplets are, however, characteristically Visigothic; see Deshusses, "Supplément," 53–57. This prayer and most of the others are treated in Juan Llopis Sarrío, "La sagrada escritura, fuente de inspiración de la liturgia de difuntos del antiguo rito hispánico," *Hispania Sacra* 17 (1964): 349–91.
57. Supplement, no. 1402: "Fac quaesumus domine . . . ut factorum suorum in poenis non recipiat uicem, qui tuam in uotis tenuit uoluntatem, ut sicut hic eum uera fides iunxit fidelium turmis, ita eum illic tua miseratio societ angelicis choris." Llopis Sarrío, "Sagrada escritura," 374, points out the typically Visigothic structure of this prayer. Note also its rhymed couplets.
58. Hadrianum, nos. 1015–17, Supplement, nos. 1402–4. Bishop, *Liturgica Historica*, 90, mistakenly supposed that they represented a "Roman burial service" corresponding to the rites in the Vatican Gelasian and eighth-century Gelasian sacramentaries.
59. Sicard, *Liturgie*, 392; Chavasse, *Sacramentaire gélasien*, 592, dated them to the years 680–720.

the region of peace and light, and order it to be the consort of your saints."[60] The second and third beg absolution for the sins of the dead person: "Absolve, Lord, the soul of your servant N. from all the fetters of sin, so that, brought back to life in the glory of the resurrection, she may breathe again among your saints. Grant to us, Lord, that the soul of your servant N. may receive remission of its sins, for which it always hoped."[61]

The source for the first of these prayers is Psalm 87:3. Sicard has noted the tone of distress in this psalm, and wondered if these prayers do not imply a movement away from the confidence expressed in the older Roman *ordo defunctorum.*[62] I think that they do. The prayer *Inclina domine* also appears in the Vatican Gelasian as part of a mass for the dead.[63] Its appearance in the *Hadrianum* as a prayer immediately after death implies that the Roman church had begun by the eighth century to stress the need for supplication over the confidence of salvation that so marks the old Roman *ordo defunctorum.* Some such change of attitude must lie behind the otherwise inexplicable omission of references to the psalms and antiphons of the *ordo* in the Roman sacramentaries of the period. In any case, the language and tone of the three Roman prayers from the *Hadrianum* conformed to that of the other prayers Benedict chose for his ritual.

Most of the Gelasian rituals contain a short group of spoken psalm verses, beginning with Psalm 111:7: "The just man will be remembered in eternity."[64] They appear at various times in the rites, but most often before or after the washing of the corpse. Benedict's placement of these verses, just before the rubric concerning prayers after the washing of the body, implies that they completed the ceremony of the laying out.[65] Characteristically,

60. Hadrianum, no. 1015: "Inclina domine aurem tuam ad preces nostras, quibus misericordiam tuam supplices deprecamur, ut animam famuli tui *ill. uel illam* quem de hoc saeculo migrare iussisti, in pacis ac lucis regione constituas, et sanctorum tuorum iubeas esse consortem."

61. Hadrianum, nos. 1016–17: "Absolue domine animam famuli tui *ill. vel illa* ab omni uinculo delictorum, ut in resurrectionis gloriam inter sanctos tuos resuscitari respiret. Annuae nobis domine ut anima famuli tui *ill.* remissionem quam semper optauit mereatur percipere, peccatorum."

62. Sicard, *Liturgie,* 399: "L'évocation elle-même du psaume 87 et de sa détresse n'impliquait-elle pas une transformation progressive du climat festif et pacifié des origines?"

63. Gelasian, no. 1686.

64. E.g., Gelasian, no. 1615; Autun, no. 1916; Rheinau, no. 1337a. Cf. Sicard, *Liturgie,* 115–16, 135–37, 319–20.

65. Supplement, no. 1406: "Post haec" (that is, the prayers in response to death) "continuatim canantur psalmi et postea dicantur capitula."

however, Benedict altered the arrangement of his sources, pulling out two verses that spoke of exultation and replacing them with the words that began one of the preceding Visigothic prayers, "Do not enter into judgment with your servant," and the Visigothic verse "Grant him, O Lord, eternal peace."[66]

The two Visigothic prayers to be said after the washing of the corpse return to the images of the afterlife as a prison which appear in the initial response to death; they beg God to "free the soul from the torments of the netherworld . . . so that, removed from the infernal prisons, it may be found worthy to be united in the company of the saints."[67] The two Visigothic prayers before burial develop these images further, asking God to spare the soul from various forms of suffering: "let not the shadows of death dominate it, or the chaos and gloom of darkness cover it. . . . Let not the torment of death touch it, the pain of the horrendous vision afflict it, the fear of punishment torture it, or the last chain of his offenses constrain it." Death is followed by darkness and chaos, the possibility of horrendous visions, torments, and fear of punishment. But it is all under the control of God, who can spare the soul the torments and the visions. The prayers present the soul suffering spiritual and psychological torments after death until its sins are forgiven by God and it is admitted into those "promised joys of the repose for which it hoped."[68]

The prayers that end the ceremony are both prayers of commen-

---

66. The omitted verses, *Exultabunt sancti in Gloria* (Ps. 149:5) and *Exultent iusti in conspectu dei* (Ps. 67:4), are replaced by *Non intres in iudicio cum seruo tuo* and *Requiem aeternam dona ei domine;* cf. Ritual 6 and, e.g., Gellone, no. 2897. Sicard's manuscript analysis (*Liturgie,* 72–74, 76–78) establishes Benedict's role in introducing the *Requiem aeternam* into the death ritual but neglects to consider its origins in the Visigothic death ritual; see Liber ordinum, 111–12. Its ultimate source, like much that has to do with death and burial for which Spain was the agent of transmission, may be North Africa, where the expression has been found on hundreds of late antique tombs; see Erwin Panofsky, *Tomb Sculpture: Four Lectures on Its Changing Aspects from Ancient Egypt to Bernini* (New York, n.d.), 45, 47.

67. Supplement, nos. 1407–8: "liberare eam ab inferorum cruciatibus . . . ut segregata ab infernalibus claustris, sanctorum mereatur adunari consortiis."

68. Ibid., no. 1409: "non ei dominentur umbrae mortis, nec tegat eum chaos et caligo tenebrarum . . ."; 1410: "non eum tormentum mortis attingat, non dolor horrendae uisionis afficiat, non poenalis timor excruciet, non reorum proxima catena constringat, sed concessa sibi delictorum omnium uenia optatae quietis consequatur gaudia repromissa." This latter prayer, which begins "Deus apud quem mortuorum spiritus uiuunt," appears in a Visigothic liturgical manuscript of the ninth to tenth centuries, Toledo, Bib. Cap. 35.7 (CLLA 394; printed in Liber ordinum, 757), as part of an *ordo ad commendandum corpora defunctorum.*

dation. The first is Visigothic.[69] It is interesting in that it discusses the ritual action of commendation itself, and not without a sense of irony: "It is indeed [a mark] of temerity, Lord, that a human, mortal, dust, dares to commend to you our Lord God another human, mortal, dust."[70] The tone is similar to that of the other prayers—a tone of radical abasement in the face of the high God. God is conceived in imperial images; his mercy takes on the qualities of imperial *misericordia*—a gift of pure grace to the undeserving, a display of the goodness not of the recipient but of the giver, in whom all goodness resides. God appears as incomprehensible judge, and Christ shares in that judgeship. The final prayer also appears in the Rheinau sacramentary, written some fifteen years before Benedict's work. Of all the prayers of commendation it is, in its simplicity of expression, the most eloquent. As so often before, Benedict altered the wording of his source. By deleting the reference to sin as a condition of the weakness of the flesh, he heightened responsibility for sinfulness after death: "We commend to you, Lord, the soul of your servant N., so that, dead to the world, he may be alive to you; although he has committed sins through the fragility of worldly converse, do, by the grace of your most merciful piety, wipe them away."[71]

Unlike the rituals we have looked at so far, the rite for death and burial in the Supplement is the work of one man, whose authorial hand is evident in nearly every prayer. Thus Benedict's rite has a striking continuity of structure, imagery, and language. In general, it is a simple and consistent plea for the forgiveness of the sins of the dead person, the release of the soul from the suffering that follows death, its reception in the bosom of Abraham, and its eventual inclusion in the company of the elect at the final judgment. It represents the son of God as high judge, distancing him from humans while making his mercy both incomprehensible and all-encompassing. A faithful and favored servant of the emperor Louis,

---

69. Supplement, no. 1414. This prayer appears in the same place in the burial service in the Visigothic *Liber ordinum* (Liber ordinum, 125), which otherwise seems not to have been a source for Benedict.

70. Supplement, no. 1414: "Temeritatis quidem est domine, ut homo hominem, mortalis mortalem, cinis cinerem, tibi domino deo nostro audeat commendare."

71. Supplement, no. 1415; Sicard, *Liturgie*, 355–56: "Tibi domine commendamus animam famuli tui *illius*, ut defunctus seculo tibi uiuat, et si qua per fragilitatem mundanae conuersationis peccata ammisit, tu uenia misericordissimae pietatis absterge." Cf. Rheinau, no. 1341b: "per fragilitatem carnis errorum peccata in mundi conuersatione cummisit."

Benedict refashioned the God of the Franks in an imperial mode.[72] Relying heavily on a vocabulary of legal terms, Benedict underlined the juridical relationship between God and his people while maintaining the absolute unworthiness of those people. In his stress on indulgence and supplication Benedict was at one with the spirit of the times. In the arrangement of the ritual as a whole, however, he was out of step, for he made no provisions for the antemortem phase of the ritual process. Nevertheless, his images of the after-death state of the unredeemed soul amplify those of the Frankish sources, adding a dimension of psychological suffering from which only the mercy of God could lift the soul. Furthermore, by bringing many old Spanish prayers into currency, with their vivid images of the after-death state, he added to the eventual elaboration of the *exitus* and its immediate aftermath, and brought the world view of the Visigothic death liturgy into the mainstream of Frankish tradition.

A Reform Rite for Anointing the Sick

The insistence of the Carolingian reformers on the institution of anointing the sick demanded a form by which it would be carried out.[73] But what form? Biblical texts gave a framework of ritual action—the anointing itself, the laying on of hands, and the act of prayer by priests—and Merovingian sources suggest that all these rituals had some currency, but the Frankish church itself seems not to have developed a clerical rite of anointing. With the introduction of Roman traditions in the Gelasian and Gregorian sacramentaries, the Franks had become familiar with the Roman episcopal rite of blessing the oil for the sick on Holy Thursday, and had begun to insist that priests obtain the necessary oil on that day, but the Roman tradition had no rite for administering unction. Clerical rites of anointing were current among reform circles in the Irish church, but they were ritual preparations for death, not rites for the restoration of health. A Carolingian reformer could look only to Spain, and perhaps northern Italy, for models of anointing rituals in conformity with the Roman emphasis on physical healing.

Benedict of Aniane was well placed to respond to the need for a

72. See the discussion of the general change in images of God in the Carolingian period in André Vauchez, *La spiritualité du moyen âge occidental: viii*e*–xii*e *siècles* (Paris, 1975), 25–26.

73. A problem first noted by H. B. Porter, "The Origin of the Medieval Rite for Anointing the Sick or Dying," JTS, n.s. 7 (1956): 212.

ritual form of anointing the sick. But did he? We have seen his handling of the death ritual in the Supplement to the *Hadrianum*. Do the ritual provisions for the sick in the Supplement exhibit similar characteristics? It does not seem so. Benedict compiled a group of prayers for use in visits to the sick, a set of mass prayers, and a general prayer for the return of health, all from the *Hadrianum* and the eighth-century Gelasian tradition (Ritual 6). For the most part, the visitation prayers express unadulterated Roman attitudes—the desire for a cure and concentration on the physical condition of the sick person. The two purely Gallican prayers in the group represent a more spiritualized approach, but they had become part of the wider Frankish Gelasian tradition by Benedict's time.[74] The mass for the sick and the prayer for the return of health, taken directly from an eighth-century Gelasian source, also preserve old Roman ritual responses to sickness. They present a straightforward petition for cure so that the sick person may reenter the community of the living and worship God.[75]

Thus, while Benedict's prayers and ritual indications for the treatment of the sick in the Supplement are generally in accord with the tenor of the reform, nothing there suggests that he had taken up the challenge of creating a ritual for anointing.[76] But a Carolingian reform rite for anointing the sick did appear in the ninth century, as H. B. Porter showed some years ago.[77] The earliest and best witness to this ritual is the sacramentary of Rodradus, written at the monastery of Corbie shortly after 853, but Porter based his analysis on the text of a sacramentary from the church of St. Eligius of Noyon, which, although written some time later, was available to his readers in a convenient printed edition.[78] Although

74. Supplement, nos. 1388–89.
75. Supplement, nos. 1392–95, 1732.
76. Benedict did give his own stamp to an old rite for purification of the home, in which water and salt were exorcised and blessed; Supplement, nos. 1451–58. Such a rite could be, and was (see below), used when the clergy visited and anointed the sick. The prayer for the mixing and blessing of both elements in this rite (Supplement, no. 1455) appears to be a personal composition of Benedict, as Deshusses points out (note to no. 1455). The final formula has Benedict's characteristic wording: "Per dominum nostrum iesum christum filium tuum qui tecum uiuit et regnat deus in unitate eiusdem spiritus sancti, per omnia saecula saeculorum."
77. Porter, "Origin," 214–23.
78. Sacramentary of Rodradus (Paris, B.N. MS lat. 12050; CLLA, 742); Sacramentary of St. Eligius (Paris, B.N. MS lat. 12051; CLLA, 901), also written at Corbie. The rite in the St. Eligius sacramentary was published by Hugo Ménard in the seventeenth century and reprinted by Migne (PL 78.231–36); the rite in the Rodradus book has now been edited by Deshusses as text no. 433 in Gregorian, 3.145–46, MS Q.

neither book preserves the ritual in its original form, comparison of the sacramentaries of Rodradus and St. Eligius reveals that the rite in Rodradus is closer to the original than the other. In the St. Eligius book, the first rubric has been altered to introduce a rite of purification of the home, some benedictions, an extra unction formula, and Benedict of Aniane's prayers for the visitation of the sick—all, except the unction formula, taken from a *Hadrianum* with Benedict's Supplement.[79] That this was not the work of the original author of the ritual is apparent from the inclusion of the benedictions, which have nothing to do with the sick, but were apparently included because they were intended for use in the home during clerical visitations and immediately followed the purification rite in the Supplement.[80] The sacramentary of Rodradus has a gloss on one of the rubrics and an additional final prayer that reflect a different understanding of the meaning of the ritual. When all these elements are excluded, what remains is essentially the seventh-century Visigothic rite for anointing the sick, at which we looked earlier (Ritual 3).[81] The Visigothic ritual provided for a simple visitation focusing on the cure of the sick person. It began with an unction of the head, after which came a series of antiphons and psalms, a prayer, and a final benediction. The creator of the Carolingian rite in the sacramentaries of Rodradus and St. Eligius used all of the Visigothic material, to which he added rubrics directing the ritual action, a new unction formula in a new place, and some new prayers (Ritual 7).

Porter dated this ritual to the years 815–845—that is, after the appearance of the Supplement to the *Hadrianum* and before the time of Rodradus. He suggested that its author may have been working in the south, because of his dependence on Visigothic sources, and that the ritual "was originally compiled for use in the clerical environment of a monastery or canonical abbey"; but he

---

79. In the Rodradus book, the rubric is "In primis faciant sacerdotes aquam benedictam et spargant eam cum antiphona et oratione super ipsum infirmum et domum eius. Deinde haec oratio dicatur, Domine Deus qui per apostolum"; Gregorian, 3.145. The St. Eligius book has "In primis faciant asperso sale aquam benedictam, et aspergant eam cum antiphona et Orationibus super ipsum infirmum, et super domus ejus" (PL 78.231), followed by Supplement, nos. 1451–58 (PL 78.231c–232d), 1462–65 (PL 78.232d–233b); Hadrianum 991, 993 (233b–c); the unction formula (233c); and Supplement, nos. 1386–91 (233d–234b).

80. On the extra unction formula, "Inungo te de oleo sancto, sicut iunxit Samuel David," see Porter, "Origin," 213.

81. Cf. Liber ordinum, 71–73, and Porter, "Origin," 215–18, 222; for the gloss and the final prayer, see below nn. 116, 118–20.

Ritual 7. Carolingian reform ritual for anointing the sick

First the priests should bless water and sprinkle it over the sick person and the house to the accompaniment of an antiphon and a prayer.

Prayer	Domine deus qui per apostolum tuum

Afterward the sick person should genuflect and stand to the right of the priest and these antiphons are sung:

Antiphons	Dominus locutus est discipulis suis . . . [Liber ordinum 72]

At this point all the priests and their ministers should place their hands on the sick person.

Verse	Deus deorum dominus locutus est	[Liber ordinum 72]
Repeat	In nomine meo	[Liber ordinum 72]
Prayer	Oremus dominum nostrum	[Liber ordinum sacerdotal 44]
Antiphon	Succurre domine infirmi	
Prayer	Deus qui famulo tuo	[Hadrianum 987]
Antiphon	Sana domine infirmum	[Liber ordinum 71]

And he should anoint the sick person so, making a cross with sanctified oil, on the neck, on the throat, between the shoulders, on the chest, or where the pain is greatest, and while the sick person is being anointed, one of the priests should say, supplicating, this prayer:

Prayer	Inungo te in nomine patris	
Prayer	Domine deus qui es uera salus	[Liber ordinum 72]
Prayer	Sana quoque quaesumus	[Liber ordinum 72]
Prayer	Propicietur dominus	[Liber ordinum 73]

Then the sick person should receive communion with the body and the blood of the Lord, and the rite should be repeated for seven days if necessary, both the communion and the other service, "and the Lord will raise him up, and if he has sinned, his sins will be forgiven." The priests and the ministers of God of the holy church should sing each day vespers and matins for the sick person with all reverence with the hymn *Christe caelestis medicina* and the rest, antiphons and responses as well as the lessons and prayers that pertain to the offices.

SOURCE: *Le sacramentaire grégorien*, ed. Jean Deshusses, vol. 3 (Fribourg, 1971), 145–46.

cautioned that "greater precision does not seem justified."[82] I think that we are now justified in being more precise, for all available evidence points to Benedict of Aniane as the author of this ritual. Benedict was closely connected with the general reform of the church in the Frankish realms and the leader of the reform of the monasteries and canonical abbeys under Louis the Pious. He

---

82. Porter, "Origin," 223.

was also an important liturgist with close links to the Visigothic
south. As such, he fits Porter's general profile. But the most compelling evidence lies in the prayers of the ritual itself. Internal
analysis reveals the same characteristic handling of sources and
turns of phrase that mark the death ritual in the Supplement to the
Hadrianum as the personal composition of Benedict of Aniane.

When discussing the new prayer that opens the anointing
ritual—a composition based on the language of the Visigothic antiphons in the *Libri ordinum* and the one prayer from the Gelasian
mass for the sick not taken into the Supplement—Porter remarked
that it was the work of whoever created the rite as a whole.[83] That
this person was Benedict of Aniane is suggested by the peculiar
wording of the text. The prayer is addressed to Jesus as Lord God in
the same manner as the prayers of the death ritual in the Supplement.[84] Similar changes appear elsewhere in the rite. The Visigothic ritual books contain no unction formula, only a rubric directing the anointing, yet the Carolingian ritual has one. Not
surprisingly, it is modeled on an Irish formula, like that which
appears in the eighth-century Gelasian from St. Gall. Here again,
however, the reference to Christ has been changed—from "the
power of Christ, the Son of God the most high," to "the power of
Christ the most high."[85] A similar alteration appears in the Visigothic prayer that follows the unction, which addresses Christ as
"Lord God" rather than the original "Jesus, our Saviour."[86] The
final prayer has been given an explicitly orthodox trinitarian ending.[87] Both the manner of referring to Christ as *Deus* and the trinitarian emphasis in the final formula are signatures of Benedict's
peculiar reworking of his liturgical inheritance, as we saw in the
analysis of his death ritual. Since there is no trace of the rite in the

83. Ibid., 218–19.
84. A Visigothic benediction of the oil for the sick in the *Liber ordinum sacerdotal* (no. 139), which may have been Benedict's source, is introduced by the words
"Lord Jesus Christ [*Domine Ihesu Christe*], who said through your apostle"; in the
Carolingian prayer the address is simply "Lord God" (*Domine Deus*).
85. St. Gall, no. 233: *virtus Christi, Filii Dei altissimi;* Gregorian, no. 4001:
uirtus Christi altissimi. Cf. also Bobbio, no. 243, and Stowe, p. 31.
86. Cf. Liber ordinum, 72, *Ihesu salvator noster et Domine,* and Gregorian,
3.128, 146, no. 3990. Porter argued ("Origin," 219) that it made sense to change the
address *Iesu saluator noster,* which would have been "offensive to ears north of the
Pyrenees," but that the expected result would have been the Gallican form *Domine
Iesu* rather than *Domine Deus.*
87. Liber ordinum, 73, *Propitietur Dominus,* ends simply with *Amen.* In the
Carolingian reform rite it ends "qui solus in trinitate unus deus uiuit per immor-
talia saecula saeculorum. Amen"; Gregorian, 3.146 and no. 3992.

Supplement itself, which Benedict had finished around 815, it must have been composed sometime between then and his death in 821, no doubt for a monastic community in the north.[88]

The first rubric in Benedict's anointing ritual directed the officiating priests to enter the house of the sick person and sprinkle it and him with holy water (accompanied by an unspecified antiphon and prayer).[89] Then a priest intoned the following prayer: "Lord God who spoke through your apostle [he recites James 5:14–15], cure, our redeemer, we beseech you, through the grace of the Holy Spirit, this sick person, heal his wounds, forgive his sins, expel all other pains from his heart and body, mercifully grant him complete health within and without, so that restored and healed through the work of your mercy, he may return to his previous service."[90] This prayer, as Porter pointed out, includes the text of the letter of St. James on which "the Carolingian revival of sick unction rested."[91] Next, the sick person was directed to genuflect and stand to the right of the priest, after which the first of the Visigothic antiphons was sung as all the priests and their attendants placed their hands on him.[92] After two prayers and antiphons from the *Libri ordinum* and the *Hadrianum*, a rubric directs the anointing, which a priest was to perform by making the sign of the cross with the oil on the neck, the throat, between the shoulders, on the chest, or at the place of greatest pain, and which was to be accompanied by the following formula: "I anoint you in the name of the Father and the Son and the Holy Spirit so that no unclean spirit may remain either in your limbs, marrow, or joints, but that the power of Christ the most high and the Holy Spirit may live in

88. This supposition accords well with its pattern of transmission around Corbie, St-Amand, and Tours in the second half of the ninth century, when it was circulated along with the Supplement and Gregorian material; see Gregorian, 3.148–54, and below, chap. 5.

89. A later witness supplies what are perhaps the intended prayer and antiphon: *Pax huic domui; Asperges me domine hysopo* (Gregorian, 3.150).

90. Gregorian, 3.127–28, no. 3988: "Domine Deus qui per apostolum tuum locutus es [James 5:14–15] cura quaesumus redemptor noster gratia spiritus sancti languores istius infirmi, sua sana uulnera, eiusque dimitte peccata, atque dolores cunctos cordis et corporis ab eo expelle, plenamque ei interius exteriusque sanitatem misericorditer redde, ut ope misericordiae tuae restitutus et sanatus, ad pristina reparetur officia."

91. Porter, "Origin," 218.

92. Gregorian, 3.146 and no. 4021: "Et postea flectat genu uel genua qui est languidus. Et stet ad dexteram sacerdotis, et sic decantetur haec antiphona. Dominus locutus est discipulis suis, In nomine meo daemonia eicite et super aegros manus' uestras imponite et bene habebunt. Hic ponant manus super infirmum omnes sacerdotes et ministri eorum."

you, so that through the operation of this mystery, and through the anointing with holy oil and our prayer, cured or comforted by the power of the Holy Trinity, you will merit the restoration and improvement of your health."[93] After two prayers—*Domine deus qui es uera salus*, with its address to Christ as high God, and *Sana quoque*—both based on the Visigothic source, and the final Visigothic benediction, the ritual ended with a rubric directing communion and the repetition of the whole ritual for seven days along with the singing of the office for the sick with a Visigothic hymn, "Christ, medicine of the heavenly father."[94]

The creation of this rite provided a means of fulfilling the decrees of the reform councils on the importance of anointing the sick. It also gave expression to the old Roman ritual approach to the sick, which was shared by the Visigothic church, if not always by the Franks and the Irish. Though Benedict of Aniane's reform rite of anointing and caring for the sick did not ignore the spiritual benefits of prayer and unction, it nonetheless emphasized their healing power, and expressed hope that a cure would be achieved and the sick person could rejoin the Christian community in this world.

The Reception of Benedict's Rites

Diversity in Ninth-Century Ritual Books

Benedict of Aniane made no small contribution to ritual development in the early ninth century. Yet, although his death ritual had the advantage of association with the Gregorian sacramentary and his rite of anointing the sick was a consumate expression of the goals of the reform, they did not sweep everything before them. Working against his death ritual was its failure to give expression

---

93. Gregorian, 3.146 and no. 4001: "Et sic perunguat infirmum de oleo sanctificato crucem faciendo in collo, in gutture et inter scapulas, et in pectore, seu in loco ubi dolor imminet amplius perunguatur, et supplicando dum inunguitur infirmus dicat unus ex sacerdotibus hanc orationem. Inungo te oleo in nomine patris et filii et spiritus sancti, ut non lateat in te spiritus immundus, neque in membris uel medullis, neque in ulla compage membrorum, sed habitet in te uirtus christi altissimi et spiritus sancti, quatinus per huius operationem mysterii, et per hanc sacrati olei unctionem atque nostram deprecationem, uirtute sanctae trinitatis medicatus siue fotus, pristinam et inmelioratam recipere merearis sanitatem."

94. Gregorian, 3.146 and no. 4026; cf. Liber ordinum, 377–85; on the hymn, *Christe caelestis medicina*, see Porter, "Origin," 217. There is a later addition to the final rubric; see Porter, 220, and below, n. 116.

to or to take account of contemporary elaborations of rites in preparation for death and around the agony. Working against the unction rite was the apparent fact that it was created too late to be included in the Supplement proper, and so depended on an independent transmission for its dissemination and use. Working against both was the persistence of older layers of ritual expression and gesture deeply embedded in the ritual books and religious life of the Frankish church and people: the old Gallican prayers, with their rich imagery of the afterlife and their penitential flavor; and the Irish and Gallican tendency to regard sickness as a spiritual preparation for death and unction as a purifying and transformative agent for ritual passage.

Thus the Carolingian reform did not put an end to the two approaches to the ritual care of the sick which we observed in the period before Pippin's reign. The reformers favored the old Roman and Visigothic approach. The ritual materials closest to the centers of the reform testify to this preference most clearly; the decrees of the reform councils, the prayers and rites in the *Hadrianum* and its Supplement, and Benedict's rite for anointing the sick are all directed at ritual healing and the return of physical health. The other stream, representing tendencies expressed in the old Gallican liturgy and in Irish circles, survived in texts that predate the high reform period or that were created in areas with strong Irish or Irish-Gallican traditions. Such texts include the eighth-century Gelasian sacramentaries, which first brought together the rituals for the sick, the dying, and the dead. The sacramentaries of St. Gall and Rheinau especially show signs of a conscious recognition of the different emphases in the two traditions and of the use with the dying of rites and prayers from the liturgy for the sick which envisioned the spiritual transformation of the recipients and their preparation for death.

A similar situation prevailed around the rites for death and burial. The Gelasian books did not go away, but continued in active use throughout the first half of the ninth century and beyond. This was a consequence of the expense of book production and dissemination in the Carolingian world as well as the enduring meaning and appropriateness of the rituals and prayers indigenous to the Frankish church, which these books preserved. Some idea of the relative popularity of the different traditions can be gained from the catalogue of liturgical books in the monastery of St-Riquier in Picardy dating to the year 831. It records the possession of three Gregorian sacramentaries but fourteen Gelasian books—that is, eighth-century Gelasians.[95] The continued use of these books along with the newer Gregorians kept any one ritual pattern from becoming the standard during the first half of the ninth century.

Ritual diversity was fostered not only by the coexistence of the various traditions but by differences within them as well. Benedict of Aniane was not the only one to take an interest in the *Hadrianum* and its deficiencies. As soon as the Gregorian sacramentary began to be regularly copied and disseminated in the Frankish realms, scribes took liberties with its structure and content, breaking it up, adding material where it was needed, and gradually transforming it into a new type of book: the mixed or Gelasianized Gregorian.[96] Jean Deshusses, in his comparative edition of the Gregorian sacramentaries of the ninth century, lists only one *Hadrianum* manuscript out of thirty-five which was created without any significant supplementary material, that is, in the form it had when it arrived at the court of Charlemagne.[97] Only nine manuscripts containing the *Hadrianum* with a Supplement in the form Benedict left it survive, and many of these manuscripts were further supplemented when they were created.[98] A number of others were supplemented with material from the Gelasian tradition not mediated by Benedict of Aniane.[99] The largest group (fourteen manuscripts) is characterized by a more or less free restructuring of the Gregorian tradition, combining portions of the *Hadrianum* and its Supplement and adding new material.[100] Although witnesses to each of these groups continued to be produced throughout the ninth century, the tendency over time was toward increasingly free adaptation.

Non-Anianian Supplements

The treatment of copies of the *Hadrianum* made independently of Benedict's supplemented version is a good indication of the per-

95. Vogel, "Réforme liturgique," 228.
96. On these books see Vogel, *Medieval Liturgy*, 102–5; Deshusses, "Sacramentaires," 85–86.
97. Gregorian, 3.19–59, MS A; three others have minor additions: N, Z4, and Omega.
98. Ibid., MSS H, J–M, O–Q, Y.
99. Ibid., MSS B1–2, C1–2, D–G.
100. Ibid., MSS R–X, TU1–2. It is unfortunate that Deshusses did not make use of the Sacramentary of St. Eligius for vols. 2 and 3 of his edition, which are devoted to additions made to the common stock of the *Hadrianum* and the Supplement. It is no less interesting than the other "mixed Gregorians" that he excluded from consideration in vol. 1 but included in the later volumes; cf. Gregorian, 1.45–47, 2.21–23.

sistence of earlier rituals and ritual traditions into the mid–ninth century, and of the continued freedom taken at local centers in developing appropriate rites. As clerics at the court in Aachen realized, copies of the *Hadrianum* needed supplementary material to render them usable, and scribes sometimes added rites for the sick and the dead at the end of their manuscripts. Such books fall into two groups, one distinctly North Italian, the other centered around Reichenau and St. Gall.[101] Since the North Italian group has the more extensive coverage of rites for the sick, dying, and dead, it can illustrate the process of supplementation.

The oldest independently supplemented *Hadrianum* is an early ninth-century book created in Verona.[102] It presents rubrics and prayers for the visitation of the sick, the reconciliation of penitents, and death and burial in the sequence established by the eighth-century Gelasian sacramentaries (Table 1).[103] The compiler of this ritual complex dealt with the lack of prayers and rites for the sick, the dying, and the dead in the Roman sacramentary by merging material from the Gelasian tradition with some unique prayers, no doubt of local North Italian stock. The visitation rite opens with an old Gallican prayer asking for the medicine of God's grace.[104] The following two prayers are foreign to the Gelasian tradition. The first recalls the biblical episode in which Peter brought a young girl back to life (Acts 9:36–41); the second begs God to put his hand in that of the officiant and order the sickness to depart, almost certainly implying the laying on of hands, which was characteristic of North Italian rites for the sick.[105] There is no mention of an anointing, and the simple ritual ends with the old Gelasian prayer for the return of health.[106]

The penitential ritual in the Verona book exhibits some ambiguity. The old Gelasian prayers for the deathbed reconciliation follow a separate rite for penance, reconciliation, and communion based on the Gelasian tradition.[107] This arrangement may indicate a rite for penance in the home before or after the laying on of hands or a

101. Gregorian, 3.19–59, MSS B1–2, G (North Italian), C1–2, D–F (Reichenau and St. Gall).

102. Verona, Biblioteca Capitolare 91 (CLLA 725; Gregorian, 1.42, 3.20–21, MS B1), written 800–825.

103. Gregorian, 3.145, 121, 168–69, provides editions of ritual materials on fols. 118v–125v of the manuscript.

104. Gelasian, no. 1535: *Deus qui facturae tuae;* this prayer is discussed in chap. 2.

105. Gregorian, 3.130, nos. 3999–4000.

106. Gelasian, no. 1543: *Domine, sanctae pater, omnipotens aeterne deus, qui benedictionis.*

107. Gregorian, 3.121.

deathbed ritual in which the communion received after reconciliation became the viaticum. The death ritual comprises a prayer of commendation over the dead body, the *Deus apud quem,* and a short graveside service.[108] The burial service opens with a Gallican bidding, and after a prayer begging absolution taken from the *Hadrianum* and a simple request that the soul of the dead person be granted a place among the elect in eternal light, ends with the commendation from the Rheinau sacramentary.[109] This ritual sequence is simple but coherent, and well suited to parish work.

A different ritual complex was added to a *Hadrianum* manuscript written sometime later for Modena or Reggio d'Emilia.[110] The treatment of the rites for the sick and penitents is undeveloped in this book, and it contains no indications of ritual preparations for death in the form of either deathbed penance or a rite for the dying.[111] Its burial service, which is based on an eighth-century Gelasian model, is, however, extraordinary.[112] Its originator apparently had some portion of the old Roman *ordo* in front of him, for he wove its rubrics and psalmody into the structure of his ritual. His ignorance of (or failure to use) the first two rubrics prescribing the ritual acts before death maintained the link with the eighth-century Gelasian tradition. While in no way directly influential, this peculiar combination of elements—a mixture of prayers from the Gelasian tradition with Roman rubrics and psalmody—would soon become a common feature of postmortem rituals in the Frankish church.[113]

108. Gregorian, 3.168–69. The *Deus apud quem* is preceded by the rubric *Oratio super defunctum uel commendatio animae.*

109. Gregorian, no. 4068 = Rheinau, no. 1341b.

110. Modena, Biblioteca Capitolare, MS O.II.7 (CLLA 777 [2d ed. 729]; Gregorian, 1.38, 3.26–27, MS G), written 830–860.

111. Gregorian, 3.145 (sick), 121–22 (penance). There are only two prayers for the sick (Hadrianum, nos. 987–88) and none for deathbed penance, only three prayers for general use with penitents (Hadrianum, no. 989, Gelasian, nos. 78, 362, 368). Moreover, the rites do not appear in sequence, and the penance prayers follow the death ritual.

112. Gregorian, 3.169–71. As can be seen in Deshusses's edition, the Modena ritual is an expanded form of that in Padua, Biblioteca Capitolare, MS D 47 (CLLA 880; Gregorian, 1.39–40, 57; 3.54–55, MS Pa). Sicard, *Liturgie,* 340–42, 348, presents the prayers in Padua D 47 as a member of his family *B* of Gelasian rites for death and burial, but he does not seem to have been aware of the Modena manuscript.

113. This manuscript has one other unusual feature: six of a group of nine prayers appended to the rite show a close relation to the prayers in the death ritual in the Supplement which do not derive from earlier Roman or Frankish sources (see Gregorian, 3.171 n.). The six prayers correspond to Supplement, nos. 1401, 1407–10, and 1414. The addition of these prayers to the Modena manuscript may indicate that an old Visigothic burial service was still circulating in some form in northern Italy in the mid–ninth century.

The Transmission of Benedict's Rituals

The more numerous manuscripts that transmitted the *Hadrianum* along with Benedict's Supplement did have a complete ritual order for the sick and for death and burial, as Benedict conceived of them, and so would have been adequate for most circumstances. Consequently they are not generally enlarged by the addition of other rituals and prayers. Examples survive from the first half of the ninth century from Marmoutier, Lyons, and St-Amand, and from the second half from southern France, Paris, Corbie, and northern Italy.[114] One of this group is the sacramentary of Rodradus, with which we have already dealt. The Rodradus book has no added material on death. Since the manuscript contains a full *Hadrianum* and a complete text of the Supplement, the implication is that Benedict's death ritual was accepted and used as it appeared in the Supplement. At the very end of the manuscript, however, Rodradus included that oldest witness to Benedict of Aniane's rite of anointing the sick, which was written sometime after the Supplement and not contained in it.[115]

The anointing rite in the sacramentary of Rodradus, as we saw earlier, is the purest form of Benedict's new ritual extant, but it shows evidence of adaptation. At some time between the original transcription of the rite and its inclusion in the sacramentary of Rodradus someone added a gloss to the final rubric, which reads: "Many priests, however, anoint the sick over the five senses of the body, that is on the eyebrows, the inside of the ears, on the end of or within the nostrils, on the outside of the lips, and on the backs of the hands. . . . They do this so that if any impurity of the soul and the body adheres to the five senses, the medicine of God will wipe it away."[116] This addition is noteworthy for two reasons. First of all, although there is no way of knowing whether Rodradus himself

114. Gregorian, 3.28–30, MSS H, J–L; 31–33, MSS O–Q; 52–53, MS Y.
115. Ibid., 3.33; edited, 145–47; and see above Ritual 7. The ritual for the anointing of the sick appears on fols. 246r–248v of the manuscript.
116. Gregorian, 3.146: "Multi enim sacerdotum infirmos perunguant insuper quinque sensus corporis, id est in superciliis oculorum, et in auribus deintus, et in narium summitate siue interius, et in labiis exterius, et in manibus exterius id est de foris. In omnibus ergo his membris crucem faciant de oleo sacrato dicentes In nomine patris et filii et spiritus sancti. Hoc enim ideo faciant ut si in quinque sensus mentis et corporis aliqua macula inhaesit, hac medicina dei sanetur." On this rubric, see Porter, "Origin," 220–21; and Murray, "Liturgical History," 34–35. For the sense of *sanare* as "to remove," see Lewis and Short, *A Latin Dictionary* (New York, 1879), s.v. *sano*, referring to *sanare nidorem*, to remove an odor; in the sense of "to clean," see Du Cange, *Glossarium mediae et infimae latinitatis*, s.v. *sanare*, where he remarks that a French word for a tool used to clean stables, *saynière*, derives from the Latin *sanare*.

composed the gloss or copied it into the text from his exemplar, it reveals a variety of practices among Frankish clerics in the middle of the ninth century. Second, the anointing of the five senses instead of the place where the sickness was concentrated denotes a shift in emphasis away from physical healing and toward spiritual purification.[117] Another addition to Benedict's original rite appears in the sacramentary of Rodradus—a prayer to be said "at the end of the ritual."[118] Porter believed that this prayer reflected mid-ninth-century practice.[119] Internal analysis bears him out, for the prayer introduces a new note into Benedict's rite of healing. The prayer asks God to send an angel to aid the sick person in her struggle, so that she may gain the "eternal remedy."[120] That remedy is not physical health but purification of sin and salvation in heaven.

Thus by the middle of the ninth century Benedict of Aniane's anointing rite had come to be colored by attitudes rather different from those that originally informed it. As in all such liturgical developments, the changes came by addition, so that the original shape of the healing ritual remained, but with new indications that opened it up to other situations and interpretations. The new indications, moreover, have the flavor of the old Irish-Gallican ritual approach to the sick. Their presence in the sacramentary of Rodradus, which is as close to the mainstream of Carolingian reform sacramentaries as it could be, suggests that by the mid–ninth

117. On the anointing of the five senses, see Chavasse, "Prières," 585. Porter, "Origin," 221n, refers to a prayer in the Leofric Missal for blessing chrism which "specifies the purifying and mollification of the five senses as among the principal effects of chrismation." The text of that prayer is interesting also for its military images, which recall the unction formula that first appeared in the St. Gall sacramentary around 800 (see above, chap. 3): "Dominator, domine deus, rex unctus, auctor unguenti, speciosas forma, speciosor unctione. . . . In tuo ergo nomine fiat haec creatura iam crisma, forma crucis, signum fontis, sacri titulus bellatoris, ut hoc crismate mulceatur auditus, purificetur uisus, odoratus suauescat, soporetur gustus, tactus in trinitate solidus sit; ut talibus stipendiis domini milites decorati, atque ambrosio rore madidi, imperanti scruiant non suadenti, et signati hoc crismate sancto, signiferi esse mereantur caelestes"; The Leofric Missal, ed. F E. Warren (Oxford, 1883), 260. The anointing ritual was spiritualized whenever it drew on baptismal imagery, because in baptism the ritual action is related solely to the spiritual condition of the recipient.

118. Gregorian, 3.146: *Oratio in consummatione huius officii.*

119. Porter, "Origin," 220, 223.

120. Gregorian, 3.129, no. 3993: "Omnipotens sempiterne deus qui subuenis in periculis et necessitate laborantibus, maiestatem tuam supplices exoramus ut mittere digneris sanctum angelum tuum, qui famulum tuum *illum* in angustiis et necessitatibus laborantem consolationibus tuis attollat, quibus et de praesenti consequatur auxilium, et aeterna remedia comprehendat." This prayer also has its roots in the baptismal liturgy; see the *exorcismus super electos* in the Vatican Gelasian, no. 291.

century certain cultural pressures had begun to reshape the reform rite of anointing the sick. The next generation would see the culmination of this process as both Benedict's anointing rite and his prayer service over the dead body and for the laying out and burial were brought together in a ritual synthesis to accompany the final days, death, and burial of a Christian.

CHAPTER FIVE

Synthesis and Dissemination: The Death
Ritual in the Later Ninth Century

Rites for the Dying in Mid-century

The year 817 was the high-water mark for the forces of unity in the Frankish church and the Carolingian empire. The creation of a unified episcopacy realized by Charlemagne had been matched by the reorganization and centralization of monks, nuns, and canons at the great reform councils of 816–817. The continuation of the empire seemed assured by the solemn design of the *Ordinatio imperii*, by which Louis's eldest son, Lothar, would succeed to the empire over his two younger brothers, who would receive kingdoms.[1] The Gregorian sacramentary supplemented by Benedict of Aniane provided a firm foundation for worship and ritual life. Impressive as these successes were, they did not signal the end to particularism. The difficulties of book production and the changing needs of the Frankish church kept older books in circulation and ensured that with time the Gregorian sacramentary would be altered, adapted, and expanded to accommodate local traditions and new experiments. The birth of Louis's fourth son, Charles, in 825 upset the balance achieved in the *Ordinatio imperii* and eventually led to civil war and a permanent end to the unity of the Carolingian world. Bishops came to challenge the authority

---

1. On the reform councils of 816–817 and the significance of the *Ordinatio imperii*, see McKitterick, *Frankish Kingdoms*, 112–24 and 135–36.

of kings and powerful laymen established control over many religious foundations, whose rich lands and dependencies made
them tempting prizes for expanding lordships.[2] By the middle of
the ninth century, East and West had irrevocably split, and the
initiative in religious reform had passed from the royal courts to
the bishops and abbots of the Frankish realms. The clerics continued to meet in council to discuss and legislate on matters of
Christian living and dying. Their decrees reveal some of the same
uncertainty over the ritual treatment of the sick and the dying
apparent in the rites in the sacramentary of Rodradus. Yet they also
hint at an emerging consensus. Anointing, confession and reconciliation, and viaticum were increasingly being regarded as necessary preparations for Christian passage.

Benedict of Aniane's reform rite of anointing the sick, in which
hope of a cure was the dominant theme, added to the diversity of
ritual responses to sickness and death in the Carolingian church.
The decrees of episcopal capitularies and church councils of the
mid–ninth century reveal, however, that in general the reform rite
for anointing the sick had made little headway, and that in some
cases anointing was being explicitly recommended as a ritual preparation for death. In 836, a council held at Aachen attempted to
address the first of these problems by making the Thursday of
Easter week the one and only day when bishops could bless the oil
for the sick and distribute it to their clergy. "It is decreed that once
a year, on Holy Thursday, the blessing of the oil that is believed to
heal the sick is not to be neglected by bishops throughout all the
cities, as it now is, but is to be performed in all devotion in accordance with the apostolic tradition and the instructions on that
subject in the statutes of the decretals."[3] Clearly, the Roman blessing of the oil for the sick on Holy Thursday, despite the presence of
the rite in both the Gelasian and the Gregorian sacramentary traditions, had not become standard practice. The restrictive language
of the decree implies a desire to gain control over ritual practice in
this regard, which appears to have moved out of conformity with
the official understanding of ritual anointing.[4]

2. Ibid., 169–99.
3. MGH, Concilia 2.710, c. (20) viii: "Statutum etiam est, ut vel semel in anno,
id est in quinta feria, quae est in caena Domini, unctio sancti olei, in quo salvatio
infirmorum creditur, per omnes civitates ab episcopis non neglegatur, sicut nunc
usque neglectum est, sed omni devotione iuxta traditionem apostolicam ac statuta
decretalium, in quo de eadem re praecipitur, peragatur." The term *unctio sancti olei*
is certainly a corruption of *benedictio sancti olei.*
4. Cf. c. 46 of the councils of Meaux-Paris, 845–846, MGH, Concilia 3.107: "Ut

About the same time, Bishop Jonas of Orléans (818–43), in a discussion of the care of the sick, attempted an explanation for the lack of interest in the ritual.

> This anointing with oil has declined in use among many out of ignorance and many others out of negligence. Those who do not use it, however, should do so. Whence it is necessary that when someone gets sick, she should seek a remedy not from magicians, who are certainly possessed by demons, but from the Church and her priests, and by the anointing of sanctified oil she should beg for herself from the Lord Jesus Christ a remedy not only for the body but also for the soul.[5]

Echoes of earlier texts reverberate through Jonas's words, but it is no doubt true that the traditional medicine of the folk culture was as common and attractive in the mid–ninth century as it had been in the time of Caesarius of Arles. The herbal medicine of the countryside was too deeply rooted to be readily replaced by an ecclesiastical rite that was no less magical, after all, than the offerings of the local healer—and no more or less likely to lead to a cure.

A long canon from a synod held at Pavia in 850 illustrates both the reasons for the unpopularity of the rite of anointing the sick and the regard in which it was held by its supporters. It reads in part:

> That salutary sacrament, which the apostle James recommended . . . ought to be made known to the people through skillful preaching. Great and worthy of request is this mystery through which, if it is asked for in faith, sins are remitted and consequently the health of the body is restored. But because it frequently so happens that someone who is sick either does not know the power of the sacrament, or thinking the sickness not too serious feigns to work for his health, or forgets the violence of the disease, the local priest

---

nemo sacrum chrisma nisi in quinta feria maioris septimanę, id est in cena, quę specialiter appellatur dominica, conficere praesumat."

5. *De institutione laicali,* bk. 3, chap. 14 (PL 106.261B): "Multis namque propter ignorantiam, multis propter incuriam, haec olei unctio ab usu recessit. Quibus autem in usu non est, necesse est ut in usu veniat. Unde oportet ut quando quis infirmatur, non a divinis et divinatricibus, quae utique habitationes sunt daemonum, sed ab Ecclesia, ejusque sacerdotibus, et unctione sanctificati olei, sibi remedium non solum in corpore, sed etiam in anima a Domino Jesu Christo postulet adfuturum."

should admonish him fittingly and, insofar as it is possible, invite the neighboring priests to this spiritual cure.[6]

The intimate knowledge of the impediments to general use and acceptance of the reform rite of anointing expressed in this decree reveals the degree to which some bishops actively concerned themselves with the problems involved in bringing the rites of the church to local parishes. There are hints of desperation here, too. No other Carolingian text makes such bold claims for the curative power of the ritual. And no other draws a causal link (*consequenter*) between the forgiveness of sins and the restoration of health, which was never the orthodox understanding of ritual anointing.[7] If priests really did follow through with the order to include fellow clerics in rites of sacramental healing through oil, their low rate of success might almost inevitably lead them to stress the spiritual over the physical aspects of the ritual.

Other texts reveal that rites of anointing were more normally understood as spiritual aids, and often were joined with other sacramental acts in a larger process of ritual preparation for death. The same council that reminded bishops to perform the blessing of the oil on Holy Thursday passed the following decree concerning the treatment of the sick: "If anyone is borne down by sickness, he should not lack, through priestly negligence, either confession and the sacerdotal prayer or anointing with the sanctified oil. And finally if he sees the end near, he [the priest] shall commend the Christian soul to the Lord his God in the sacerdotal manner with the reception of holy communion. . . ."[8] In this text, confession

6. MGH, Concilia 3.223, c. viii: "Illud quoque salutare sacramentum, quod commendat Iacobus apostolus dicens: *Infirmatur . . . ei* [i.e., James 5:14–15] sollerti predicatione populis innotescendum est. Magnum sane et valde appetendum misterium, per quod, si fideliter poscitur, et peccata remittuntur et consequenter corporalis salus restituitur. Sed quia frequenter contingit, ut ęgrotans aliquis aut sacramenti vim nesciat aut minus periculosam reputans infirmitatem salutem suam operari dissimulet aut certe morbi violentia obliviscatur, debet eum loci presbiter congruenter admonere, quatinus ad hanc spiritalem curam secundum proprię possibilitatis vires vicinos quoque presbiteros invitet."

7. Some clerics must have recognized that this canon broke with precedent, for those who prepared one of the two contemporary North Italian manuscripts in which it appears omitted the word linking forgiveness of sin and the return of health; see ibid., n. e-e, referring to Wolfenbüttel, Herzog-August-Bibliothek, MS Blankenburg 130.

8. MGH, Concilia 2.712 (29), c. v: "Si autem infirmitate depressus fuerit, ne confessione atque oratione sacerdotali necnon unctione sacrificati olei per eius neglegentiam careat. Denique si finem urgentem perspexerit, commendet animam

and forgiveness of sins are clearly delineated from anointing and no causal connection is drawn between forgiveness and cure. Indeed, physical healing is not mentioned at all. If the illness were serious, both confession and anointing would naturally tend to be brought together with the commendation of the soul and the reception of communion as viaticum, as this decree implies. This succession of ritual acts mirrors the textual arrangement of the sacramentaries from the later eighth century on, in which the prayers and rites for the sick regularly precede those for death and funerals, and suggests that use of such sacramentaries in religious communities was, by the middle of the ninth century, beginning to determine the context of decrees aimed at the population in general.

When Archbishop Hincmar of Reims wrote on the subject in 852, in a capitulary to his diocesan clergy, his language was suggestive: "Each priest should learn by heart the rite of reconciliation, according to the manner canonically reserved to themselves, and the anointing of the sick, as well as the corresponding prayers for that same rite. Similarly [he should know] the rite and prayers for funerals and at the deathbed as well as the exorcisms and blessings of water and salt."[9] The fathers of the council presided over by Hrabanus Maurus at Mainz a few years earlier (847) were more explicit. Recalling ancient canons regarding deathbed penance, canon 26 of the Mainz council unambiguously includes ritual anointing as one of the "consolations of the church" to the dying.

> Priests should seek a simple confession of sins from the sick who are in danger of death; not, however, imposing on them a quantity of penance, but making it known, and the weight of penance should be alleviated through the prayers and devotion to almsgiving of friends, so if by chance the sick should die soon, they will not be excluded from the fellowship of pardon through the obligation of excommunication. If, divinely delivered from danger, they should get well, they must carefully observe the manner of penance placed upon them by their confessor. And thus, in accordance with canonical authority, so that the door of piety should not seem to them closed, they should

---

Christianam domino Deo suo more sacerdotali cum acceptione sacrae communionis. . . ."

9. PL 125.773–74: "Ordinem reconciliandi, juxta modum sibi canonice reservatum, atque ungendi infirmos, orationes quoque eidem necessitati competentes memoriter discat. Similiter ordinem et preces in exsequiis atque agendis defunctorum, nec minus exorcismos et benedictiones aquae et salis." Cf. Hincmar's capitulary to his deans, c. 10 (PL 125.779): "Si ipse presbyter visitet infirmos, et inungat oleo sancto, et communicet per se, et non per quemlibet. . . ."

be refreshed while still alive with the prayers and consolations of the church, with the sacred anointing, and with communion of viaticum in accordance with the statutes of the holy fathers.[10]

Here, for the first time, anointing is unambiguously prescribed as a response to imminent death. It may have been given earlier, during the illness, but this canon recognizes and states its appropriateness as an aid to the dying. Along with confession and reconciliation, the anointing is a means of preparing the dying for the agony and *exitus*. Indeed, the needs of the dying are at the center of this decree, all of whose provisions are aimed at lessening the anxiety surrounding death. The penitential obligations of the last confession are taken over by friends and relatives, who will see to them in the days following the funeral.[11] The dying are to receive all possible care and solace.

An anonymous diocesan capitulary from the same period (ca. 850) contains a canon that also associates the anointing of the sick and the rites for the dying. It directs the diocesan clergy to perform the anointing according to the apostolic tradition and the *commendatio animae* as the deathbed rite.[12] In 858, however, when Bishop Herard of Tours drew on this capitulary for one of his own, he went further: "Those who become ill are to be reconciled without delay; they should receive the viaticum while still alive and they should not lack the benediction of sanctified oil."[13] In Herard's view, there was to be no hesitation; as soon as someone became ill (one assumes gravely), he or she was to be reconciled—

10. MGH, Concilia 3.173–74, c. 26: "Ab infirmis in mortis periculo positis per presbiteros pura inquirenda est confessio peccatorum, non tamen est illis imponenda quantitas penitentiae, sed innotescenda, et cum amicorum orationibus et elimosinarum studiis pondus penitentiae sublevandum, ut, si forte migraverint, ne obligati excommunicatione alieni ex consortio venie fiant. A quo periculo si divinitus erepti convaluerint, penitentiae modum a suo confessore impositum diligenter observent. Et ideo secundum canonicam auctoritatem, ne illis ianua pietatis clausa videatur, orationibus et consolationibus aecclesiasticis sacra cum unctione olei animati secundum statuta sanctorum patrum communione viatici reficiantur." See also W. Hartmann, "Die Mainzer Synoden des Hrabanus Maurus," in *Hrabanus Maurus: Lehrer, Abt und Bischof*, ed. R. Kottje and H. Zimmermann (Mainz, 1982), 130–44.

11. Cf. Angenendt, "Theologie und Liturgie," 165–66.

12. Troyes, Bibliothèque Publique, MS 1979; de Clercq, *Législation*, vol. 2 (Angers, 1958), 414: "Ut unctio olei infirmis iuxta apostoli preceptum tribuatur. Similiter et morientibus commendationem animae ecclesiastico more impendite."

13. PL 121.765–66: "Ut in infirmitate positi absque dilatione reconcilientur, et viaticum viventes accipiant, et benedictione sacrati olei non careant." On the use of the Troyes statutes by Herard, see de Clercq, *Législation*, 2.351.

that is, given penance—and anointed. The language makes it clear that these are preparations for death, not parts of a healing ritual.

These examples show that adjustments to the practice of anointing the sick were not confined to sacramentaries, such as Rodradus's book for Corbie. Efforts to maintain the reform rite of anointing the sick and to keep it separate from the rites for the dying, by then generally referred to as the *commendatio animae*, were losing ground to a general trend to include anointing within the structure of rites in preparation for death, along with confession and reconciliation. Indeed, the pressure in that direction was so strong that one text connects the anointing of the dying with the authority and prestige of Charlemagne. The apocryphal First Capitulary of Charlemagne, which may be the work of Benedict the Levite, compiler of the False Capitularies, makes this claim: "The dying should lack neither the unction of blessed oil, reconciliation, nor viaticum."[14] After the year 850, anointing, confession and reconciliation, and viaticum were beginning to define the ritual response to dying.

The growing attention given to the needs of the dying and the dead in Carolingian culture favored the use of anointing as a transformative and purificatory agent within rites in preparation for death. Against the tide of local religious practice the reformers had managed to erect legal precedents and new rites that sought to preserve a model of ritual healing inherited from the Roman church. But the disintegration of the unified administration of Pippin, Charles, and Louis entailed the failure of the long-term effects of their efforts. Individual provinces and dioceses had to make their own way in the wake of the civil strife of the 830s and early 840s, and with the shattering of the dream of unity sought at the great reform councils of the period 813–817, local traditions could assert themselves more vigorously than before. Under such circumstances, the situation observed at mid-century is perfectly understandable. The legislative texts show that in some places—Mainz, Reims, Tours—the development of the ritual process had gone so far by then that many clerics regarded anointing, along with confession, as a necessary prelude to death. The changes made to the Carolingian reform rite of anointing the sick in the

14. MGH, Capitularia 1.45, c. 10: "Similiter de infirmis et poenitentibus, ut morientes sine sacrati olei unctione et reconciliatione et viatico non deficiant." This so-called *Capitulare primum* of Charlemagne, dated 769, has long been regarded as a later fabrication, perhaps by Benedict; see Porter, "Origin," 50–51; de Clercq, *Législation*, 1.157–58.

sacramentary of Rodradus hint at this development but are far from explicit. A change in ritual form could not maintain itself until it had taken definitive shape in ritual books, for it was these books— the models for generations of scribes and practitioners—that provided the basis for the acts and the attitudes of the clerics who orchestrated Christian living and dying.

Experiment and Synthesis at St-Amand

The monastery of St-Amand, near Tournai, was founded in the seventh century on an endowment from the Merovingian king Dagobert.[15] By the middle of the ninth century it had become one of the most important abbeys of the Frankish realm, and its lands and dependencies could be found throughout present-day northeastern France and Belgium. Loyal to the West Frankish king, Charles the Bald, the abbots of St-Amand placed the considerable resources of the monastery's library and scriptorium at his disposal.[16] Thus it is that in the third quarter of the ninth century, no fewer than seven extant sacramentaries were produced at St-Amand, probably at the request of the court, for presentation as gifts to other communities.[17] The identification of these sacramentaries as the work of a single scriptorium provides a unique opportunity to observe in detail changes in the rituals around death and dying at a critical stage, for the St-Amand sacramentaries reveal the culmination of the process of ritual creation which had begun in the previous century. On the basis of the tentative chronology put forward by Deshusses,[18] it is apparent that, after a

15. Henri Leclercq, "Saint-Amand-Les-Eaux," DACL 15.462–82; Henri Platelle, *Le temporel de l'abbaye de Saint-Amand des origines à 1340* (Paris, 1962).

16. The reign of Charles the Bald has only recently begun to get the attention it deserves; see McKitterick, *Frankish Kingdoms*, chaps. 7–8; *Charles the Bald: Court and Kingdom*, ed. M. T. Gibson and J. T. Nelson, BAR International Series 101 (Oxford, 1981); and the collected essays of Janet Nelson in her *Politics and Ritual in Early Medieval Europe* (London and Ronceverte, 1986).

17. Jean Deshusses, "Chronologie des grands sacramentaires de Saint-Amand," RB 87 (1977): 230–37, and "Encore les sacramentaires de Saint-Amand," RB 89 (1979): 310–12; see also Wallace-Hadrill, *Frankish Church*, 244–52, and Rosamond McKitterick, "Charles the Bald (823–877) and His Library: The Patronage of Learning," *English Historical Review* 95 (1980): 28–47, esp. 42–46.

18. Deshusses, "Chronologie" and "Encore les sacramentaires." I have followed Deshusses's dating in all cases except the sacramentary of St-Denis, which Deshusses dates ca. 867, with some apprehensions ("Chronologie," 232–35). Although the precise dating of such manuscripts is notoriously difficult, dating it closer to 875 (as proposed by Bernhard Bischoff and followed by Sicard, *Liturgie*, 45n) is more in accordance with its presentation of the rituals in question (Table 2).

number of experiments, the liturgists of St-Amand succeeded in bringing together and synthesizing all the various streams of tradition into a coherent ritual complex whose activities stretched from grave illness through the agony to the postmortem ceremonies and burial. Their achievement, in one form or another, laid the foundation for the ritual response to death and dying for the rest of the Latin Middle Ages.

The Sacramentaries of Le Mans, Chelles, and Tournai

The remarkable series of sacramentaries from the scriptorium of St-Amand begins with a pure copy of the *Hadrianum*, with Benedict of Aniane's Supplement, created for Le Mans around 851.[19] If, as Deshusses suggests, this book represents the usage of St-Amand in mid-century, the abbey's liturgists did not remain happy with it for long. The next two books in the series, one produced for Chelles around 855 and the other for Tournai around 863, present a considerable change from the sacramentary of Le Mans.[20] The prefaces from the Supplement have been woven into the individual masses of the liturgical year; certain of the ritual additions in the Supplement, such as its baptismal ceremonies, have been inserted into the appropriate sections of the sacramentary; and much of the Supplement itself has been left out or replaced with other material.[21] This organization, however, had little effect on the presentation of rites for the sick, the dying, and the dead, which were left in the form given them by Benedict in the Supplement.[22]

19. Le Mans, Bibliothèque Municipale, MS 77. See Gregorian, 3.29 (MS J), for a description; Deshusses, "Chronologie," 234–35, for thoughts on the date and circumstances of production.

20. Chelles = New York, Pierpont Morgan Library, MS G 57; Gregorian, 3.36–37 (MS T1). Tournai = Leningrad, Publichnaia Biblioteka im. M. E. Saltykova-Shchredrina, MS lat. Q.v.I.41; Gregorian, 3.43–45 (MS T5). Cf. Deshusses, "Chronologie," 235.

21. Deshusses, "Chronologie," 231.

22. The only change made was the addition of Benedict's preface for the sick (Supplement, no. 1732) in the mass for the sick in the books for Chelles and Tournai. Deshusses's manuscript descriptions—Gregorian, 3.37, at fols. 147r–148r (Chelles), and 3.44, at fols. 184r–185r (Tournai)—need to be emended on two points here. The prayers for the visitation of the sick in these two manuscripts do not accord with his edition (3.148–49, no. 437), as indicated, but rather with Supplement, nos. 1386–91; and the prayer for the return of health (Supplement, no. 1395) follows the mass for the sick (= Supplement 1391–95 + 1732). See New York, Pierpont Morgan Library, MS G 57, fols. 147r–148v, and Antonio Staerk, *Les manuscrits latins du ve au xiie siècle conservés à la Bibliothèque Imperiale de Saint-Petersbourg*, vol. 1 (St. Petersburg, 1910), 123.

The Sacramentaries of St-Thierry and St-Germain

The next two sacramentaries in the series maintain the basic structure of the rituals for Chelles and Tournai, but introduce some new elements. The first of the pair was given to the monastery of St-Thierry around 869; the second to St-Germain-des-Prés around 875–876.[23] In these books, the general process of reorganization and enrichment was taken a step further than before. After the sacramentary proper the St-Thierry manuscript has a collection of extra prayers, prefaces, and benedictions for the masses of the liturgical year taken from eighth-century Gelasian books; the St-Germain manuscript weaves all of these elements into the corresponding section of the sacramentary, and new supplementary material has nearly doubled the size of the whole.[24] New material also appears in the rites for the sick, the dying, and the dead (Table 2).

The additions made to the stock of Benedict's Supplement in the sacramentaries of St-Thierry and St-Germain illustrate the same tendencies visible in contemporary decrees by bishops and councils. The rite of visitation of the sick in these books opens with the antiphon *Deus in adiutorium meum intende* (Ps. 69:2), which is followed by the first of the seven penitential psalms, Psalm 6, *Domine ne in furore tuo*.[25] There follow, as in the previous books, the prayers from the Supplement. Unlike their predecessors, however, these ritual books include an anointing. Although there is no indication that the St-Amand liturgists yet had access to a copy of Benedict of Aniane's reform rite of anointing, the wording of the formula and its clear separation from the deathbed reconciliation suggest support for the reform tradition of anointing the sick. The formula spoken during the anointing, although different from that in the reform rite of Benedict of Aniane, breathes its spirit: "God, omnipotent father of our lord Jesus Christ, have mercy on this your servant by the power of the Holy Spirit, and grant him remission of all his sins and recuperation from his threatening illness, through this holy anointing and our suppliant prayer."[26] The creators of the

23. St-Thierry = Reims, Bibliothèque Municipale, MS 213; Gregorian, 3.38–39 (MS T2). St-Germain = Paris, Bibliothèque Nationale, MS lat. 2291; Gregorian, 3.39–41 (MS T3). Dating and circumstances of production in Deshusses, "Chronologie," 235–36; but see his "Encore les sacramentaires," 310, where he revised the date of the second manuscript from ca. 871 to ca. 875–76.
24. Deshusses, "Chronologie," 231–32, and Gregorian 3.38–41.
25. Gregorian, 3.147; the edition refers only to Paris, MS 2291 (St-Germain), but the St-Thierry book contains the same ritual; cf. ibid., 38–40.
26. Gregorian, 3.131, no. 4005: "Deus omnipotens pater domini nostri iesu

Table 2. Experiment and synthesis in the sacramentaries of St-Amand,
ca. 851–ca. 877

Le Mans (ca. 851), Chelles (ca. 855), and Tournai (ca. 863)	St-Thierry (ca. 869) and St-Germain (ca. 875–876)	St-Denis (ca. 875)	Sens (ca. 876–877)
Sick visitation prayers (S)	Sick visitation prayers (S) + unction and introductory psalm	Sick visitation prayers (S) + unction	New rite for anointing, confession, and reconciliation of sick and dying
		Deathbed reconciliation (S)	
Mass for sick (S)	Mass for sick (S) Mass for dying	Masses for sick	Mass for sick (S) Mass for dying
Prayer for return of health (S)	Prayer for return of health (S)	Prayer for return of health (S)	
Deathbed reconciliation (S)	Deathbed reconciliation (S)		
Rite for death and burial (S)	Rite for death and burial (S)	Synthesis of Frankish rite for agony, Roman psalmody and rubrics, prayers for death and burial from S	Synthesis of Frankish rite for agony, Roman psalmody and rubrics, prayers for death and burial from S

S = Supplement.
SOURCE: *Le sacramentaire grégorien*, ed. Jean Deshusses, vol. 3 (Fribourg, 1982), 36–45.

St-Thierry and St-Germain books did not neglect the needs of the dying, however, for they introduced one other new item into the ritual complex—a mass specifically written for them.[27] The prayers of this mass, not surprisingly, make use of old Gallican concepts of spiritual medicine, which had always suggested their use in rites for the dying. "Omnipotent and eternal God, conserva-

---

christi, in uirtute spiritus sancti miserere huic famulo tuo, et tribue ei remissionem omnium peccatorum et recuperationem ab imminenti aegritudine, per hanc sanctam unctionem et nostram supplicem deprecationem."

27. Gregorian, 2.195–96, sec. 210, nos. 2794–97, *Pro infirmo qui proximus est morti;* I have been unable to find any sources for this mass, which may be a St-Amand composition.

tor of souls . . . we call upon you, Lord, to grant your cure to the soul of your servant . . . give her your heavenly grace, Lord, so that in the hour of death her soul, without stain of sin, may deserve to be returned by the hands of the holy angels to you, its own giver."[28] "Be present, Lord . . . receive this sacrifice which we offer to you for the soul of your servant lying on his pallet, seeking the health not of his body but of his soul."[29] "We pray that you have mercy on your servant, may the adversary not prevail against him in the hour of his death, but may he merit transit to life."[30] While bestowing new meaning on the Gallican lexicon of spiritual cure, this mass gives expression to the growing sense in the Frankish church that the power of the devil, from whom the soul was in grave danger at the critical moment of death, could be overcome by the power of communal prayer. Purified and aided by the prayers and masses offered for it, the soul of the moribund would escape the dangers of death and its immediate aftermath and return with the angels to its original home in heaven.

That, however, is the limit of the experimentation in these two sacramentaries. Their rites for death and burial remain unchanged from the earlier St-Amand sacramentaries and comprise simply the prayers and rubrics from Benedict of Aniane's Supplement to the *Hadrianum*.[31]

The Sacramentary of St-Denis

In 867, Charles the Bald appointed himself abbot of the monastery of St-Denis in Paris. As Deshusses surmises, that may have been the impetus for the creation of the next sacramentary, which came to St-Denis from the scriptorium of St-Amand.[32] It is so different from the other books in the series that Deshusses has

28. Gregorian, no. 2794: "Omnipotens sempiterne deus conseruator animarum . . . te inuocamus domine, ut medelam tuam conferre digneris in animam famuli tui . . . da ei domine gratiam tuam, ut in hora exitus illius de corpore, absque peccati macula, tibi datori proprio per manus sanctorum angelorum eius anima repraesentari mereatur."

29. Gregorian, no. 2795: "Adesto domine . . . suscipe hostiam quam tibi offerimus pro famulo tuo iacente in grabatto, salutem non corporis sed animae suae petenti. . . ."

30. Gregorian, no. 2796: "precamur, ut misereri digneris famulo tuo, ne praeualeat aduersus eum aduersarius in hora exitus illius de corpore, sed transitum habere mereatur ad uitam."

31. Cf. Gregorian, 3.40 and 3.175, and see Table 2.

32. Paris, Bibliothèque Nationale, MS lat. 2290; Gregorian, 3.34–35 (MS R); Deshusses, "Chronologie," 235. On my dating, see n. 18 above.

suggested that the monks of St-Denis supplied some of their own materials for incorporation in the final product.[33] If that is the case, then St-Denis is responsible for a considerable increase in the level of experimentation at St-Amand in regard to the rites for the dying and the dead. The rituals in the St-Denis book, like those in the previous sacramentaries, open with the prayers for the visitation of the sick in Benedict's Supplement. The sacramentary of St-Denis differs from its predecessors, however, in the use of the first part of the unction formula from St. Gall: "I anoint you with blessed oil in the name of the Lord, so that, in the manner of a warrior prepared through anointing for battle, you will be able to prevail over the aery hordes."[34] As in the St. Gall book, this formula introduces a tension into the visitation ritual. While the prayers speak of the health of the body along with the salvation of the soul, the anointing in this manner suggests not the return of physical health but the preparation of the sick person for death and the *migratio* to the other world through the realms of the demons of the air. This impression is strengthened by the arrangement of the rites, for the prayers immediately following the anointing comprise the deathbed reconciliation (Table 2). Then, rather oddly, come the masses for the sick and the traditional prayer for the return of health. This is not the most satisfactory arrangement, but the tendency is clear. The monks of St-Denis were experimenting with ways to bring the act of anointing together with the reconciliation as a ritual preparation for death.

The second innovation in the St-Denis sacramentary involves the prayers and actions accompanying death and burial. We have seen how the existence of manuscripts of both Gelasian and Gregorian sacramentaries in the first half of the ninth century guaranteed that different ritual traditions circulated in the Frankish realm. The eighth-century Gelasians, on the one hand, transmitted many old Gallican prayers, and in some cases a new rite for the agony and/or some of the psalms and rubrics of the old Roman *ordo defunctorum*. The Gregorian books, on the other hand, usually carried Benedict's prayers for death and burial in the Supplement. The tendency to reorganize liturgical books already apparent in the treatment given to the sacramentaries of Chelles and Tournai by the liturgists of St-Amand had the effect of bringing these

33. Deshusses, "Chronologie," 233.
34. Gregorian, 3.147, no. 4002; cf. above, chap. 3.

two traditions into direct contact. The result was synthesis. The Frankish *commendatio animae* was used to introduce the prayers in the Supplement, which were themselves woven together with the psalmody and rubrics of the Roman *ordo*. The earliest example of such a synthesis is the sacramentary of St-Denis (Ritual 8).[35]

The rites for death and burial in the St-Denis sacramentary follow the masses for the sick and the prayer for the return of health. The initial rubric immediately establishes both the communal and the penitential nature of the ritual action: when a person is known to be at death's door, monks or others of the faithful should take pains to get to the bedside and immediately begin singing the seven penitential psalms.[36] The psalms are to be followed by a litany, during which it is hoped that the dying person will pass away.[37] Like earlier Frankish rituals that used the old Roman *ordo*, the rite in St-Denis lacks the Roman rubrics directing the reception of the viaticum and the reading of the Passion of Christ. It also lacks the chant prayers of the eighth-century Gelasians—the *Proficiscere* and *Libera*—but the litany performed the same service and had the same effect. The assembled persons called upon the saints in heaven to attend to the death of their brother or sister. Like the rites of anointing and reconciliation, the rite for the agony acted both to separate the dying person from the community of the living and to aid in effecting the incorporation of the soul in the community of the dead.

The immediate response to death in the St-Denis book is the antiphon-psalm chant from the old Roman *ordo* followed by the prayer of commendation that Benedict used to end his ritual in the Supplement. In addition there is a new prayer that concentrates on aid to the soul on its journey to the other world. Built from pieces

35. Sicard (*Liturgie*, 44–49) called this ritual "un *ordo* gallican de la mort." He treated it, however, only to contrast its prescriptions for the agony with those of the Roman *ordo*. What he missed is that, though it omits the first three rubrics of the Roman *ordo*—which guide the ritual action before death—it nevertheless retains much of the psalmody of the old Roman rite.

36. MS Paris, B.N. lat. 2290, fol. 160r; Gregorian, 3.171: "Cum anima in agone sui exitus dissolutione corporis sui uisa fuerit laborare, conuenire studebunt fratres uel ceteri quique fideles. Et canendi sunt vii paenitentiac psalmi."

37. The first rubric continues, after prescribing the psalms: "atque agenda est laetania prout permiserit ratio temporis, et secundum quod in causa egressuri perspici poterit uel aestimari." The St-Denis ritual provides for cases in which death does not occur during the litany: "Si autem quiddam superuixerit canantur alii psalmi uel agatur laetania usquequo anima terrenae corruptionis absoluatur" (MS fol. 161r; Gregorian, 3.172).

Ritual 8. Rites for death and burial in the St-Denis sacramentary

When a soul in the dissolution from its body is seen to labor in the death agony, the brothers and any others of the faithful will make every effort to attend. And they should sing the seven penitential psalms and the litany as time allows, in accordance with the estimated time of death. At the end of the litany, after the words "we beseech you to deign to lead us to eternal joy," they add, for the one who is dying, "we beseech you to deign to grant to this our brother returning to you from Egyptian captivity a place of light and refreshment and perpetual beatitude." As soon as the litany is finished, all should begin the response *Subuenite sancti dei* [OR]. When they finish, a priest says this prayer or commendation for him.

Prayer	Tibi domine commendamus	[Supplement 1415]
Prayer	Misericordiam tuam domine	[new]

If, however, the person should continue to live, they should sing the other seven psalms and a litany until the soul is freed from earthly corruption. As the soul leaves the body, they intone the antiphon *Suscipiat te christus qui te uocauit, et in sinum abrahae angeli deducant te* [OR] and the psalm *In exitu israhel de aegypto* [113] [OR].

Prayer	Omnipotens sempiterne deus qui	[new]
Antiphon	Chorus angelorum te suscipiat	[OR]
Psalms	Dilexi quoniam—Beati [114–18]	[OR, new]
Prayer	Diri uulneris nouitate	[Gelasian 1608]

Then the priest should pray and ask the others to pray for him:

Et ne nos inducas in tentationem. Requiem aeternam dona ei domine. Anima eius in bonis demorabitur. Et non intres in iudicium. A porta inferi.

Prayer	Partem beatae resurrectionis	[new]
Prayer	Deus cui soli competit	[Verona 1147]

Then the body of the dead person is washed. Prayer after the body is washed before it is removed from the house:

Prayer	Suscipe domine animam serui tui	[Supplement 1400]

Then, accompanied by the response *Subuenite sancti dei* [OR] and other responses of the dead, the body is carried in procession. When they near the church Psalm 50 is sung with the antiphon *Requiem aeternam* [Rheinau]. The body is laid in the church until a mass for his soul is sung. And it should be offered by all who wish to participate. After the celebration of the mass, a priest stands next to the bier and says this prayer:

Prayer	Non intres in iudicium	[Supplement 1401]
Response	Subuenite sancti dei	[OR]
Verse	Chorus angelorum	[OR]
	Kyrie eleison	
Prayer	Deus cui omnia uiuunt	[Supplement 1399]
Response	Antequam nascerer nouisti me	[new]
Verse	Commissa mea pauesco	[new]
	Kyrie eleison	
Prayer	Fac quaesumus	[Supplement 1402]

Ritual 8. (Continued)

Then the priest asks the others to pray for him.

Et ne nos inducas in tentationem. Requiem aeternam. A porta inferi.

Prayer   Inclina domine aurem tuam   [Supplement 1403]

And then the body is carried from the church accompanied by the antiphon *Aperite mihi portas iustitiae* [OR] and Psalm 117, *Confitemini* [OR], and carried to the grave.

Prayers at the grave:
Prayer	Pio recordationis affectu	[Supplement 1398]
Antiphon	Ingrediar in locum tabernaculi	[Rheinau]
Psalm	Quemadmodum [41]	[OR, Rheinau]
Prayer	Obsecramus	[Supplement 1409]
Antiphon	Haec requies mea	[new]
Psalm	Memento domine dauid [131]	[new]
Prayer	Deus apud quem mortuorum	[Supplement 1410]
Antiphon	De terra plasmasti me	[OR]
Psalm	Domine probasti me [138]	[new]

And the body of the dead person is placed in the grave.

Prayers after burial: [Supplement 1411–12, 1407–8
                                         (Gregorian 4074), 1414, 1413]

Then the priest asks the priests to pray for him, and he says each of the prayers as above.

Partem beatae resurrectionis. Requiem aeternam. Psalm [50], Miserere mei.

Prayer   Absolue domine   [Supplement 1404]

OR = Roman *ordo.*
SOURCES: *Le sacramentaire grégorien,* ed. Jean Deshusses, vol. 3 (Fribourg, 1982), 171–75; Paris, Bibliothèque Nationale, MS 2290, fols. 160r–166v.

of many earlier prayers, it evokes a picture of the afterlife which recalls the images and cadences of the oldest Gallican responses to death. After the petitioners admit their unworthiness on account of their own sins, they beg God to receive the soul of the dead person.

Let Michael, the angel of your testament, be present with the soul of your servant, and through the hands of your holy angels, deign to gather it up among the saints and the elect in the bosoms of your patriarchs Abraham, Isaac, and Jacob, freed from the princes of darkness and the places of punishment, so that it be confounded by no errors of its first birth, whether of ignorance, weakness, or its own iniquity, but rather may it be acknowledged by yours and enjoy to the fullest the peace of holy beatitude, so that when the great day of judgment comes, revived among your saints and elect, it may be sated forever in the glory of your vision now made known.[38]

This prayer is noteworthy for its vivid evocation of the *migratio* as well as for the evidence it gives of the tenacity of ancient conceptions regarding the after-death state. Its presence in the new ritual reveals a conscious concern to keep alive older Gallican attitudes toward death, especially in the face of the prayers of Benedict of Aniane, in which the old images were considerably pared down.[39] After a Roman antiphon and psalm, now extended into a group of five psalms, the St-Denis rite returns the old Gallican prayer *Diri uulneris*, with its supplications for the forgiveness of the sins of the deceased and the purification of his soul, to the place it held in the pre-Anianian sacramentaries.[40] This prayer is followed by a brief entreaty for eternal life, and a prayer from one of the masses for the dead in the Verona sacramentary which conforms to the old Gallican understanding of spiritual medicine: "God who alone is competent to offer medicine after death, grant, we beseech you, that the soul of your servant N., stripped of earthly contagion, be numbered among the lot of your redemption."[41]

This portion of the ritual stands directly in the Frankish Gela-

---

38. MS fols. 160v–161r; Gregorian, no. 4071: "Misericordiam tuam domine . . . rogare pro aliis cogimur, qui pro nostris supplicare peccatis nequaquam sufficimus. . . . Adsit ei angelus testamenti tui michahel, et per manus sanctorum angelorum tuorum inter sanctos et electos tuos in sinibus abrahae isaac et iacob patriarcharum tuorum eam collocare digneris, quatinus liberata de principibus tenebrarum et de locis poenarum, nullis iam primae natiuitatis uel ignorantiae aut propriae iniquitatis seu fragilitatis confundatur erroribus, sed potius agnoscatur a tuis, et sanctae beatitudinis requie perfruatur, ut cum magni iudicii dies aduenerit, inter sanctos et electos tuos resuscitatus gloria manifestate contemplationis tuae perpetuo satietur." Cf. this prayer with the *Te domine* (above, chap. 2) in the rite of Caesarius of Arles, and those in the Bobbio Missal (no. 539), the Vatican Gelasian (nos. 1617, 1621), and the eighth-century Gelasians (Gellone, no. 2914, and Autun, no. 1923).

39. This concern is also apparent in the prayer in response to death after the second litany, which reuses the old *Suscipe* prayer (Gelasian, no. 1610), ignored by Benedict, with a new beginning presenting the soul as the breath and image of God, which returns to its maker when the flesh has reverted to dust; MS fol. 161r and Gregorian, no. 4077: "Omnipotens sempiterne deus qui humano corpori animam ad similitudinem tuam inspirare dignatus es, dum te iubente puluis in puluerem reuertitur, tu imaginem tuam cum sanctis et electis tuis, aeternis sedibus praecipias sociari."

40. MS fol. 161v; Gregorian, no. 4059. Cf. Gelasian, no. 1608; Gellone, no. 2901; and Autun, no. 1924.

41. MS fol. 162r; Gregorian, no. 4073: "Deus cui soli competit medicinam praestare post mortem, praesta quaesumus ut anima famuli tui *illius* terrenis exuta contagiis, in tuae redemptionis parte numeretur."

sian tradition. It ignores the antemortem portions of the Roman
ordo; it uses communal chant as an aid to the dying in the same
manner as the eighth-century Gelasians; and it returns to the imagery and flavor of the old Gallican prayers in response to death,
while rejecting all of Benedict of Aniane's prayers for that moment
in the ritual process. The remainder of the service alternates
psalmody from the Roman *ordo* (or modeled on it) with the prayers
from Benedict's Supplement.[42] After the corpse was washed, it was
to be carried in procession to the church to the accompaniment of
Psalm 50 and the antiphon *Requiem aeternam*. While the body
was present in the church, a mass was to be said, after which the
priest recited a number of Benedict's prayers with accompanying
psalmody. After a procession to the grave, Benedict's prayers for
that moment in the ritual were recited. The rest of the prayers from
the Supplement were recited at the grave after the burial. The
ritual ended with a repetition of Psalm 50 with its antiphon and a
short petition originally from the *Hadrianum*, "Absolve, Lord, the
soul of your servant from all the chains of sin and let him draw
breath again in the glory of the resurrection resuscitated among
your saints."[43]

The Sacramentary of Sens

The liturgical products of St-Amand between 850 and 875 point
up the need to resolve the state of tension among the differing
approaches to sickness, death, and dying which had emerged during the preceding three centuries. Although there had long been a
tendency to associate rites of penance and anointing with the
prayers and acts accompanying death and burial, no unambiguous
ritual complex containing them had emerged. The impulse toward
synthesis evident in the late eighth-century Gelasian books had
been sidetracked by the work of Benedict of Aniane. Since Benedict's time, liturgists had had to deal with the merging of Gregorian and Gelasian ritual books. At St-Amand we can see this
work proceeding in stages during the third quarter of the century.
By 875, the creators of the sacramentary of St-Denis had synthe-

---

42. The apparatus in Sicard, *Liturgie,* establishes the St-Denis sacramentary as
the oldest witness to those antiphons and psalms identified as [new] in Ritual 8; see
Sicard's index on pp. 419–20.

43. MS fol. 166v; Gregorian, no. 4035 (= Hadrianum, no. 1016): "Absolue
domine animam famuli tui *illius*, ab omni uinculo delictorum, ut in resurrectionis
gloria, inter sanctos tuos resuscitatus respiret."

sized the Frankish rite for the agony with the prayers of Benedict's Supplement and the psalmody of the old Roman *ordo*, but without resolving the precise place of anointing and penance in the rites of preparation for death.

The last of the great sacramentaries of St-Amand, a book that may have been given to Ansegisus, archbishop of Sens in 877, represents the culmination of this process of ritual development and the resolution of all of these problems. The sacramentary of Sens contains a complete ritual complex for death comprising a form of the unction rite of Benedict of Aniane, altered to make it appropriate as a purificatory ritual for the dying; a mass for the sick and a mass for the dying; and the death and burial rite that first appeared in the St-Denis sacramentary.[44] In presenting such a ritual complex, the St-Amand liturgists managed to stay within the letter of the law of the reform decrees while definitively creating a place for anointing within the larger structure of rites in preparation for death. The result was the beginning of a ritual tradition in the Latin West for the final illness, death, and burial of a Christian within a cohesive sequence of prayers and gestures. Along with the confraternity system and the general extension of commemorative practices to the whole Christian community, this ritual complex became the foundation of all later rituals of death, dying, and the dead in medieval Europe. The structure of the whole is seen in Table 2. The directions and prayers for death and burial are those of the St-Denis sacramentary (Ritual 8). Ritual 9 presents the innovative reworking of Benedict of Aniane's anointing ritual for use with the dying.

The basis for the ritual of anointing in the sacramentary of Sens is clearly the reform rite devised by Benedict of Aniane which first appeared in the sacramentary of Rodradus (Ritual 7). As we have seen, even in the Rodradus book, the ritual had undergone some changes since its creation. The changes here are more extensive and more revealing. What was a rite of ritual healing, directed at the restoration of physical health, has become primarily a rite of penance and spiritual purification. The rubric that precedes the

---

44. Stockholm, Kungliga Biblioteket, Holm. A136, fols. 197r–212v. For a description of this manuscript, see Gregorian, 3.41–43 (MS T4); for the date and circumstances of its origin, see Deshusses, "Chronologie," 236, and "Encore les sacramentaires," 310. The discovery of pages from another sacramentary from St-Amand in the Huntington Library in San Marino, Calif., shows that the activity of the scriptorium was not limited to the manuscripts that have come down to us (Deshusses, "Encore les sacramentaires," 310–12).

Ritual 9. Rites for the dying or sick in the sacramentary of Sens

Before the sick person is anointed he should confess wholly to God and his priest purely all his sins, and he should receive complete reconciliation from him, so that with the ulcers of his vices first opened through confession the spiritual anointing may more suitably aid him by correcting the putrescence of sin lying deep within.

Rite for visiting and anointing the sick

As the priests enter the house of the sick person they should sing the seven penitential psalms with the litany presented below.

Litany	Parce domine parce populo tuo	[St-Denis]
Prayer	Omnipotens mitissime deus respice	[new]
Prayer	Deus qui illuminas omnem hominem	[new]
Prayer	Dimitte domine peccata nostra	[new]

After finishing these the priest-confessor should ask the other priests to say these prayers over him, namely, the reconciliation of penitents at death:

Prayer	Deus misericors deus clemens	[St-Denis]
Prayer	Maiestatem tuam domine	[St-Denis]
Prayer	Maiestatem tuam quaesumus	[St-Denis]

Next, making holy water mixed with salt, they sprinkle it over the sick person and the house to the accompaniment of an antiphon and prayers. Then the priest says this prayer:

Prayer	Domine deus qui per apostolum tuum	[Rodradus]

And the person who is sick genuflects and stands to the right of the priest, and the following antiphon is sung:

Antiphon	Sana domine infirmum istum	[Rodradus]
Psalm	Domine ne in furore tuo II [37]	
Prayer	Oremus dominum nostrum	[Rodradus]
Antiphon	Dominus locutus est	[Rodradus]
Prayer	Deus qui famulo tuo	[Rodradus]
Antiphon	Cor contritum	[new]
Prayer	Respice domine	[Supplement]
Antiphon	Succurre domine	[Rodradus]
Prayer	Adesto domine	[Supplement]

And the priests should each anoint the sick person with the blessed oil, making the sign of the cross on the neck, and throat, and chest, and between the shoulders, and on the five corporeal senses, on the eyebrows, on the ears inside and out, on the end of or within the nostrils, on the outside of the lips, and similarly on the outside of the hands, so that the stains that have in any way adhered through the five senses of the mind and body by the fragility of the flesh of the body, these may be cast out by the spiritual medicine and the mercy of the Lord. While the officiating priest anoints the sick person the others say these prayers carefully.

Vnguo te oleo sanctificato	[St-Denis]
In nomine patris et filii	

(Continued)

Ritual 9. (Continued)

Vnguo to oleo sancto inuocata	[Rodradus]
Vnguo te oleo sancto in nomine	
Deus omnipotens pater domini nostri	[St-Thierry/St-Germain]

After the sick person has been anointed, these prayers are recited by the attendant priests.

Domine iesu christe qui es saluatio	[Rodradus]
Propitietur	[Rodradus]
Deus qui facturae tuae	[Supplement]
Deus qui humano generi	[Supplement]
Virtutum caelestium deus	[Supplement]
Domine sancte pater	[Supplement]

Then the sick person should receive communion with the body and the blood of the Lord, and the rite should be repeated for seven days if necessary, both the communion and the other service, and the Lord in his clemency will restore him to health, and if he has sinned, his sins will be forgiven, as the apostle says. The priests and the ministers of the holy church of God should sing each day vespers and matins for the sick person with all reverence with the hymn *christe caelestis medicina* and the rest, namely, the antiphons and responses as well as the lessons and prayers that pertain to these offices.

Prayer in consummation of this office:

Omnipotens sempiterne deus qui subuenis	[Rodradus]
Domine sancte pater omnipotens aeterne deus	[Supplement]

When those are finished the priests say these benedictions over the sick person, each doing one. If, however, a bishop is present, this will be his duty. [Five benedictions.]

SOURCES: Stockholm, Kungliga Biblioteket, MS Holm. A136, fols. 197r–212v; *Le sacramentaire grégorien,* ed. Jean Deshusses, vol. 3 (Fribourg, 1982), 148–49.

ritual proper betrays a completely spiritualized understanding of the anointing, one that represents the ritual activity in the language of a surgical procedure for the cure of the soul. With the wounds of sin opened by confession, the oil of anointing can seep deep within to cleanse and purify the soul of the recipient.[45] The penitential theme struck here is present from the very start of the ritual action, which begins in exactly the same manner as the

45. Stockholm, Kungliga Biblioteket, MS Holm. A136, fol. 197r; Gregorian, 3.148: "Antequam unguatur infirmus confiteatur omnimodis deo et sacerdoti suo puriter omnia peccata sua, et reconciliationem ab eo percipiat plenam, ut ulceribus uitiorum per confessionem prius adapertis dignius proficiat et unctio spiritalis medendo nequitiarum putredinem interius latitantem."

deathbed ritual in the St-Denis sacramentary, with the seven penitential psalms and a litany.[46]

The most striking aspect of the anointing ritual is the presence
within it of the deathbed reconciliation. The reconciliation is preceded by three prayers derived from material added to Gregorians
during the ninth century. The first two are from one of Alcuin's
votive masses, "requesting the grace of the holy spirit."[47] The last
is from a mass "for those in trouble or undergoing pressure."[48]
They are calls to God to free the heart of the recipient from evil
thoughts, to illuminate it, and to forgive the dying person's sins.
These prayers introduce the three from the St-Denis sacramentary
for the deathbed reconciliation.[49] Whether or not the recipient is
nearing death or merely sick, this ritual will prepare him or her for
death. Anointing and deathbed penance have been assimilated into
one ritual structure.

After the reconciliation, the prayers and directions of Benedict of
Aniane's reform rite of anointing begin.[50] Consequently, the remainder of the ritual unfolds along two parallel lines. The prayers
and anointing formulas from the reform tradition maintain their
emphasis on the return of physical health, while the more recent
additions and compositions express the exclusive desire for spiritual cleansing and the purification of the soul. Thus the anointing
ritual in the sacramentary of Sens could do double duty as a rite
either for the sick or for the dying. The intent of the authors of the
ritual was not to replace the anointing of the sick by an anointing
of the dying, but to adapt the former to the latter purpose. Thus the
original prayers and antiphons remain. The result is ambiguous,
but so must have been most prognoses in the ninth century. What

46. That the litany in Sens is the same as that called for in the St-Denis death
ritual is implied by the presence of the petition "Ut ad gaudia aeterna eum per-
ducere digneris te rogamus," after which, at St-Denis, a new petition was added, "Vt
huic fratri nostro de aegyptia captiuitate ad te reuertentem, locum refrigerii lucis-
que et perpetuae beatitudinis donare digneris, te rogamus." See Ritual 8. The sacramentary of Sens has two litanies, one for the anointing ritual and one during the
agony; in the second the new petition is present in the place called for in the St-
Denis manuscript. Cf. Gregorian, 3.139, 168.

47. Gregorian, 3.131, nos. 4006–7; cf. 2.126–27, *Missa ad postulandam gratiam
spiritus sancti*, nos. 2330, 2334.

48. Gregorian, 3.132, no. 4008; cf. 2.150, *Missa pro tribulantibus uel pressuram
sustinentibus*, no. 2451. Both this and the previous mass appear (elsewhere) in the
sacramentary of Rodradus.

49. MS fol. 200r–v; Gregorian, 3.148: "His ita expletis roget sacerdos confessor
infirmi alios sacerdotes ut dicant has orationes super ipsum quae sunt de reconciliatione paenitentis ad mortem."

50. Cf. Gregorian, 3.148 and 145–46.

is important here is the clear intention to provide the dying with the benefits of anointing.

I noted above that the rubric on the anointing in the sacramentary of Rodradus gave evidence of the confluence of two different understandings of the anointing—one emphasizing physical healing and the other the purification of the senses. The sacramentary of Sens expresses only the second of those understandings. The reference in the Rodradus book to anointing the place "where the pain is greatest" has been excised and replaced by what had previously been the gloss explaining that many priests anointed the five senses. The final phrase, "he will be healed by this medicine of God," has been altered to express a different view of anointing: "so that the stains that have in any way adhered through the five senses of the mind and body by the fragility of the flesh, these may be cast out by the spiritual medicine and the mercy of the Lord."[51] Understood in this way, anointing is a ritual of purification before death and part of a larger rite of separation.[52]

The rubric directing the anointing prescribes nine separate crosses made with oil and five different accompanying formulas.[53] The first was the same as that used at St-Denis: "I anoint you with sanctified oil in the name of the Lord, so that, in the manner of a warrior prepared through anointing for battle, you will prevail over the aery hordes"; the third is a variation of the formula in the sacramentary of Rodradus; and the last was taken over from the rite in the sacramentaries of St-Thierry and St-Germain. Though most of them speak only of spiritual healing, the last unequivocally refers to physical recovery. So do the prayers that complete the ritual, which were taken for the most part from the visitation of the sick in the Supplement.[54] After the prayers from Benedict's

51. MS fol. 201v; Gregorian, 3.149: "Et sic perunguant singuli sacerdotes infirmum de oleo sanctificato, facientes cruces in collum, et guttur, et pectus, et inter scapulas et super quinque sensus corporeos, et in supercilia oculorum, et in aures intus et foris et in narium summitatem siue interius et in labia exterius, et in manus similiter exterius id est de foris, ut maculae quae per quinque sensus mentis et corporis fragilitate carnis aliquo modo inhaeserunt, haec medicina spiritali et domini misericordia pellantur."

52. Note the emphasis on cleansing (*maculae* and *inhaeserunt*) and the same use of the old Gallican sense of *medicina* that appears in the some of the new prayers in the St-Denis rite for death and burial. On purification within rites of separation, cf. van Gennep, *Rites of Passage*, 164.

53. MS fol. 202r; Gregorian, 3.149.

54. The first prayer of the series is remarkable. It is the original form of the Visigothic prayer *Ihesu saluator noster*, which Benedict of Aniane rewrote for the anointing ritual. Benedict changed the typically Visigothic address *Ihesu Saluator*, but, as Porter noticed ("Origin," 219), instead of changing it to the Gallican form

rite, the old directive for communion and repetition of the rite for seven days is given as well as the full text of the hymn *Christe caelestis medicina patris.*

The presence of the various anointing formulas, the prayers from the Supplement, and the last rubric do not mean that the rite had not become a preparation for death, but illustrate the dual nature of the ritual. Although it makes the claim that God will cure the sick person within seven days, the structure and placement of the rite recommends its use not for the merely sick but especially for those in danger of death. This dual emphasis is reinforced by the two masses that follow the anointing and reconciliation. The first is a mass for the sick for whom a cure might be expected and the second is the mass for the dying which first appeared in the sacramentaries of St-Thierry and St-Germain.[55] Immediately following the anointing ritual in Sens is a copy of the synthetic rite for death and burial taken over from the sacramentary of St-Denis (Ritual 8).[56] In the absence of other prayers for death and dying in this sacramentary, the juxtaposition of these two rituals creates a complete ritual complex, extending from penance, reconciliation, anointing, and communion through the agony, the laying out of the corpse, the processions, vigil and mass, and burial.

Experiment and Synthesis at Lorsch

The abbey of St-Amand was not the only center of ritual experimentation in the third quarter of the ninth century; nor was it alone in achieving a solution to the problems created by the various ritual traditions around death and dying. In the East Frankish kingdom, at the monastery of Lorsch, a similar solution was found. Deriving in large part from different sources, the ritual at Lorsch maintained and transmitted its own synthesis of Roman, Gregorian-Anianian, and Frankish-Gelasian materials in a ritual structure that included anointing and penance as rites of preparation for death within a larger ritual sequence stretching from final illness to burial.

Domine Iesu, Benedict used *Domine Deus.* The sacramentary of Sens restores the original text of the Visigothic prayer, except for the address, which reads *Domine Iesu!* MS fol. 202v; Gregorian, 3.132–33, no. 4012.

55. MS fol. 204v–206v; Gregorian, 2.194–96, secs. 209, 210.
56. MS fols. 206v–212v; Gregorian, 3.171–75.

The monastery of Lorsch was established in 764 as a family foundation, but later became a royal abbey under the direct authority of the Frankish kings.[57] Situated just east of the Rhine and north of the Neckar, Lorsch lay at a major junction of routes to and across Germany. Its lands and dependencies grew throughout the late eighth and all of the ninth centuries, both by endowment and by planned colonization of the uplands of the Odenwald, to the east.[58] After the settlement among the sons of Louis the Pious, Lorsch maintained close ties with the East Frankish kings, especially Louis the German, who, along with his son Louis the Younger, was buried in the monastery's crypt. The scriptorium and library of Lorsch were among the finest in the Carolingian realm; here works of classical antiquity, both pagan and Christian, and contemporary history were copied and transmitted.[59] Yet the liturgical remains of Lorsch are not large. No complete sacramentaries or other liturgical books survive from its holdings, but a portion of the liturgy of Lorsch from the later ninth century has been preserved in a composite manuscript now in the Vatican, whose various pieces were written at Lorsch between 860 and 875.[60] This manuscript in its present form is a carefully constructed book put together at Lorsch near the end of the century as a manual for the instruction of priests.[61] It provides well-edited versions of important early ninth-century episcopal capitularies (by Theodulf of Orléans, Gerbald and Waltcaud of Liège); basic canonical texts on clerical life and responsibilities (the Nicene and "Apostolic" canons); a number of important penitentials (attributed to or associated with Egbert, Bede, Cummean, and Theodore); poetic, expository, and lexigraphical guides to the computus, the rites of baptism, and the mass; and prayers and rubrics for a complete ritual order for sickness, death, and burial.

57. The best source for information on Lorsch is *Die Reichsabtei Lorsch: Festschrift zum Gedanken an ihre Stiftung 764*, ed. Friedrich Knöpp, 2 vols. (Darmstadt, 1973, 1977).

58. H.-J. Nitz, "The Church as Colonist: The Benedictine Abbey of Lorsch and Planned Waldhufen Colonisation in the Odenwald," *Journal of Historical Geography* 9 (1983): 105–26.

59. Bernhard Bischoff, "Lorsch im Spiegel seiner Handschriften," *Reichsabtei Lorsch*, 2.7–127; Wallace–Hadrill, *Frankish Church*, 338–40.

60. Vatican, MS Pal. lat. 485; CLLA, 1582; on the dating see Bischoff, "Lorsch im Spiegel seiner Handschriften," 46–47; and Frederick S. Paxton, "Bonus liber: A Late Carolingian Clerical Manual from Lorsch (Bibliotheca Vaticana Pal. lat. 485)," in *The Two Laws: Studies in Medieval Legal History Dedicated to Stephan Kuttner*, ed. Laurent Mayali and Stephanie A. J. Tibbetts, Studies in Medieval and Early Modern Canon Law 1 (Washington, D.C., 1990), 1–30.

61. Paxton, "Bonus liber."

Historians of the medieval liturgy have independently published and commented on the anointing rituals and the rite for death and burial in the Lorsch manuscript, but it is only when the Lorsch rituals are viewed in their entirety and against the background of ritual developments in the Frankish lands over the preceding 135 years that their originality and significance stand out.[62] Working from different sources, yet exhibiting the same freedom and experimentation apparent in the contemporary products of the scriptorium of St-Amand, the monks of Lorsch devised their own solutions to the conflicting tendencies around rites of anointing and to the competing traditions around the prayers and obsequies for the dead. They devised two separate anointing rituals, one for the sick and another for the dying, and they successfully brought together the prayers for death and burial in the Supplement with the rubrics and psalmody of the old Roman *ordo defunctorum*.

The ritual material in the Lorsch manuscript fills three quires in the middle of the book (Ritual 10).[63] Quire 8 is devoted to baptismal rituals, especially the baptism of the sick. After the prayers for the blessing of the paschal candles with which the Supplement of Benedict of Aniane begins, an inscription identifies the source for what follows as the authentic sacramentary of Pope Gregory.[64] Some such inscription came at the head of most of the mixed Gregorian sacramentaries of the later ninth century, although they were increasingly a mixture of Gregorian and non-Gregorian elements. Such is the case for what follows. While much of it comes from the *Hadrianum* and its Supplement, just as much does not. Quire 9 contains the complete ritual synthesis in which we are primarily interested. The short quire 10 adds the rite of purification of the home from the Supplement, which had come to be associated with the visitation of the sick.[65]

There are three separate anointing rituals in the Lorsch manual.

---

62. Carlo de Clercq, "'Ordines unctionis infirmi' des ixe et xe siècles," EL 44 (1930): 100–122, published the rites for the visitation and anointing of the sick on fols. 53v–54r, 55v–56v, and 58r–58v. Sicard (*Liturgie,* 22–25) has published the rites for death and burial; cf. Frank, "Älteste erhaltene *ordo defunctorum,*" 379–81. None of these authors, however, looked at the manuscript as a whole and so missed the significance of the placement and interdependence of the rites. Although the same prayers appear in the two anointing rituals on fols. 53v–54r and 58r–58v, they differ in the manner in which they are presented. Both could be preparations for death, but the second is explicitly presented as such.

63. Paxton, "Bonus liber," 15–18.

64. Vatican, MS Pal. lat. 485, fol. 49r: "Ex authentico libro sacramentorum sancti Gregorii papae urbis rome."

65. Supplement, nos. 1451–56.

Ritual 10. Rites for the sick, dying, and dead in Vatican MS Pal. lat. 485

Quire and folio nos.	Rite	Source
Quire 8		
48r–49r	Blessing of candles	Supplement
49r–50r	Baptism of sick	*Hadrianum*
50v–53v	Benedictions	Various sources
53v–54r	Anointing of sick	Irish rites
54r–54v	Prayers for persons possessed by demons	Supplement
54v–55r	Imposition of hands on catechumens	Supplement
55r	Deathbed reconciliation prayers	Supplement
	Prayers for serenity, against storms, and over a barn	Various sources
55v	*Oratio super infirmum* from fol. 54r	Irish rites
	Blessings	
Quire 9*		
55v–56v	Visitation, confession, and anointing of sick	New
56v–57r	Deathbed reconciliation prayers	Supplement
57r–58r	Mass for the sick, with readings	Frankish Gelasians
58r–58v	Anointing of dying	Anointing rite in quire 8
58v–61r	Synthesis: Rubrics and psalmody	Roman *ordo*
	Prayers for death and burial	Supplement
Quire 10		
62r–63v	Purification and blessing of a home	Supplement

*Quire 9 begins on 56r, but the change of hand and the beginning of the ritual complex begins on the reverse of the last folio of quire 8.
SOURCE: Vatican, MS Pal. lat. 485.

The first is in quire 8, on folios 53v–54r, and may originally have been inscribed in the context of the collection of baptismal rites for the sick. It is a short ritual with a bidding, a petitional prayer, a credo to be spoken by the sick person, anointing, confession, the giving of the pax, and communion.[66] Both the structure and the prayers of the ritual are derived from Irish sources, and the whole most resembles the rituals in the Book of Mulling and the Book of Deer. Like those rituals, the one in Lorsch uses often ambiguous images and language that direct the emphasis both toward physical healing and toward purification and preparation for eternal life. The opening bidding begs God to cure the sick person with "celes-

66. Cf. de Clercq, "'Ordines unctionis infirmi,'" 102–4.

tial medicines," so that "he who gives the soul may also give health."[67] The second asks God to "conserve this your servant whom you brought to life and redeemed by the great price of your son's blood."[68] The formulas for anointing and communion look to eternal life and salvation: "I anoint you with sanctified oil in the name of the holy Trinity so that you may be saved [*saluus*] for all time. May the peace and communion of the body and blood of our lord Jesus Christ preserve your soul unto eternal life."[69] The final prayer, which recalls the miracle by which Peter brought the child Tabitha back to life, appears elsewhere only in an early ninth-century manuscript from Verona, and seems to express a desire for the return of physical health.[70] In the context of the other prayers, however, Peter's miracle has the character more of a type of the resurrection than of a miraculous healing.

The material in quire 8 is in a rather haphazard state. The rites do not appear in any clear order; important rubrics have not been filled in; and material is repeated. Unlike the rest of the manuscript, which is rather polished, quire 8 has the quality of a liturgical worksheet rather than a definitive collection of rituals. That impression disappears, however, on the reverse of the last folio of quire 8, where, in the finest hand of the manuscript, with extensive rubrics inscribed in carefully executed uncials, a full ritual order for sickness, death, and burial begins. This ritual complex fills the whole of quire 9 except for part of the last folio, which was left

67. MS fol. 53v; cf. de Clercq, "'Ordines unctionis infirmi,'" 102: "Oremus fratres dominum nostrum pro fratre nostro quem dure ad praesens malum languoris adfligit ut eum domini pietas caelestibus dignetur curare medicinis, qui dedit animam det et salutem."

68. MS fol. 53v; cf. de Clercq, "'Ordines unctionis infirmi,'" 102: "Domine sancte, pater omnipotens, aeterne deus, qui es via, et veritas, et vita, exaudi et conserua famulum tuum hunc quem uiuificasti et redemisti pretio magno sancti sanguinis filii tui."

69. MS fols. 53v–54r; cf. de Clercq, "'Ordines unctionis infirmi,'" 103: "Ungueo te oleo sanctificato in nomine sanctae trinitatis ut saluus sis in perpetuum. . . . Pax et communicatio corporis et sanguinis domini nostri ihesu christi conservet animam tuam in uitam aeternam."

70. MS fol. 54r; cf. de Clercq, "'Ordines unctionis infirmi,'" 104: "Deus qui beatum petrum apostolum tuum misisti ad thabitam famulam tuam ut eius precibus resuscitaretur ad uitam, exaudi nos pro famulo tuo quem in tuo nemine [*sic*] uisitat nostra fragilitas ut exorata medicina tuae medele subueniat." The Verona manuscript is discussed in chap. 4. This prayer is repeated at the end of the quire followed by a series of blessings similar to the *benedictio hominis* preceding the anointing in the book of Mulling. Cf. MS fol. 55v, "Sanat te deus pater qui te creauit. Sanat te iesus christus qui pro te passus est. Sanat te spiritus sanctus qui in te effusus est. . . . Benedicat te dominus. Custodiat te Christus. Ostendatque dominus faciem suam et misereatur tui," and Warren, *Liturgy and Ritual*, 172 (Mulling).

blank. The sequence of rites begins with a new visitation ritual.
The new visitation, while showing no trace of Benedict of Anianc's
reform rite of anointing, nevertheless conforms to conciliar demands for a rite of anointing the sick and is built around the structure of Irish rituals of anointing and the prayers for the sick in
Benedict's Supplement. It opens with the old prayer *Deus qui facturae tuae,* which Benedict took from the Gelasian tradition.[71]
Next the recipient was to make a confession, after which the visitors sang Psalm 53 with the antiphon *In veritate tua exaudi me
domine* (Ps. 142:1) and the sick person recited the Lord's Prayer and
a series of verses from the psalms.[72] Then come two prayers from
the Supplement and the anointing:

> After this the holy unction is applied with the extended right hand,
> first on the chest and above the heart, then between the shoulders,
> and then in the shape of a cross in the place of greatest pain, while the
> priest says, "I anoint you with divinely sanctified oil, allotted to us as
> a celestial gift, in the name of the holy and undivided Trinity, so that
> [the Trinity] which holds its whole creation lest it perish may by
> healing you within and without give you life."[73]

The rite ends with a slightly rewritten prayer from the Irish rite
and six prayers from the Supplement.[74] This is a pure visitation
ritual not meant in any way for the dying. The confession is not a
prelude to deathbed reconciliation, but simple private confession.
There is no communion and the anointing is directed to the place
of greatest pain.

But there is another anointing ritual in this ritual sequence.
After the prayers for deathbed reconciliation and a mass for the
sick, the anointing ritual from quire 8 is repeated, but with the

---

71. MS fol. 55v; Gelasian, no. 1535. The prayer also appears in Stowe and Dimma: Stowe, 34; Warren, *Liturgy and Ritual,* 168 (Dimma).

72. MS fol. 55v: "Tunc detur locus secretior confitendi. Inde post acceptam
paenitentiam et fidem explicatam redeant uisitantes et incipiant psalmum . . . cum
antiphona. . . . Tunc finita oratione dominica cum his uersibus."

73. MS fol. 56r; Supplement, nos. 1386, 1393, followed by: "Post hec sancta
adponatur unctio dextera sacerdotis palma extensa: primum in pectore et cordis
loco, inde et inter scapulas, indeque in modum crucis in loco maximi doloris et sic
dicendo incipiat: Ungueo te oleo diuinitus sanctificato caelesti munere nobis
adtributo, in nomine sanctae et indiuiduae trinitatis, ut ipsa te interius exteriusque
sanando uiuificet quae uniuersam conditionem suam ne pereat continet."

74. MS fol. 56r–v: "Domine sancte pater omnipotens aeterne deus qui es via,
veritas et vita exaudi et conserua hunc famulum tuum quem pretio magno redi-
mendo uiuificasti sacro sanguine filii tui" (cf. above, n. 68); and Supplement, nos.
1473, 1480, 1387, 1389–91.

rubric "Prayers and requests over a sick person before death."[75] With this introduction the prayers and actions of the ritual shed any ambiguity. They are meant as a preparation for death. The liturgists at Lorsch had found another elegant solution to the alternate understandings of the rite of anointing. Instead of creating a hybrid rite such as that in the sacramentary of Sens, which could be used for either the merely sick or the moribund, the monks of Lorsch created two separate rituals. Not surprisingly, they built the rite of anointing the sick around the visitation prayers of the Supplement and the anointing of the dying around that Irish model in which it had first developed over a century before.

The last piece in the ritual complex in the Lorsch manuscript is a rite for death and burial which is a blend of the old Roman *ordo* with the prayers of the Supplement, preserving, as the St-Denis rite did not, the rubrics of the Roman *ordo* as well as its ritual prescriptions for the agony—communion and the reading of the Passion.[76] After the first three rubrics of the old Roman *ordo*, the Lorsch rite prescribes the prayers "when the soul has gone out from the body" from Benedict's Supplement.[77] Then come the rubrics of the Roman *ordo*, with their accompanying psalmody, which direct the washing of the corpse, its placement on a bier, and then the bier's placement in church, followed by Benedict's prayers "after the washing of the body."[78] A new rubric directs the chant to be sung in church; it is followed by Benedict's prayers "before burial."[79] The ritual ends with the prayers "after the burial of the body" from the Supplement.[80]

The Lorsch manuscript contains a complete ritual complex for the sick, the dying, and the dead. It is the earliest witness to a tradition of two separate rites for anointing the sick—one for use with any sickness and designed as a healing ritual in conformity

75. MS fol. 58r: *Oratio et preces super infirmum antequam moriatur.* Cf. de Clercq, "'Ordines unctionis infirmi,'" 102–4. The *Missa pro infirmis* = Gellone, nos. 2882–86, and the readings are the same as those in the sacramentary of Sens, Stockholm, Kungliga Biblioteket, Holm. A136, fol. 205r.

76. Edited in Sicard, *Liturgie,* 22–25; cf. Frank, "Älteste erhaltene *ordo defunctorum,*" 379–82. Vatican Pal. lat. 485 is the oldest witness to the antemortem rubrics of the old Roman *ordo.*

77. Supplement, nos. 1398–1406. There are a few additions and variations in Pal. lat. 485. For example, the *capitula* (no. 1406 in the Supplement) are moved so that they come exactly in the middle of the series of eight prayers (MS fol. 58v). They are, moreover, preceded by a series of responses/verses/antiphons and a Kyrie.

78. Supplement, nos. 1407–8.

79. Ibid., nos. 1409–10. The rubrics in the manuscript are *Incipit cantor hanc cantare* and *Et antequam sepeliatur dicat has orationes.*

80. Ibid., nos. 1411–15.

with Carolingian reform goals; and the other for dying individuals. The visitation rite uses Gregorian—that is, Roman—prayers that express the desire for physical healing which is their distinguishing characteristic. The second uses both the structure— confession, anointing, and communion—and the prayers of the Irish anointing rituals. A ritual devised by priests to compensate for their absence at the moment of death had been consolidated into a larger structure including not only preparatory rites but those for death and burial as well. By following this rite of preparation for death with a synthesis of the old Roman *ordo* and the prayers from the Supplement, the creators of the Lorsch ritual reached a solution to the competing streams of ritual around death and burial nearly the same as that reached at St-Amand at the same time. The Lorsch rite is distinguished from that of St-Amand by its use of the antemortem aids to the dying from the old Roman *ordo* in place of the litanies and chants of the Frankish rite for the agony, but structurally they amount to the same thing—a coherent set of ritual actions and prayers accompanying the last illness, death, and burial of a Christian. Together the two ritual syntheses drew on all the streams of tradition which had flowed into the Frankish realm under the Carolingians: Irish and Anglo-Saxon, Gallican, Roman, and Spanish.

Patterns of Dissemination

The syntheses achieved at St-Amand and Lorsch represent the culmination of over a century of development in the ritual response to death and dying in the Carolingian world. In their different ways, they resolved the tensions created by the confluence in the Frankish kingdoms of old ritual traditions from Rome, Spain, and Ireland, and new creations such as the *commendatio animae,* the reform rite of anointing the sick, and the rite for death and burial created by Benedict of Aniane. In the ritual care of the sick, the Lorsch ritual took up where the liturgists of the Rheinau sacramentary left off, separating the two streams and channeling Roman-reform traditions into visitation rituals for the merely sick and Irish-Gallican traditions into a separate and distinct ritual for anointing the dying. At St-Amand the reform rite of anointing the sick became the basis for a ritual that could be used as a healing rite but was fundamentally directed toward purification, spiritual transformation, and preparation for death. At both centers confession and reconciliation accompanied anointing. At St-Amand the communion received in the anointing ritual became the viaticum; at Lorsch, where the antemortem phase of the old Roman *ordo* was reintroduced, a separate viaticum was given to the dying shortly before death. At both centers, a new rite for death and burial was fashioned from the essentially Visigothic prayers of Benedict of Aniane and the psalmody of the old Roman *ordo*.

The importance of the ritual syntheses of St-Amand and Lorsch was not lost on the following generations. The new rites were local products, of course, and not disseminated according to any centralized plan. It is therefore all the more remarkable that the St-Amand rituals were added in the tenth century to the end of the famous sacramentary of Hildoard of Cambrai, the oldest extant copy (811–812) of the Gregorian sent to Charlemagne by Pope Hadrian.[81] Ruggero Dalla Mutta has already shown that the sacramentary of Sens was the link between the Carolingian reform rite of anointing the sick and the most important ritual books of the tenth and eleventh centuries, including the mid-tenth-century Roman-German pontifical, which was the ancestor of the Roman pontificals of the twelfth and thirteenth centuries and the post-Tridentine *Rituale Romanum* of Paul V.[82] But the situation is more complex than Dalla Mutta realized. The Roman-German pontifical has two rituals for the sick, as does the manuscript from Lorsch.[83] The first consists of a visitation with laying on of hands followed by a mass for the sick and the old prayer for the return of health.[84] The second ritual is a blend of material from Lorsch and St-Amand. While in general it follows closely the anointing rite from St-Amand, it includes the communion formula from the Lorsch ritual.[85] This second ritual is linked with the rites for death and burial via new rites for deathbed penance and reconciliation, a priest's mass for the forgiveness of his sins, and the mass for the dying from the St-Amand tradition.[86] The ritual for death and burial which

81. Cambrai, Bibliothèque Municipale, MS 164, fols. 222r–239v; Gregorian, 3.20.

82. Ruggero Dalla Mutta, "Un rituel de l'onction des malades du ixe siècle en Flandre chaînon important entre le rituel 'carolingien' et les rituels des xe–xie S.," in *Mens concordet voci: Mélanges A. G. Martimort* (Tournai, 1983), 609–18.

83. *Le pontifical romano-germanique du dixième siècle*, ed. Cyrille Vogel and Reinhard Elze, 3 vols. (Vatican City, 1963–1972), 2.246–56 and 258–70.

84. *Pontifical romano-germanique*, 2.246–57.

85. Ibid., 2.258–70, at 265, l. 32: "Pax et communicatio corporis et sanguinis domini nostri Iesu Christi custodiat animam tuam in uitam aeternam."

86. Ibid., 2.270–75, *Ordo poenitentis ad mortem;* 275–77, *Reconciliatio ad mortem;* 277–79, *Missa quam sacerdos pro sibi confesso canere debet;* and 280, *Missa pro infirmis qui proximus est morti.*

follows is also a blend of the solutions of both Lorsch and St-Amand.[87] It begins with the first rubric of the old Roman *ordo* directing communion as soon as the sick person appears to be approaching death, but it retains the singing of the seven penitential psalms and litany during the agony. It goes beyond its ninth-century predecessors, however, in gathering into itself many of the old Gelasian prayers that had fallen by the wayside as clerics sought to combine the prayers of the Supplement with the psalmody of the Roman *ordo*. Like so many of the rituals in the pontifical, it is a compendium of material that had circulated in the Frankish lands over the previous two hundred years.

What is most remarkable here is the continuation and furtherance of the achievements of the late ninth century. The Roman-German pontifical reveals that the creation of two separate rites for the sick, first achieved at Lorsch, was to be the wave of the future. There was no reason to give up the ritual care of the sick, with or without anointing; but there was just as little reason to deny the appropriateness of rituals of anointing as preparation for death and as part of the larger ritual complex around death, dying, and incorporation in the other world. When the Council of Trent placed the rites of confession, communion, and anointing under the rubric "Extreme Unction" as the last rites of the church, it gave official recognition to the synthesis first achieved in the late ninth century.[88] The Roman ritual of Pope Paul V, published in 1614, has separate sections on the visitation of the sick, anointing the dying (extreme unction), the *commendatio animae*, and the burial service.[89] Both the creation and the articulation of those rituals were the work of the Carolingian church.

Even in the later ninth century, only monasteries and other cloistered communities could have taken full advantage of these rites. They were, and would remain for centuries, a specialty of clerical elites. The specialization of the clergy in these matters is evident in the institution of deathbed clothing in a monastic habit, which entailed entry into a cloistered community during a final illness, so that one might die as a monk or a nun. One of the first to do so was the emperor Lothar, son of Louis the Pious, who took

87. Ibid., 2.281–305.
88. François-A. Isambert, "Les transformations du rituel catholique des mourants," *Archives de sciences sociales des religions* 20 (1975): 90.
89. See, e.g., *Rituale Romanum Pauli V. Pont. Max. Iussu Editum*, newest ed. (Paris, 1641), 114–30, *Visitatione et cura infirmorum*; 89–96, *Ordo ministrandi sacramentum extremae unctionis*; 133–59, *Ordo commendationis animae*; and 160–79, funeral service.

monastic vows and spent his last days at the abbey of Prüm in
855.[90] The reasons for such an act must have been complex, but it
is noteworthy that the early instances are contemporaneous with
the full development of the rituals around death, dying, and the
dead.

The extent to which different groups of clergy made use of the
full panoply of rites for the sick, the dying, and the dead can be
seen in a curious document that survives today in the municipal
library in Bern, Switzerland.[91] This document describes the practices of a group of clerics who formed a type of confraternity for the
purpose of mutual amity and the provision of ritual care for its
members in the event of sickness or death.[92] Under the guidelines
laid out in the document, when one of the fraternity fell ill, the
others were to congregate at his house, sing the seven penitential
psalms along with a litany and prayers, and bless holy water.[93]
Afterward the visitors were to go to church and offer mass for him
and then return to the house to share bread and water.[94] If the
sickness continued, the joint visitations were to continue for
twelve nights, after which only one of the group would remain. If
death seemed imminent, the whole group was to come together
once again and anoint the sick man.[95] When death actually arrived,
the one on vigil at the time was to perform the *commendatio* and
prepare the body for burial. After a funeral attended by all, each
member was to dedicate the offices of matins and vespers and all
masses for thirty days to the soul of the dead man. Until the anniversary of the death, a daily mass would be said for him, and after

90. Louis Gougaud, *Devotional and Ascetic Practices in the Middle Ages*, trans.
G. C. Bateman (London, 1927), 135.
91. André Wilmart, "Le règlement ecclésiastique de Berne," RB 51 (1939): 37–52.
92. The charter of confraternity drawn up by the communities of St-Denis and
St-Remy of Reims in 840 is the earliest record of the extension of the benefits of
communal prayer to the sick and the dying along with the dead. See *Obituaires de
la province de Sens*, ed. Auguste Molinier, Recueil des historiens de la France,
obituaires 1 (Paris, 1902), 1.1023: "Si vero quidam ex eis aliqua corporis commodi-
tate occupatus fuerit, mox ut nobis nuntiatum fuerit, omni die, quousque con-
valescet aut ab hac luce discedat, unusquisque v psalmos pro eo sollicite compleat."
93. Wilmart, "Règlement," 49: "Item ammoneo uos fratres, ut si aliquis ex uobis
fratribus infirmatur, elegite unum ex uobis qui alios nontiat, et ite itaque cunctis ad
domum eius, et cum omni diligentia uisitate eum, ibique septem psalmos peniten-
tiales decantate, cum letania et capitularum et orationibus, deinde aqua benedicta
facite."
94. The reference to bread and water as part of a visitation ritual gives a living
context to the prayers for the blessing of bread and water in the visitation rite in the
St. Gall sacramentary; see above, chap. 3.
95. Wilmart, "Règlement," 50: "Com [sic] uero morti proximus fuerit, ite cuncti
ad domum eius, et ungite eum oleo sancto in nomine domini."

the anniversary he would be remembered in the regular commemorations of the dead members of the fraternity.[96]

André Wilmart believed that the document described the practices of a group of Irish clerics of the eighth century.[97] It certainly accords well with the attitudes and behavior of the Célí Dé. The interest in care of the sick, the practice of anointing the dying, even the reluctance to be present at the death or have contact with the body—note that it was the one time when the whole group did not participate—recall Irish practice. G. G. Meersseman has convincingly shown, however, that the document in its present form dates from the last quarter of the ninth century and describes the arrangements of a group of Parisian clerics attached to the cathedral, and known as the Society of the Twelve Apostles (*societas duodecim apostolorum*).[98] Nonetheless, the link with Ireland is important, for Ireland was the source not only of so much of the commemorative activity of the eighth and ninth centuries, but also of the use of anointing with the dying. Like the transmission of the Irish anointing rite to Lorsch, the connection between Ireland and the continent apparent in the "rule" of the Society of the Twelve Apostles goes a long way toward an explanation of the consistent pressure in the Frankish church to include anointing among the rites for the dying.

But the ritual synthesis was never meant for the clergy alone. The culmination of the development of the ritual process was marked not only by the possibility of joining a religious community to take full advantage of its ritual services, but also by significant moves to include the laity in the ritual process. Carolingian bishops had always meant their priests to bring the comforts of the sacraments to the people. Almost every one of the extant conciliar and episcopal decrees on the rites for the sick and the dying is framed in the context of a discussion of the education of the parish

96. Ibid.: "Post anniuersarium uero, unus quisque ex uobis fratribus per totas epdomadas de anno quicumque cartellum secum habuerit, de sua epdomade cotidiae memoriam pro fratribus uestris defuntis agite."

97. The atrocious orthography of this document led Wilmart to conclude that it had been transcribed around the year 830 from an insular original dating back to 700; ibid., 38.

98. G. G. Meersseman, *Ordo fraternitatis: Confraternite e pietà dei laici nel medioevo*, 2 vols. (Rome, 1977), 1.150–69. The names of the group appear among a commemorative list added to the mid-ninth-century Gregorian sacramentary of the Cathedral of Paris; ibid., 150–52, 166–68; cf. Gregorian, 3.33, and Vatican, Biblioteca Apostolica Vaticana, MS Ottoboni 313, fols. 110r–11v. Meersseman suggests that the names of the society's members were written into the longer list from the *cartellum* used for the society's commemorative services.

clergy and the proper performance of pastoral work. In rare cases, texts directly refer to the participation of the laity. Bishop Jonas of Orléans, for example, in his treatise "On the Laity," urged everyone to visit the sick.[99] Jonas complained that the rich and powerful did not visit the poor and refused to accept poor visitors. Both rich and poor stayed away from the sick out of fear of contagion, "as if they might escape death if it were to come to find them." Jonas saw sickness as an admonishment from God and an aid to salvation. He felt that when someone fell sick, priests should be called to perform the anointing, but, on the authority of Pope Innocent I, gave the laity the right to do so as well. Jonas also urged attendance at funerals, not just those of the rich, but of all Christians.[100] Not only should Christians see to the burial of rich and poor alike, but they should also bring hope to the spirits of the dead through prayers and alms. Thus the whole community would be involved in the care of its members in sickness, death, and the after life.

The inclusion of the laity in the new rituals for the dying is indicated by the reference, first appearing in the sacramentary of St-Denis, to both monks "and others of the faithful" (ceteri quique fideles) in the rubric urging attendance at the deathbed for the commendatio animae.[101] The phrase suggests that although the ritual was devised primarily by and for the members of religious communities, it was not meant to be restricted to them. The "others of the faithful" could be lay visitors to the cloister or relatives of the dying person, but in any case their inclusion would tend to make the rituals known to a wider circle. Indeed, the appearance of this phrase in ritual orders from the later ninth through the eleventh centuries reveals the continued relevance of the goal of joint lay-clerical participation in deathbed rituals.[102]

The situation seems to have been more advanced at Lorsch, so that the ritual itself was meant for parish use. That intention would accord with its Irish roots, for the Irish visitation of the sick

99. Jonas of Orléans, De institutione laicali, bk. 3, chap. 14, "De infirmis uisitandis oleoque sancto perungendis," PL 106.258–61.

100. Ibid., chap. 15, "De mortuis sepeliendi et cura pro eorum animibus," PL 106.261–65.

101. Paris, B.N. MS lat. 2290, fol. 160r; Gregorian, 3.171: "Cum anima in agone sui exitus dissolutione corporis sui uisa fuerit laborare, conuenire studebunt fratres uel ceteri quique fideles."

102. It appears regularly in deathbed rituals in the tenth and eleventh centuries. In the eleventh century a few books omit the phrase, and the fourteenth-century pontifical of Amiens replaces it with "only priests and clerics"; Sicard, Liturgie, 45–46, apparatus.

had evolved in a pastoral rather than an institutional context. As I noted earlier, the Lorsch manuscript is not a sacramentary but a manual for the instruction of the secular clergy. Thus, though we cannot know if the ritual was actually used outside of the abbey, it was clearly meant to be. Indeed, the manner of its inscription in the manuscript, filling, but not quite completely, one whole quire, suggests that it was copied from (or was the model for) a separate *libellus* intended for use by individual priests. Moreover, it is precisely in the last quarter of the ninth century and the beginning of the tenth that small *libelli* with the rites for the sick and the dying begin to appear in significant numbers.[103]

Just such a ritual booklet has been partially preserved in the Vatican library. It is a little manuscript of twenty-four folios which Hieronymus Frank identified as representative of a ritual type.[104] It is incomplete at both beginning and end, but Frank was able to fill in the missing parts by means of a later witness to the same ritual.[105] Although it does not include an anointing, the ritual type in this manuscript exhibits the same synthetic quality as the rites for the agony and for burial in the sacramentaries of St-Denis and St-Amand and the Lorsch manual.[106] Frank hesitated to trace the ritual type in this manuscript to Lorsch, "even if the manuscript was written there and belonged to the abbey library," because it includes the laity (*populus*) and repeatedly refers to the home of the deceased as the scene of ritual activity, and thus, he felt, could not have been written in a monastic scriptorium.[107] But the context of the rites in the Lorsch manuscript nullify that objection. The monks of Lorsch did not hesitate to create rituals for the use of the secular clergy and the laity. Indeed, it was at Lorsch and at St-Amand in the late ninth century that the earliest religious texts in

103. Vogel, *Medieval Liturgy*, 261–62; P.-M. Gy, "Collectaire, rituel, processional," *Revue des sciences philosophiques et théologiques* 44 (1960): 454–57; Walter von Arx, "Zur Entstehungsgeschichte des Rituale," *Zeitschrift für schweizerische Kirchengeschichte* 63 (1969): 51.

104. Vatican, MS Pal. lat. 550; Frank, "Älteste erhaltene *ordo defunctorum*," 387–402.

105. Rome, Biblioteca Vallicelliana, MS B 141.

106. This ritual includes much old Gelasian material left out of the rites in the sacramentary of Sens and the Lorsch manual; see Frank, "Älteste erhaltene *ordo defunctorum*," 391–98. The prayers reintroduced here can be found in Gellone, nos. 2896, 2898, 2900, 2902, 2906, 2910, 2911, 2914, 2917, 2918. The Gelasian prayers that this manuscript preserves—above all the *Proficiscere*—survived and were transmitted to the Roman pontifical of the twelfth century, through which they became a permanent part of the Latin death rites; Andrieu, *Pontifical Romain*, 1.279–85.

107. Frank, "Älteste erhaltene *ordo defunctorum*," 388; and see 390–98.

the vernacular languages appear. The French vernacular "Sequence of St. Eulalie," a short poem on the martyrdom of the saint adapted from Prudentius, first appears in a St-Amand manuscript dated to about 880, and St-Amand was also the home of the "Fragment of Valenciennes," which contains a priest's notes for a sermon mingling French and Latin.[108] Similarly, the Lorsch manuscript contains not only the ritual sequence for death and dying but also the famous *Lorscher Beichte*, an old High German confession formula for the laity, which is one of the oldest pieces of German prose literature to come down to us.[109] The fact is that the great foundations of the later ninth century, such as Lorsch and St-Amand, were not completely inward-looking. They oversaw increasingly large networks of farms and villages for which they had responsibility, both secular and spiritual.[110] It should come as no surprise that their monastic scriptoria should produce materials for the use of the laity and the secular clergy. After all, their abbots were as often as not bishops. Bishop Adalbero of Augsburg and Bishop Haito of Mainz were successive abbots of Lorsch at the turn of the tenth century.[111]

There is also evidence that the specialized commemorative services of the monastic and clerical confraternities were becoming increasingly available to the laity in the late ninth century. By that time, no one doubted the efficacy of prayer for the dead. Most people, clergy and laity alike, believed that even persons who died without penance could be aided or even saved from hell by the prayers of the faithful.[112] In such an atmosphere of belief, it was only natural that members of clerical confraternities would wish to extend the benefits of commemorative prayer to their relatives. This practice is already apparent in memorial books such as the early ninth-century *Liber memorialis* of Remiremont.[113] The earliest expression in a charter of confraternity comes from the monastery of Fulda in 863. The terms of the agreement encompass the living, for whom ten psalters and ten masses were to be offered yearly; the sick, who were to be visited by any members in the

108. Jeanette M. A. Beer, "Picard Literature," DMA 9:633; cf. DMA 4:521; 5:233–34.
109. Paxton, "Bonus liber," 9.
110. Nitz, "Church as Colonist," 113, 118–19.
111. Paxton, "Bonus liber," 29–30.
112. Megan McLaughlin, "The Limits of Theology: Prayer for the Dead in Carolingian Society," paper read at the annual meeting of the American Historical Society, December 28, 1988, Washington, D.C.
113. *Liber Memorialis von Remiremont*, ed. Hlawitschka et al.

vicinity, and for whom five psalms would be offered daily; and the dead, who would receive three masses, three psalters, and twelve vespers and vigils.[114] For the parents, brothers, and sisters of the members fifty psalms and a vespers and vigil would be specially sung (other relatives would receive thirty psalms) and all the dead would be commemorated each year with twelve masses and as many psalters.[115] By the end of the century noble clans such as the Liudolfings had entered into special relations with certain religious foundations for commemoration of their members, and in the early tenth century they began to establish houses for the express purpose of familial commemoration.[116] Such practices did not become generally available until the twelfth century, but the basic work was done by the year 900. Christian Europe had forged a complete ritual response to death, dying, and the needs of the dead.

114. *Die Klostergemeinschaft von Fulda*, ed. Karl Schmid, 3 vols., Münstersche Mittelalter-Schriften 8 (Munich, 1978), 1.207: "complacuit inter illos quorum nomina inferius scripta sunt, ut unusquisque illorum singulis annis generaliter pro omnibus uiuis X psalteria uel X missas cantet uel perficiat. Si aliquis eorum languore correptus infirmetur, ceteri qui potentes sunt uiribus, si in uicinitate positi, uisitent eum et solacia praebeant. Atque si in tanta infirmitate teneatur, . . . unusquisque . . . V psalmos pro eo Domino reddere curet. Si quis eorum metam huius uite reliqueret, unusquisque superstitum pro anima defuncti infra XXX diebus postquam audierit tria psalteria et tres missas, uigilias quoque XII totidemque uesperas cantet uel cantari faciat."

115. Ibid.: "Pro patre quidem et matre, fratribus sororibusque psalmos L, uigiliam quoque uesperamque impendat. Pro ceteris uero defunctis eadem affinitate coniunctis ordinem XXX psalmorum persoluat. In circulo uero anni pro animabus defunctorum unusquisque XII missas aut XII psalteria cantet uel perficiat."

116. Althoff, *Adels- und Königsfamilien*, 11–30, 242–43.

Conclusion

The ritual complex around death, dying, and the dead, whose genesis has been traced to the eighth and ninth centuries, is a product of the material and the spiritual cultures of early medieval Europe. It is an expression of concrete historical circumstances as well as less tangible conceptions, attitudes, hopes, and fears. The Carolingian rulers and their clerical advisers attempted to control directly the creation and dissemination of ritual. Through councils and capitularies, schools and scriptoria, they sought to create a Christian society united by common forms of worship and a common understanding of the Christian way of life and death. But the unspoken understandings of the majority of people, even among the clergy, could not be strictly contained. The mechanisms of power were inefficient, inchoate, and fragile. The rituals—the gestures and prayers—with which people had attended the dying and the dead in the various cultural traditions that merged in Carolingian Francia had lasting power and appeal. During the high reform period, when some clerical and secular rulers sought to standardize ritual life around Roman models, other ritual traditions were obscured. When they were given the chance, however—when the mechanisms of centralization failed—they resurfaced. If they were to survive within an increasingly literate culture, they needed the material basis created by the Carolingian renaissance; but if they were to express the real cultural unity that had been achieved, they had to subvert and re-form the Carolingian program.

To express the state of culture in Europe, they had to emerge from the shadow of Rome—and of Aachen.

In the Roman church under the late empire sickness was regarded as a natural part of life, a small reminder from God of human mortality. The Roman ritual response to sickness comprised the prayers of the community for the health of the sick person and the informal application of blessed oil as a spiritual medicament. In the sixth century, Caesarius of Arles preached on the anointing of the sick in accordance with the exhortation of the apostle James. He encouraged the sick to seek anointing from priests as an alternative to non-Christian healing practices of a magical-popular sort. His argument that Christians would receive both health for their bodies and indulgence for their sins at the hands of priests led clerics to begin to create rituals of visitation and anointing. The remains of the earliest such rituals reveal two separate approaches to the care of the sick. The Spanish church of the Visigothic period conformed to and extended the Roman response to sickness. Its ritual tended to focus on bodily healing, and presented the oil (or chrism) blessed by the bishop as a curative salve. The Gallican and Irish sources display another approach. What was sought for the sick was primarily the purification of the soul and the "health" of eternal salvation. The ritual action aimed at spiritual healing at least as much as and often more than physical healing.

The remains of the most ancient Western rituals around the deathbed reveal a similar bifurcation in the ritual response to death. The Christian communities of late Roman antiquity celebrated death. The old Roman *ordo defunctorum* was based on psalms of joy and triumph as the soul entered into the celestial Jerusalem. It ritualized death as a passage of the triumphant soul to the celestial regions and it gave the dying the viaticum as the token by which their souls would join the community of saints at the final resurrection. Yet the emphasis in the old Roman rite was almost solely on the soul's passage and resurrection. There was little concern with the dying person and little participation by the people in attendance. Baptism and viaticum ensured salvation. And death marked the entry into the real life of a Christian.

To the new communities of Christians in the early medieval West, however, death held more terror. Salvation was not ensured by virtue of membership in the community, or in the imperial religion of the fourth and fifth centuries. In a world of disorder, among people for whom Christianity was an alien faith conveyed in a foreign tongue, the question of personal salvation had less easy answers. Humankind's fallen condition demanded penitence; converse with the world necessarily brought pollution. The forms of penance multiplied and rites of purification played an increasing role, as the proliferation of rites of deathbed penance in Gaul and Visigothic Spain in the sixth and seventh centuries makes abundantly clear.

This shift, which might seem to be retrogressive, a fall from a natural and primitive Christian attitude toward death, has a significant psychological and social importance. Whereas the old Roman death ritual focused attention almost exclusively on the state of the soul and its passage to the other world, rites of deathbed penance tended to focus attention on the state of the dying person. By confession and reconciliation with the community, the dying were taken through a set of ritual moments that prepared them for their death. Separated from the community, absolved, reclothed, and brought back into the fold as new persons, they received a second baptism. The dying were purified and strengthened for death while simultaneously they were presented with a model of the community's response to their death and of their own after-death experiences. The ritual process paralleled the experience of death. The dying would leave the community, which would accompany their passage with prayer; and they would, by the mercy of God, enter the community of the saints in the other world. The ritual process created bonds between the living and the dead. It met the fear of death with expressions of communal solidarity and care, and with symbols of Christian transformation as powerful as those of baptism, the first of the Christian rites of passage. It is not fortuitous that this type of ritual was most highly developed in the liturgy of Visigothic Spain. The Visigothic church was rooted in Roman and Eastern traditions, yet its barbarian constituency could not bear the ancient penitential discipline, or do without it. Before they could meet death with any equanimity, they had to be ritually "passed on" while they still lived.

Irish Christianity gave a peculiar twist to the rites of preparation for death by the inclusion of anointing as part of the ritual process. Since sickness was an opportunity to attend to the state of one's soul, Irish visitation rites, like deathbed penance, emphasized purification and salvation, *salvatio* rather than *salus*. During the eighth century, under the influence of Old Testament prohibitions of priestly contact with the dead, Irish reformers reinscribed older services for the taking of oil and communion to the sick as rites for the dying. The new rituals focused more on the dying person and his or her need for purification and strengthening than on the passage of the soul. Not that the Irish neglected the postmortem fate of the soul. From Ireland also came new forms of aid to souls in the afterlife—votive masses, commutations of penances, and informal fraternities of prayer for the dead. Such practices spread to England and the continent with the migration of Irish monks in the seventh and eighth centuries. In late Merovingian Gaul, they merged with local Gallican deathways in a process of mutual adaptation. Although the exact patterns of influence remains obscure, the pre-Carolingian Gallican liturgy often articulated ritual responses to sickness and death in ways similar to those of the Irish.

All these traditions became the common inheritance of the new Christian society developing in northern Europe in the eighth and ninth centuries. Since the field of cultural transmission comprised the court, the monasteries, and the churches of the Carolingian realm, it was in these places that the different traditions met, influenced one another, and were shaped to meet the needs of the people of the time. The Frankish realm reached its greatest extent during the last half of the eighth century. Charlemagne's acceptance of the title Emperor of the Romans, bestowed on him by the pope and the people of Rome in the year 800, marked the culmination of the forces set in motion by his father's coronation almost fifty years before. The Saxons had been forcibly brought into the Christian community of the West, Frankish power reached from the Pyrenees to the Elbe, and the Frankish church applied itself ever more vigorously to the education of clergy and laity in the precepts of Christian living. One means of promulgating those precepts was the production of ritual books, many of which were modeled on Roman sacramentaries. But the introduction into the Frankish church of Roman traditions founded on the very different cultural and social conditions of the late empire conflicted with many of the devotional practices that had been developing independently in the monasteries and other communities of the late Merovingian period, where Irish, Goths, Franks, and Anglo-Saxons met and shared their experiments in Christian living and dying. It was a fruitful conflict, however, for it led to developments in ritual life which set the stage for the synthesis of ritual traditions in the next century. Some of these developments are hidden from us, but enough traces have been left to indicate the overall pattern of change.

The Roman attitude toward sickness and its expression in

prayers and rites for the sick made deep inroads into northern spirituality by means of the Gregorian sacramentary. The old Gallican prayers for the sick remained in the Frankish Gelasian sacramentaries, however, especially in areas where Irish influence was strong. The old Roman *ordo defunctorum*, which might have been the natural starting point for a turn to Roman traditions around death and burial, played a curious role in the ritual history of the Frankish church. The evidence in Roman sacramentaries suggests that it was no longer current in Rome in the eighth century, and the Frankish monastic communities that picked it up adapted it freely to their needs. Although it was available to the Carolingian clerics, they made little use of it. When they did use it, they dropped its indications for preparation and vigil before death and added an element of penitential supplication, more or less developed. The restructuring of the antemortem stage of the ritual process was a result of the vitality of Irish-Gallican traditions. By regarding sickness as a preparation for death, they had fostered a tendency, visible in the Frankish Gelasian liturgical books, to connect the rites and prayers for the sick with those for the dead. The creation of this ritual continuity led to the elaboration of rites of separation that had not existed in late antiquity.

Yet the Frankish church did not take over from the Irish their peculiar relationship with Mosaic law. Whereas Irish priests shunned the moment of death, Frankish churchmen worked to heighten the participation of the attendants at a death. By the late eighth century, preparation for death regularly included some form of penance, a circumstance signaled by the universal agreement among the eighth-century Gelasian ritual books in the placement of the prayers for the reconciliation *ad mortem* immediately before those for death and burial. That such a practice had been taken over from the Spanish church seems highly probable, given the developed state of rites of deathbed penance in Visigothic Spain in the seventh and eighth centuries. But it is equally probable that, insofar as that was the case, no special significance was attached to that penance. The currency of Irish and Anglo-Saxon penitential practices, which integrated confession and penance into the fabric of everyday life, ensured that a deathbed confession would be expected—it would hardly have been extraordinary. Thus no special rubrics accompany the prayers for reconciliation to guide the ritual process. What was special to the deathbed rituals in late eighth-century Francia was the emergence of the *commendatio animae,* consisting of prayers and a chanted litany. Not so much a commending of the soul to God as a ritual of aid to the dying, the *commendatio* at one and the same time begged God to release the soul from the flesh; elicited the aid of the saints, martyrs, and all the blessed in that endeavor; and shielded the dying individual from the attacks of the demons who might hinder its passage. This Frankish contribution to deathbed rituals completed the change of emphasis from the exclusive concern with the fate of the soul to the needs of the dying person. As to the fate of the soul, the Franks turned informal Irish and Anglo-Saxon commemorative practices into an institution, beginning the process by which prayer for the dead would become an increasingly central concern of religious communities in the West.

It was into this situation that Benedict of Aniane inserted his liturgical creations. In his Supplement to the *Hadrianum*, Benedict introduced a new death rite based on prayers from the Visigothic liturgy and the three Roman prayers found in the sacramentary he was supplementing. His ritual was coherent and well structured. Through subtle manipulation of Visigothic texts, he created a new vision of death and judgment reflecting the imperial court culture that was his world. He drew on legal terminology to express the relationship of the dead soul to God as one of petitioner before a royal judge, dependent on mercy and fearful of royal justice. Benedict focused on the needs of the soul in the period immediately following death (as opposed to images of the afterlife). The prayers of his ritual accompany the soul's *migratio* not with psalms of entry into the celestial Jerusalem but with descriptions of the terrors of the journey and entreaties to God to deliver the soul from the powers of demons and to the angels to show the soul the way to life. Benedict took no cognizance of the rites for the dying being developed in the Frankish realm. Nor did his work replace the other death rituals in circulation and in use. Although his ritual's position in the Supplement to the Gregorian sacramentary ensured its eventual influence, the continued existence and relevance of other ritual models in Frankish Gelasian books guaranteed that it would not be the final word on death and dying in the ninth century.

The Carolingian reformers hoped to encourage ritual care of the sick along the lines laid down in the epistle of James and the Roman prayers of the Gregorian sacramentary. Since no formal ritual had emerged from within the Roman tradition, one needed to be created—a task that was taken up by Benedict of Aniane. Again he turned to the Visigothic liturgy, creating a ritual context for the biblical text on which the Carolingian reformers based their support for the unction of the sick by integrating it with the old Spanish anointing ritual. The resulting ritual was completely within the old Roman tradition and was meant to effect the physical and spiritual relief of the sick, not to prepare them for death. Like his death ritual, however, it was just one of several competing ritual forms. Both were destined to be transformed by later ninth-century liturgists, who achieved the unification the reformers had sought but failed to find. It was a unification that conformed not to Roman models but to a deeper, more general cultural disposition. The medieval Latin death ritual took definitive shape not when the Roman *ordo* or any other ritual was introduced, but when the liturgical material created or put into circulation during the reform period (750–820) was synthesized into a ritual process that accompanied final illness, death, and burial in a coherent series of ritual moments, a ritual complex that gave shape and voice to all the streams flowing into the Christian culture of the north—Roman, Gallican, Irish, and Visigothic.

The later ninth century, a time of invasion, confusion, and breakdown on the political scene, was a time of energetic creation and synthesis in ritual life. On one level the reform had not succeeded; conformity to an imagined ideal had not been achieved. But the reformers' lack of success set up the preconditions for a different type of unity. They created a literate clergy; they created libraries and scriptoria where those clerics could recognize, work with, and transmit the ritual material of the past; and they established a carrier—the Gregorian sacramentary—that would give authority and longevity to any rite that could become part of it. The impetus they gave to efforts to organize and standardize ritual life led ultimately to a synthesis of all the various traditions on death and dying in early medieval Christianity, a synthesis founded on broader cultural impulses than those that lay behind the official reform. Texts from mid-century show a great deal of freedom in various locales in the creation of ritual books and the care for the dying and the dead. Gregorian sacramentaries were ever more extensively supplemented and reorganized to include indigenous materials, and existing rituals were put to new uses. Above all, the evidence suggests an increasing use of penance and anointing as rites of separation and preparation for death. Then, around the year 875, clerics at St-Amand and Lorsch brought together the various liturgical materials on sickness and death which had been created and put into circulation during the previous 500 years and synthesized them into a coherent ritual complex. With minor alterations, this ritual complex became the basic ritual response to death and dying in the medieval church, and for long afterward. It gave expression to all the cultural attitudes toward death and dying which flowed within the Frankish empire and the new Christian culture of the north. The new ritual maintained the practice of deathbed penance through inclusion of confession, absolution, and the prayers of the old *reconciliatio ad mortem*. It took the Carolingian rite of anointing the sick and altered its prayers and expanded the act of anointing so that it became a ritual purification of all the senses. Sins committed through sight, hearing, touch, and so on were wiped away. The body was gradually re-formed to prepare it for the soul's release. The new rite preserved the Frankish prayers and litanies for the aid of the dying during the agony. Finally, it combined the Frankish prose prayers in response to death, during the vigil, and for the burial, with their emphasis on penitence and the community's appeal to God's mercy for the soul of their sister or brother, with Benedict of Aniane's Visigothic compositions, which presented the soul as defendant in the imperial court of the Almighty God. To these prayers it added the triumphant and optimistic psalmody of the old Roman *ordo defunctorum*. When these contradictory impulses were blended together in a ritual structure of deep human significance, the result was a balanced response to death and dying true to the polyglot nature of early medieval culture.

The achievements of the later ninth century did not put an end to the diversity of ritual responses to death and dying in the Latin West, but they mark a significant cultural watershed. The inheritance of antiquity and of the diverse Christian communities of the early Middle Ages had been brought together, sorted through, and absorbed. The gestures and images that accompanied rites of anointing and of penance, reconciliation, and the communion that sealed it had been put at the service of the dying. The power of communal prayer had been marshaled to aid in the moments of greatest anxiety, not only for the moribund but for the attendants as well. The institution of confraternities of prayer for the dead gave expression to the intense personal bonds of Christian society and matched the expansion of aid to the dying with a system of care for the dead aimed at the ritual incorporation of souls into the body of the saved in paradise. The rites expressed both a sense of the need for penitence and forgiveness and the optimism of a Christian bound for a heavenly home. Against the basic human fear of death and the added anxiety of Christians living in a rough-

and-tumble world of precarious plenty and only occasional peace, the Frankish church erected a complex and coherent ritual process to accompany the individual through his or her last illness, agony, flight to the other world, and eventual incorporation in the community of the blessed. More than one historian has seen in the Carolingian age signs of the birth of Europe. The emergence of this ritual process in a definitive form in the late ninth century can only reinforce that impression. For, insofar as a common death ritual is a mark of a unified culture, the later ninth century marks the birth, in the Latin West, of the culture we call European.

Selected Bibliography

Primary Sources

Manuscripts

New York, Pierpont Morgan Library, MS G57.
Paris, Bibliothèque Nationale, MS lat. 2290.
Stockholm, Kungliga Biblioteket, MS Holm. A136.
Vatican, Biblioteca Apostolica Vaticana, MSS Ottob. lat. 312, Pal. lat. 485.
Zürich, Zentralbibliothek, Codex Rheinau 30.

Editions

The Bobbio Missal: A Gallican Mass-book (Ms. Paris B.N. Lat. 13246). Ed. Elias A. Lowe et al. HBS 53 (facsimile), 58 (text), 61 (notes). London, 1917, 1920, 1924.
Capitula episcoporum. Ed. Peter Brommer. MGH, Capitula episcoporum 1. Hanover, 1984.
Capitularia regum Francorum. MGH Leges, sec. 2. Vol. 1. ed. A. Boretius; vol. 2 ed. A. Boretius and V. Krause. Hanover, 1883, 1897.
Concilia aevi Karolini. MGH Leges, sec. 3, Concilia 2. Vols. 1–2 ed. A. Werminghoff; vol. 3 ed. W. Hartmann. Hanover, 1906, 1908, 1984.
Concilia aevi Merovingici. MGH Leges, sec. 3, Concilia 1. Ed. F. Maasen. Hanover, 1893.
Concilia Africae a. 345–a. 525. Ed. C. Munier. CCL 149. Turnhout, 1949.
Concilia Galliae a. 314–a. 506. Ed. C. Munier. CCL 148. Turnhout, 1963.
Concilia Galliae a. 511–a. 695. Ed. Carlo de Clercq. CCL 148A. Turnhout, 1963.
Concilios visigóticos e hispano-romanos. Ed. José Vives. España cristiana, textos 1. Barcelona/Madrid, 1963.
Didascalia et Constitutiones Apostolorum. Ed. Franz X. Funk. 2 vols. Paderborn, 1905.

Divi Gregorii papae I liber sacramentorum. Ed. H. Ménard. Paris, 1642; repr. PL 78.26–240.

Grégoire le grande. *Dialogues.* Ed. Adalbert de Vogüé. 3 vols. Sources chrétiennes 252, 260, 265. Paris, 1978–80.

Initia consuetudinis Benedictinae: Consuetudines saeculi octavi et noni. Ed. Kassius Hallinger et al. CCM 1. Siegburg, 1963.

Die irische Kanonensammlung. Ed. Hermann Wasserschleben. 2d ed. Leipzig, 1885.

The Irish Penitentials. Ed. Ludwig Bieler. Scriptores latini Hiberniae 5. Dublin, 1963.

Jonas of Bobbio. *Vitae Columbani abbatis discipulorumque eius.* Ed. Bruno Krusch. MGH, SRM 4.1–158. Hanover, 1902.

Liber Memorialis von Remiremont. Ed. Eduard Hlawitschka, Karl Schmid, and Gerd Tellenbach. MGH, Libri Memoriales 1. Dublin/Zürich, 1970.

Le liber ordinum en usage dans l'église wisigothique et mozarabe d'Espagne du cinquième au onzième siècle. Ed. Mario Férotin. Monumenta ecclesiae liturgica 5. Paris, 1904.

Liber ordinum sacerdotal (Cod. Silos Arch. monástico, 3). Ed. José Janini. Studia Silensia 7. Abadía de Silos, 1981.

Liber sacramentorum Augustudonensis. Ed. Odilo Heiming. CCL 159B. Turnhout, 1984.

Liber sacramentorum Gellonensis. Ed. Antoine Dumas. CCL 159. Turnhout, 1981. Introduction, tables, and indexes by Jean Deshusses. CCL 159A. Turnhout, 1981.

Liber sacramentorum Romanae aeclesiae ordinis anni circuli (Cod. Vat. Reg. lat. 316/Paris B.N. 7193, 41/56). Ed. Leo Cunibert Mohlberg, L. Eizenhöfer, and P. Siffrin. 3d ed. RED series maior, fontes 4. Rome, 1981; 1st ed. Rome, 1960.

Martène, Edmond. *De antiquis ecclesiae ritibus.* 3 vols. Rouen, 1700–1702. 2d ed., 4 vols., Antwerp, 1736–38; repr. Hildesheim, 1967–69.

Missale Francorum (Cod. Vat. Reg. lat. 257). Ed. Leo Cunibert Mohlberg. RED series maior, fontes 2. Rome, 1957.

Missale Gallicanum vetus. Ed. Leo Cunibert Mohlberg. RED series maior, fontes 3. Rome, 1958.

Missale Gothicum. Ed. Leo Cunibert Mohlberg. RED series maior, fontes 5. Rome, 1961.

Les "Ordines Romani" du haut moyen âge. Ed. Michel Andrieu. 5 vols. Spicilegium sacrum Lovaniense 11, 23, 24, 28, 29. Louvain, 1931–61; repr. 1960–65.

Patrologia cursus completus: series latina. Ed. J.-P. Migne. 221 vols. Paris, 1841–64.

Le pontifical romain au moyen-âge. Ed. Michel Andrieu. 4 vols. Studi e testi 86–88, 99. Vatican City, 1938–41.

Le pontifical romano-germanique du dixième siècle. Ed. Cyrille Vogel and Reinhard Elze. 3 vols. Studi e testi 226, 227, 269. Vatican City, 1963, 1972.

Das Prager Sakramentar. Vol. 2, *Prolegomena und Textausgabe.* Ed. Alban Dold and Leo Eizenhöfer. Texte und Arbeiten 38–42. Beuron, 1949.

The Rule of Tallaght. Ed. E. J. Gwynn. In *Hermathena* 24, 2d suppl. vol., 1–109. Dublin, 1927.

Le sacramentaire grégorien: Ses principales formes d'après les plus anciens manuscrits. Ed. Jean Deshusses. Comparative ed. 1, *Le sacramentaire, le supplément d'Aniane.* 2, *Textes complémentaires pour la messe.* 3, *Textes complémentaires divers.* SF 16, 24, 28. Fribourg, 1971, 1979, 1982.

Sacramentarium Rhenaugiense (Handschrift Rh 30 der Zentralbibliothek Zürich). Ed. Anton Hänggi and Alfons Schönherr. SF 15. Fribourg, 1970.

Sacramentarium Veronense (Cod. bibl. capit. veron. LXXXV [80]). Ed. Leo Cunibert Mohlberg. RED, series maior, fontes 1. Rome, 1956.

Sancti Caesarii Arelatensis opera omnia. Vol. 2, *Opera varia.* Ed. G. Morin. Marietoli, 1942.

Sancti Caesarii Arelatensis sermones. Ed. G. Morin. 2 vols. CCL 103, 104. Turnhout, 1953.

Ein St. Galler Sakramentar-Fragment (Cod. Sangall. No. 350). Ed. Georg Manz. Liturgiegeschichtliche Quellen und Forschungen 31. Münster, 1939.

The Stowe Missal (Ms. D.II.3 in the Library of the Royal Irish Academy, Dublin). Ed. George F. Warner. HBS 32. London, 1915.

Secondary Sources

Althoff, Gerd. *Adels- und Königsfamilien im Spiegel ihrer Memorialüberlieferung.* Münstersche Mittelalter-Schriften 47. Munich, 1984.

Angenendt, Arnold. "Missa Specialis: Zugleich ein Beitrag zur Entstehung der Privat-Messen." FS 17 (1983): 153–221.

——. "Theologie und Liturgie der mittelalterlichen Toten-Memoria." In *Memoria,* ed. Karl Schmid and Joachim Wollasch, 79–199. Munich, 1984.

Ariès, Philippe. *The Hour of Our Death.* Trans. Helen Weaver. New York, 1981. French ed., *L'homme devant la mort.* Paris, 1977.

Arnold, Carl Franklin. *Caesarius von Arelate und die gallische Kirche seiner Zeit.* Leipzig, 1894; repr. 1972.

Beck, Henry G. J. *The Pastoral Care of Souls in South-East France during the Sixth Century.* Analecta Gregoriana 51. Rome, 1950.

Binchey, D. A. "Penitential Texts in Old Irish." In *The Irish Penitentials,* ed. Ludwig Bieler, 47–51. Dublin, 1963.

Bischoff, Bernhard. "Lorsch im Spiegel seiner Handschriften." In *Die Reichsabtei Lorsch,* ed. Friedrich Knöpp, 2.7–127. Darmstadt, 1977.

Bishop, Edmund. *Liturgica Historica: Papers on the Liturgy and Religious Life of the Western Church.* Oxford, 1918; repr. 1962.

Boglioni, Pierre. "La scène de la mort dans les premières hagiographies latines." In *Essais sur la mort: Travaux d'un seminaire de recherche sur la mort,* ed. Guy Couturier, André Charron, and Guy Durand, 269–98. Montreal, 1985.

Brandon, S. G. F. *The Judgment of the Dead: The Idea of Life after Death in the Major Religions.* New York, 1967.

Browe, Peter. "Die letzte Ölung in der abendländischen Kirche des Mittelalters." *Zeitschrift für katholische Theologie* 55 (1931): 515–61.

Brown, Henry F. *Baptism through the Centuries.* Mountain View, Calif., and Omaha, Neb., 1965.

Brown, Peter. *The Cult of the Saints: Its Rise and Function in Latin Christianity.* Chicago, 1981.

Bullough, Donald. "Burial, Community, and Belief in the Early Medieval West." In *Ideal and Reality in Frankish and Anglo-Saxon Society: Studies Presented to J. M. Wallace-Hadrill,* ed. Patrick Wormald, 175–201. Oxford, 1983.

Chavasse, Antoine. *Etude sur l'onction des infirmes dans l'église latine du iiie au xie siècle.* Vol. 1, *Du iiie siècle à la réforme carolingienne.* Lyons, 1942.

——. "Prières pour les malades et onction sacramentelle." In *L'église en prière: Introduction à la liturgie,* ed. A. G. Martimort, 580–94. Paris/Tournai/Rome/New York, 1961.

——. *Le sacramentaire gélasien (Vatican Reginensis 316): Sacramentaire presbytéral en usage dans les titres romains au viie siècle.* Bibliothèque de théologie, Ser. 4, vol. 1. Paris/Tournai/New York/Rome, 1958.

Clercq, Carlo de. *La législation religieuse franque.* Vol. 1, *De Clovis à Charlemagne (507–814).* Louvain/Paris, 1936. Vol. 2, *De Louis le Pieux à la fin du ixe siècle (814–900).* Angers, 1958.

——. " 'Ordines unctionis infirmi' des ixe et xe siècles." EL 44 (1930): 100–122.

Death in the Middle Ages. Ed. Herman Braet and Werner Verbeke. Mediaevalia Lovaniensia, ser. 1, stud. 9. Leuven, 1983.

Deshusses, Jean. "Chronologie des grands sacramentaires de Saint-Amand." RB 87 (1977): 230–37.

——. "Encore les sacramentaires de Saint-Amand." RB 89 (1979): 310–12.

——. "Le sacramentaire de Gellone dans son contexte historique." EL 75 (1961): 193–210.

——. "Les sacramentaires: Etat actuel de la recherche." ALW 24 (1982): 19–46.

——. "Le 'Supplément' au sacramentaire grégorien: Alcuin ou Saint Benoît d'Aniane?" ALW 9 (1965): 48–71.

Dictionary of the Middle Ages. Ed. Joseph R. Strayer. 13 vols. New York, 1982–89.

Dictionnaire d'archéologie chrétienne et de liturgie. Ed. Fernand Cabrol and Henri Leclercq. 15 vols. Paris, 1907–53.

Dictionnaire d'histoire et de géographie ecclésiastiques. Ed. Alfred Baudrillart et al. Paris, 1912ff.

L'église en prière: Introduction à la liturgie. Ed. A. G. Martimort. Tournai/Paris/New York/Rome, 1961. New ed., 4 vols. Paris, 1984.

Enright, Michael. *Iona, Tara, and Soissons: The Origin of the Royal Anointing Ritual.* Berlin/New York, 1985.

Fernández Alonso, Justo. *La cura pastoral en la España romanovisigoda.* Rome, 1955.

Février, Paul-Albert. "La mort chrétienne." In *Segni e riti nella chiesa altomedievale occidentale,* 2.881–952. Settimane di studio del centro italiano di studi sull'alto medioevo 33. 2 vols. Spoleto, 1987.

——. "Vie et mort dans le 'Epigrammata Damasiana.'" In *Saeculum Damasiana,* 89–111. Studi di antichità cristiana 39. Vatican City, 1986.

Fichtner, Gerhard. "Christus als Arzt: Ursprunge und Wirkungen eines Motivs." FS 16 (1982): 1–18.

Frank, Hieronymus. "Der älteste erhaltene *Ordo defunctorum* der römischen Liturgie und sein Fortleben in Totenagenden des frühen Mittelalters." ALW 7 (1962): 360–415.

Frankenmölle, H. "Krankensalbung im Neuen Testament." In *Heilssorge für die Kranken und Hilfen zur Erneuerung eines Missverstandenen Sakraments*, ed. Manfred Probst and Klemens Richter, 28–38. Freiburg/Einsiedlen, 1975.

Freistedt, Emil. *Altchristliche Totengedächtnistage und ihre Beziehung zum Jenseitsglauben und Totenkultus der Antike.* Liturgiegeschichtliche Quellen und Forschungen 24. Münster, 1928.

Gamber, Klaus. *Codices liturgici latini antiquiores.* Spicilegii Friburgensis subsidia 1. Fribourg, 1963; 2d ed., 1968.

Geary, Patrick J. *Before France and Germany: The Creation and Transformation of the Merovingian World.* Oxford, 1988.

Gougaud, Louis. "Etude sur les *Loricae* celtiques et sur les prières qui s'en rapprochent." *Bulletin d'ancienne littérature et d'archéologie chrétiennes* 1 (1911): 265–81; 2 (1912): 33–41.

——. "Etude sur les 'Ordines commendationis animae.'" EL 49 (1935): 3–27.

Grimes, Ronald L. *Research in Ritual Studies: A Programmatic Essay and Bibliography.* ATLA Bibliographic Series 14. Metuchen, N.J., 1985.

Gros, Miquel. "Le pontifical de Narbonne." In *Liturgie et musique (ixe–xive s.)*, 97–114. Cahiers de Fanjeaux 17. Toulouse, 1982.

——. "Los ritos de la Tarraconense y Narbona." In José Janini, *Manuscritos litúrgicos de las bibliotecas de España*, vol. 2, *Aragón, Cataluña y Valencia*, 7–17. Burgos, 1980.

Gwynn, E. J., and W. J. Purton. "The Monastery of Tallaght." *Proceedings of the Royal Irish Academy* 29, sec. C (1911): 115–79.

Gy, P.-M. "La pénitence et la réconciliation." In *L'église en prière*, ed. A. G. Martimort, new ed., 3.115–31. Paris, 1984.

Heil, Wilhelm. "Der Adoptionismus, Alkuin und Spanien." In *Karl der Grosse: Lebenswerk und Nachleben*, vol. 2, *Das geistige Leben*, ed. Bernhard Bischoff, 95–155. Düsseldorf, 1965.

Hennig, John. "Liturgy, Celtic." DMA 7.613–16.

Hertz, Robert. "A Contribution to the Study of the Collective Representation of Death." In *Death and The Right Hand*, trans. R. and C. Needham, 27–86. Glencoe, Ill., 1960.

Hillgarth, J. N. "Popular Religion in Visigothic Spain." In *Visigothic Spain: New Approaches*, ed. Edward James, 3–60. Oxford, 1980.

Hopkins, Keith. *Death and Renewal.* Sociological Studies in Roman History 2. Cambridge, Eng., 1983.

Hughes, Kathleen. *The Church in Early Irish Society.* Ithaca, N.Y., 1966.

Huntington, Richard, and Peter Metcalf. *Celebrations of Death: The Anthropology of Mortuary Ritual.* Cambridge, Eng., 1979.

Janini, José. *Manuscritos litúrgicos de las bibliotecas de España.* Publaciones de la Facultad de Teología del Norte de España, Sede de Burgos 38. 2 vols. Burgos, 1977–80.

———. "Las oraciones visigóticas de los formularios penitenciales del re-ginensis 316." *Hispania Sacra* 37 (1985): 191–204.

Jungmann, Joseph A. *The Mass of the Roman Rite: Its Origins and Development (Missarum Sollemnia).* Trans. Francis A. Brunner. 2 vols. New York, 1951, 1955.

Karl der Grosse: Lebenswerk und Nachleben. Ed. Wolfgang Braunfels. 4 vols. Düsseldorf, 1965.

Kenney, J. F. *Sources for the Early History of Ireland.* Vol. 1, *Ecclesiastical.* New York, 1929.

Klauser, Theodor. "Die liturgischen Austauschbeziehungen zwischen der römischen und der fränkisch-deutschen Kirche von achten bis zum elften Jahrhundert." *Historisches Jahrbuch* 53 (1933): 169–89.

Die Klostergemeinschaft von Fulda. Ed. Karl Schmid. 3 vols. Münstersche Mittelalter-Schriften 8. Munich, 1978.

Lane Fox, Robin. *Pagans and Christians.* San Francisco, 1986.

Levison, Wilhelm. *England and the Continent in the Eighth Century.* Oxford, 1946.

Llopis Sarrío, Juan. "La sagrada escritura, fuente de inspiración de la liturgia de difuntos del antiguo rito hispánico." *Hispania Sacra* 17 (1964): 349–91.

Lozano Sebastián, F. Javier. "La legislación canónica sobre la penitencia en la España romano y visigoda (s. iv–vii)." *Burgense* 19 (1978): 399–439.

MacCormack, Sabine. *Art and Ceremony in Late Antiquity. Transformation of the Classical Heritage* 1. Berkeley/Los Angeles, 1981.

McKitterick, Rosamond. *The Frankish Church and the Carolingian Reforms, 789–895.* London, 1977.

———. *The Frankish Kingdoms under the Carolingians, 751–987.* London/New York, 1983.

McNeill, John T., and Helena M. Gamer. *Medieval Handbooks of Penance: A Translation of the Principal Libri Poenitentiales and Selections from Related Documents.* Records of Civilization 29. New York, 1938.

McWilliam Dewart, Joanne E. *Death and Resurrection.* Message of the Fathers of the Church 22. Wilmington, Del., 1986.

La maladie et la mort du chrétien dans la liturgie: Conférences Saint-Serge, XXIᵉ Semaine d'Etudes Liturgique, Paris, 1ᵉʳ–4 Juilet, 1974. Bibliotheca "Ephemerides Liturgicae," subsidia 1. Rome, 1975. Partially trans. as *The Temple of the Holy Spirit.* New York, 1983.

Malnory, A. *Saint Césaire: Evêque d'Arles, 503–543.* Paris, 1894; repr. 1978.

Martimort, A.-G. "Prières pour les malades et onction sacramentelle." In *L'église en prière,* ed. Martimort, new ed., 3.132–53. Paris, 1984.

Memoria: Der geschichtliche Zeugniswert des liturgischen Gedenkens im Mittelalter. Ed. Karl Schmid and Joachim Wollasch. Münstersche Mittelalter-Schriften 48. Munich, 1984.

Mirrors of Mortality: Studies in the Social History of Death. Ed. Joachim Whaley. Europa Social History of Human Experience 3. London, 1981.

Moreton, Bernard. *The Eighth-Century Gelasian Sacramentary: A Study in Tradition.* Oxford, 1976.

———. "The 'Liber Secundus' of the Eighth Century Gelasian Sacramentaries: A Reassessment." In *Studia Patristica* 13, ed. E. A. Livingstone, 382–86. Texte und Untersuchungen 116. Berlin, 1975.

La mort au moyen-âge. Ed. Association des Historiens Médiévistes de l'Enseignement Supérieur Publique. Publications de la Société Savante d'Alsace et des Régions de l'Est, Collection "Recherches et Documents" 25. Strasbourg, 1977.

Mundó, Anscari M. "Sur quelques manuscrits liturgiques languedociens de l'époque carolingienne." In *Liturgie et musique (ixe–xive s.)*, 81–95. Cahiers de Fanjeaux 17. Toulouse, 1982.

Murray, Placid. "The Liturgical History of Extreme Unction." In *Studies in Pastoral Liturgy,* ed. Vincent Ryan, 2.18–35. Dublin, 1963. Also in *Furrow* 11 (1960): 572–93.

Narberhaus, Josef. *Benedikt von Aniane: Werk und Persönlichkeit.* Beiträge zur Geschichte des alten Mönchtums und des Benediktinerordens 16. Münster, 1930.

New Catholic Encyclopedia. 15 vols. New York, 1967.

Niederhellmann, Annette. *Arzt und Heilkunde in den frühmittelalterlichen Leges: Ein wort- und sachkundliche Untersuchung.* Arbeiten zur Frühmittelalterforschung 12. Berlin/New York, 1983.

Nitz, H.-J. "The Church as Colonist: The Benedictine Abbey of Lorsch and Planned Waldhufen Colonisation in the Odenwald." *Journal of Historical Geography* 9 (1983): 105–26.

Ntedika, Joseph. *L'évocation de l'au-delà dans la prière pour les morts.* Recherches africaine de théologie 2. Louvain, 1971.

O'Dwyer, Peter. *Célí Dé: Spiritual Reform in Ireland, 750–900.* 2d ed. Dublin, 1981.

Oexle, Otto Gerhard. "Die Gegenwart der Toten." In *Death in the Middle Ages,* ed. Herman Braet and Werner Verbeke, 19–77. Leuven, 1983.

Ó Riain-Raedel, Dagmar. "Spuren irischer Gebetsverbrüderungen zur Zeit Virgils." In *Virgil von Salzburg: Missionar und Gelehrter,* ed. H. Dopsch and R. Juffinger, 141–46. Salzburg, 1985.

Orlandis, José, and Domingo Ramos-Lisson. *Die Synoden auf der Iberischen Halbinsel bis zum Einbruch des Islam (711).* Paderborn, 1981.

O'Shea, William J. "Liturgiology." NCE 8.919–27.

Paxton, Frederick S. "Bonus liber: A Late Carolingian Clerical Manual from Lorsch (Bibliotheca Vaticana Pal. lat. 485)." In *The Two Laws: Studies in Medieval Legal History Dedicated to Stephan Kuttner,* ed. Laurent Mayali and Stephanie A. J. Tibbetts, 1–30. Studies in Medieval and Early Modern Canon Law 1. Washington, D.C., 1990.

Porter, H. B. "The Origin of the Medieval Rite for Anointing the Sick or Dying." JTS, n.s. 7 (1956): 211–25.

Quasten, Johannes. *Music and Worship in Pagan and Christian Antiquity.* Trans. Boniface Ramsey. Washington, D.C., 1983.

Reeves, W. "On the Célí-de, Commonly Called Culdees." *Transactions of the Royal Irish Academy* 24 (1873): 119–263.

Die Reichsabtei Lorsch: Festschrift zum Gedanken an ihre Stiftung 764. Ed. Friedrich Knöpp. 2 vols. Darmstadt, 1973, 1977.

Rowell, Geoffrey. *The Liturgy of Christian Burial.* London, 1977.

Rush, Alfred C. *Death and Burial in Christian Antiquity.* Catholic University of America Studies in Christian Antiquity 1. Washington, D.C., 1941; repr. 1977.

_____. "The Eucharist: The Sacrament of the Dying in Christian Antiquity." *Jurist* 34 (1974): 10–35.

Schmid, Karl, and Otto Gerhard Oexle. "Voraussetzungen und Wirkung des Gebetsbundes von Attigny." *Francia* 2 (1974): 71–122.

Sicard, Damien. *La liturgie de la mort dans l'église latine des origines à la réforme carolingienne.* LQF 63. Münster, 1978.

Siffrin, Petrus. *Konkordanztabellen zu den römischen lateinischen Sakramentarien.* 3 vols. RED, series minor 4–6. Rome, 1958–61.

Tellenbach, Gerd. "Die historische Dimension der liturgischen Commemoratio im Mittelalter." In *Memoria*, ed. Karl Schmid and Joachim Wollasch, 200–214. Munich, 1984.

Thorndyke, Lynn. *A History of Magic and Experimental Science.* Vol. 1. New York, 1923.

Toynbee, J. M. C. *Death and Burial in the Roman World.* Ithaca, N.Y., 1971.

Turner, Victor. *Dramas, Fields, and Metaphors: Symbolic Action in Human Society.* Ithaca, N.Y., 1974.

_____. *The Forest of Symbols: Aspects of Ndembu Ritual.* Ithaca, N.Y., 1967.

Van der Meer, F. *Augustine the Bishop: Religion and Society at the Dawn of the Middle Ages.* Trans. B. Battershaw and G. R. Lamb. New York, 1961.

Van Gennep, Arnold. *The Rites of Passage.* Trans. Monika B. Vizedom and Gabrielle L. Caffee. Chicago, 1960.

Vogel, Cyril. "Deux conséquences de l'eschatologie grégorienne: La multiplication des messes privées et les moines-prêtres." In *Grégoire le Grand*, ed. Jacques Fontaine, Robert Gillet, and Stan Pellistrandi, 267–76. Colloques internationaux du Centre National de la Recherche Scientifique. Paris, 1986.

Vogel, Cyrille. *La discipline pénitentielle en Gaule des origines à la fin du viiᵉ siècle.* Paris, 1952.

_____. *Medieval Liturgy: An Introduction to the Sources.* Rev. and trans. William G. Storey and Niels Krogh Rasmussen. Washington, D.C., 1986. French ed., *Introduction aux sources de l'histoire du culte chrétien au moyen-âge.* Biblioteca degli Studia Medievali 1. Spoleto, 1966.

_____. *La réforme cultuelle sous Pepin le Bref et sous Charlemagne.* Graz, 1965. Printed in one volume with Erna Patzelt, *Die karolingische Renaissance.*

_____. "La réforme liturgique sous Charlemagne." In *Karl der Grosse*, vol. 2, *Das geistige Leben*, ed. Bernhard Bischoff, 95–155. Düsseldorf, 1965.

Vorgrimler, Herbert. *Busse und Krankensalbung.* Handbuch der Dogmengeschichte 4.3. Freiburg/Basel/Vienna, 1978.

Wallace-Hadrill, John Michael. *The Frankish Church.* Oxford, 1983.

Warren, Frederick E. *The Liturgy and Ritual of the Celtic Church.* Oxford, 1881. 2d ed., with introduction and bibliography by Jane Stevenson. Woodbridge, Suffolk, and Wolfeboro, N.H., 1987.

Watkins, O. D. *A History of Penance.* 2 vols. London, 1920.

Wilmart, André. "La règlement ecclésiastique de Berne." RB 51 (1939): 37–52.

Young, Bailey. "Exemple aristocratique et mode funéraire dans le Gaule mérovingienne." AESC 41 (1986): 379–407.

_____. "Paganisme, christianisation et rites funéraires mérovingiennes." *Archéologie médiévale* 7 (1977): 1–65.

Index

Aachen, 133, 202; councils at, 133, 135–37, 162–63
Absolue domine animam, 141, 145n
Accepto salutari diuini, 83n
Adalbero of Augsburg, 199
Admonitio generalis, 128
Adomnan, 84, 86n
Adoptionism, 139, 142
Adventus, 42. *See also* Funeral processions
Africa, 146n
Agde, council at, 48, 51
Agony, rites for, 116–22, 124–26, 131, 174–75, 191–92, 194, 208
Aix-en-Provence, 37n
Alaric II, 48
Alcuin of York, 132, 139, 183
Alexander of Tralles, 50n
Allemans, 70n
Amalarius of Metz, 136
Ambrose, St., 34
Ambrosian liturgy, 32
Andrieu, Michel, 12, 37–38
Angels: and dead, 39–40, 42, 64, 173, 206; and sick, 73, 80, 160
Angenendt, Arnold, 67–68, 98
Angilbert of St-Riquier, 134–35
Anglo-Saxon England, 14, 90–92
Anglo-Saxon missionaries, 92, 98, 100
Anglo-Saxons, 67, 99–101, 105
Angoulême, sacramentary of, 97n, 115n

Aniane, monastery of, 132. *See also* Benedict of Aniane
Annals of Ulster, 85n
Anointing, 10, 27–28, 88, 126, 157, 163, 207; formulas for, 81, 111, 152, 159–60, 174, 184; and senses, 160. *See also* Oil
—of dying, 82–83, 96, 109, 126, 163, 165–68, 180–83, 192, 196, 207; at Lorsch, 187, 190–91; in Roman-German pontifical, 193
—of sick, 10, 27–30, 32, 50–51, 55–56, 96, 171, 207; in Carolingian Francia, 104, 106, 111, 113, 128–30, 164–68; in Ireland, 78–83; at Lorsch, 187–91; reform rite for, 148–55, 159–61, 180–83, 193, 208; in Roman-German pontifical, 193; in Visigothic Spain, 70–73, 82, 85, 104, 149
Ansegisus of Sens, 180
Anthropology, 3, 5–9
Antique memores, 63n
Apostolic Constitutions, 26, 29, 43
Apostolic Tradition, 29
Archaeology, 3
Arians, 105
Ariès, Philippe, 17
Armagh, monastery of, 85
Ashes, 74–75
Attigny, council at, 100–102, 136
Augustine, St., 26–27, 29, 34–35

Library of Congress Cataloging-in-Publication Data

Paxton, Frederick S., 1951–
   Christianizing death : the creation of a ritual process in early
medieval Europe / Frederick S. Paxton.
      p.   cm.
   Includes bibliographical references.
   ISBN 0–8014–2492–5 (alk. paper)
      1. Funeral   rites   and   ceremonies—Europe—History.   2. Death—Religious
aspects—Christianity.   3. Europe—Religious life and customs.   4. Civilization,
Medieval.   I. Title.
GT3242.P39   1990
265'.85'09409021—dc20   90–34072